THE ADOPTION AND DIFFUSION OF IMPORTED TECHNOLOGY: THE CASE OF KOREA

The Adoption and Diffusion of Imported Technology

The Case of Korea

J.L. ENOS
Magdalen College, Oxford

W.-H. PARK
Seoul National University, Seoul

CROOM HELM
London • New York • Sydney

© 1988 J.L. Enos and W.-H. Park
Croom Helm Ltd, Provident House,
Burrell Row, Beckenham, Kent BR3 1AT
Croom Helm Australia, 44-50 Waterloo Road,
North Ryde, 2113, New South Wales

Published in the USA by
Croom Helm
in association with Methuen, Inc.
29 West 35th Street
New York, NY 10001

British Library Cataloguing in Publication Data

Enos, J.L.
    The adoption and diffusion of imported
technology : the case of Korea.
    1. Technological innovations — Korea
    I. Title   II. Park, W.-H.
    609′.51′9   T173.8
    ISBN 0-7099-2030-X

Library of Congress Cataloging-in-Publication Data

Enos, John L. (John Lawrence), 1924–
    The adoption and diffusion of imported technology.

    Bibliography: p.
    Includes index.
    1. Technological innovations — Economic aspects —
Korea (South) — Case studies. 2. Technology transfer —
Korea (South) — Case studies. 3. Korea (South) —
Industries — 1960– — Case studies. 4. Diffusion
of innovations — Korea (South) — Case studies.
    I. Park, U-hŭi. II. Title.
    HC470.T4E56 1987   338.9519′506   87-19894
    ISBN 0-7099-2030-X

Typeset by Leaper & Gard Ltd, Bristol, England
Printed and bound in Great Britain
by Billing & Sons Limited, Worcester.

Contents

Tables

Figures

Preface

Simple theories of production among nations assume either that
techniques are unique to each country or are shared equally by
all. Reality conforms to neither of these extremes, but displays
across countries a spectrum extending from the most modern
and sophisticated to the antique. Brave indeed is the country
which attempts to shift, within a single generation, from one end
of the spectrum to the other; and fortunate indeed is the
country which succeeds.

Such a country is the Republic of Korea, whose attempts to
adopt modern technology imported from the most economically
advanced nations are described in the following study. Yet it
was not Korea's success that led to the study but its status as an
importer of foreign techniques, in common which several other
developing countries of South and East Asia. It was the belief
that countries like India, Nepal, Sri Lanka, Bangladesh, the
Philippines and South Korea had had common objectives, faced
common difficulties, experienced common results, that led the
Canadian government, through its International Development
Research Council (IDRC), to sponsor in the mid-1970s a
common research programme on the absorption and diffusion
of imported techniques.

Subsequently, in the late 1970s, and with the financial
support of the IDRC, a preliminary study of the adoption
and diffusion of new techniques within four industries in
South Korea was carried out. Each industry was surveyed by
a team consisting of an engineer and an economist, both
familiar with their industry's technology and economy.
Organizer was the first of the authors of this book. Listing the
members of the teams in the order in which their industries
appear in the case studies in the text, the first pair, examining
the petrochemical industry, were Professor Hyun-Koo Rhee of
the Chemical Enginering Faculty of Seoul National University
and the first of the authors; the second, examining the textile
industry, were Professor Sang-Yong Kim of the Mechanical
Engineering Faculty and Professor Moo-Ki Bai of the Economics Faculty; the third, the machinery industry, were Professor Suck-Chul Yoon of the Faculty of Business Administration and the second of the authors; and the fourth, the steel

industry, were Professor Jong-Kyu Yoon of the Mechanical Engineering Faculty of Seoul National University and Professor Hyung-Yoon Byun of the Economics Faculty.

A report, summarising the results of the preliminary study, was submitted to the IDRC. There the matter rested until the mid-1980s, when the two authors of this book revised the original material, extended the analysis and, throughout the summer of 1985, brought the enquiry up to date. This last endeavour doubled the coverage of events, thereby providing a history of approximately 20 years of technical change in the four industries in South Korea, a period coinciding with that of the country's rapid economic growth.

It remains to acknowledge the many persons who have contributed to this research. The administration of the preliminary enquiry, no easy task, was supervised by Professor Hyun-Jae Lee, then Director of the Economic Research Institute of Seoul National University, and was carried out by the Institute's staff. Officials in the various departments of the South Korean government responded willingly to our requests for information and assistance. Among the parastatal organisations we obtained most helpful responses from Mr Young-Woo Kim, Executive Deputy Chairman of the Korea Industrial Technology Research Institutes, and his staff; Mr Byon-Sik Jeon, Director for the National Industrial Research Institute; Mr Young-Ok Ahn, President of the Korea Technology Advancement Corporation; Mr Chang-Dal Kim, President of the Korea Technology Development Corporation; and Mr Masanori Moritani, Deputy Director at the Nomura Research Institute of Tokyo. In each of the four companies whose absorption of technology is covered in detail in our case studies, we received a cordial welcome and extensive help. The basic data came from the companies' records; some of them were already available, others had to be abstracted and processed anew, these tasks often requiring days of work. Our appreciation of this assistance, vital as it has been to the analysis, extends beyond the polite thanks afforded in the customary preface. In expressing our gratitude we are acknowledging an interest in the issues that was just as keen as our own, an allocation of effort that exceeded our own, and contributions that were inestimable. At Han Yang Chemical Corporation, the focus of the chapter on the petrochemical industry, we were assisted by Messrs K.-K. Choi, President; U.-J. Choi,

Managing Director for Technology and Development; J.-S. Kang, General Manager, Technical Development and Management; D.-S. Yoon, Plant Manager at the Ulsan Plant; and I.-Y. Kim, Plant Manager of the Yeocheon Plant. In addition, we received guidance from Mr Do-Sim Kim, Executive Director of the Kohap Chemical Corporation.

At Kolon Industries, the focus of the chapter on the textile industry, we received financial help from Mr Dong-Chan Lee, Chairman, without whose assistance no work could have been carried out in 1985, and technical help from Messrs Min-Hae Koo, Vice President; Sang-Uk Lee, Managing Director; Kwan Kang, Managing Director of the Technical Departments; Keum-Dae Kim, Director and Manager of the Daegu Plant; Yong-Chang Cho, Director of the R & D Centre; Jung-Ho Jo, General Manager of the Technical Planning Department; Baik-Young Sung of its Technical Section; Won-Pil Lee, General Manager of the Product Department at the Daegu Plant; and Ki-Taek Park, Manager of its Technical Section.

The focus of the chapter on machinery is the diesel engine factory of Daewoo Heavy Industries Ltd, a subsidiary of the Daewoo Corporation. There we were helped by Messrs Myung-Kul Choi, Vice Chairman of the Daewoo Corporation; Jhoung-Ung Kim, President of Daewoo Motor Company; Soon-Hoon Bae, President of Daewoo Automotive Components; Mr Nag-Young Chang, Executive Managing Director of the Technical Centre at the Incheon Plant of Daewoo Heavy Industries; and Mr H.-S. Lee, Section Manager of the Engine Engineering Department at the Technical Centre.

The last of the case studies focuses on the Pohang Iron and Steel Company (POSCO), at which we were cordially received by Messrs Tae-Joon Park, Chairman, Byong-Wha Ahn, President and Mal-Soo Cho, Managing Director. There we worked with Messrs Won-Pyo Lee, General Manager of the Technology Development Department and Ki-Young Choi, Manager of the Technology Co-operation Section; Mr Y.-K. Shin, Chief Metallurgist in the Research Laboratory, and Mr Hyoung-Ky Shin, Assistant Chief Researcher. At POSCO's office in Seoul we were assisted by Messrs. S.-S. Cho, Manager of the Corporate Planning Department and Jung-Woong Chang, Deputy General Manager of the Corporate Strategic

Planning Section. It remains to say that whereas the men above should be credited with much of what is worthwhile in our study of the adoption and diffusion of imported technology in South Korea, we, the authors, must take responsibility for its deficiencies.

J.L. Enos
Magdalen College
Oxford

Woo-Hee Park
Seoul National University
Seoul

1

Outline of the Study

OBJECTIVES

In industrialising, most countries first acquire technology. Before production can begin, even before plants can be constructed and equipment installed, a minimal amount of information about the manufacturing technique must usually be imported. Up to the time of transfer, this information will reside in patents and other published documents, in blueprints, in design and operators' manuals that are the private possession of construction and producing firms abroad, and in the accumulated experience of individuals who have perfected the technique. The reservoirs of technological knowledge are many, deep and distant.

Yet, somehow or other, the fluid that resides in these distant sources must be tapped, and piped as swiftly and economically as possible to the potential users in the developing countries. Moreover, as a fluid to be supplied by one group of individuals and acquired by another group of individuals, technical knowledge is very complex, so complex that its nature is difficult to define and its transfer to describe. To categorise technological knowledge and to investigate its transfer from developed countries to the Republic of Korea are two of the objectives of this study.

It might be said that attaining these two objectives would be sufficient to justify carrying out the study, for relatively little is known about what constitutes technological knowledge and about how this knowledge is drawn upon; but the choice of the Republic of Korea provides further justification. By general agreement, the Republic of Korea has been particularly successful in industrialising: it therefore should be able to provide not only a case study of the transfer of technology — i.e. a description — but also an inquiry into how the transfer can be conducted skilfully — i.e. a prescription.

It is unlikely that Korea's achievements would have been so great had its acquisition of modern technology been slow and inefficient; so the presumption can be made that the transfer of technology to the Republic of Korea has been relatively smooth. Nevertheless, this general statement is not very revealing; it immediately leads one to ask in which activities, involved in the transfer, Korea may have excelled and in which not. It also leads one to ask fundamental questions concerning the relations between the acquisition of technology on the one hand and the production of goods on the other hand and the meaning of excellence. Economists have reasonably good ideas of what is meant by excellence in production and exchange, centring on efficiency in the static sense and on innovation and responsiveness in the dynamic sense, but they have few ideas of what is meant by excellence in the transfer of technological knowledge. In the observation of what one imagines to have been a successful transfer some ideas may emerge; to evoke these ideas is the final aim of this study.

MEANS EMPLOYED

The chief means employed in trying to meet the aims of this work were detailed case studies involving the recent acquisition of sophisticated technical knowledge by Korean companies. The historical period involved is the recent past, extending from the mid-1960s to the present; the technologies involved are chemical, metallurgical and mechanical. The sources of the technological knowledge were firms in the developed countries, specifically the United States, Japan and West Germany; the firms that utilised the imported techniques are scattered about Korea.

The choices of firms located in a developing country and owned by its citizens, of advanced products and precisely defined manufacturing techniques and of extremely detailed inquiries, were deliberate. Already there have been several studies published on the transfer of technology by the vehicle of multi-national firms (Baranson [1978], Berman [1976] and Teece [1976]), so it seemed proper to concentrate on transfers

2

to independent firms domiciled within a developing country. The advantages of applying simple techniques utilising resources abundant in the developing countries have been eloquently argued and illustrated (see Stewart [1978], and the references cited therein), so it seemed useful to concentrate on the sophisticated techniques that developing countries themselves are determined to introduce. Last of all, those studies that have been made of the acquisition of advanced technologies by developing countries, chiefly Korea, have summarised the experience of many firms in selected industries (machinery in the cases of Kim, Lin-Su and Kim, Young-Bae [forthcoming], and Ausden and Kim [1984]; and electronics in the cases of Kim, Lin-Su [1980a], Kim, Lin-Su [1980b] and Kim, Lin-Su and Utterback [1983]), achieving broad coverage but not describing the technologies acquired, so it seemed desirable to fill this gap. Technologies are so complex that to consider more than a few would be impossible for a limited number of researchers; as it was, our investigation of the acquisition of four technologies occupied our attention over a period of ten years. To have drawn a larger sample would have taxed us beyond our ability to cope, and would also, in all likelihood, have taxed the capacity of the reader of this book to absorb.

The Korean firms that acquired the technologies provided our chief fund of information. Other sources ranged widely, from government ministries and international agencies, through academic publications, manuals for engineers and businessmen, to promotional material. The academic literature appears in four overlapping fields commonly designated as 'technology transfer', 'appropriate technology', 'the multi-nationals' and 'science policy'. Where the material is germane, it will be referred to, but there will be no general attempt to survey the literature.

It may well be that the main contribution of this work on the acquisition and application of modern technology by the Republic of Korea will lie not in the objectives attained but in the information secured. In conducting the case studies the investigators were given almost complete access to all the material in Korea, thanks to the generosity of the private firms and the Korean government. Economic data on costs and prices; financial data on sources and uses of funds; personal data on backgrounds and employment; institutional data on negotiations and agreements; and general technical data on

3

products and processes were made available in detail whenever they were requested. The only data withheld were engineering specifications and operating conditions for proprietory processes and products.

Not only were data willingly provided, but they were the correct data, so far as we have been able to ascertain. In most developing countries, those who do economic research encounter information which they become accustomed to examine with great care. Our scrutiny of the information we gathered in Korea did not reveal any inconsistencies: it was, to the best of our knowledge, accurately recorded and honestly reported. We have consequently worked with it with confidence.

The long chapters forming the core of this study reveal the information that was gathered and the analysis that it permitted. The import of modern, sophisticated technologies into a developing country provides a challenge to its engineers and managers, a challenge which we presumed, at the start of our project, had been successfully met. To test this hypothesis of successful incorporation of technologies we needed much information; hence the concentration on relatively recent events, which have been recorded in greater detail and in more accessible sources.

The industries from which our cases are drawn are petrochemicals, iron and steel, heavy engineering goods and textiles. In the first three of these industries, as in most other industries in Korea utilising imported technologies, the manufacturing process is employed by a single firm which has been granted a monopoly in its use by the government. The study of the adoption of the technology is therefore almost synonymous with the study of the firm that adopts it.

Surrounding the core of the study are four other chapters; preceding it are an attempt to provide a framework within which case studies of technology can be systematically carried out (Chapter 2 on methodology) and a description of the broader economic environment within which the technologies were absorbed (Chapter 3). This third chapter presents material on the overall growth of the Korean economy and of the growth of those four industries from which the case studies were drawn. Following the case studies are a summary of the experience of Japan, a forerunner in the import of the technologies (Chapter 8), and a final chapter (9) that draws conclusions.

4

2

Methodology

DEFINITIONS

The purpose of this chapter is to describe the methodology that
has guided the four case studies on the adoption and diffusion
of imported technology in Korea. Certain parts of the methodology — the objectives, the definitions of terms and some of the
quantitative measures and relevant statistical tests — were
formulated well before the case studies were begun; other parts
— the sources of information, the division of research efforts,
many of the hypotheses and the theoretical underpinnings —
were revised after the first impressions from the industrial visits
had been gained. In the natural sciences, experiments can be
designed before laboratory work commences; in the social
sciences, design and data collection proceed together.

The objective of this enquiry has been to learn as much as
possible about the adoption and diffusion of industrial technologies imported into the Republic of Korea from more
advanced economies. Such questions were asked as: what techniques were available, and which one was chosen and why?
Through what agency was the technology transferred? Which
individuals, with which skills, of which nationalities and with
which affiliations, were involved? How rapidly and efficiently
was the technology absorbed? What changes were made in the
process and why? What improvements were subsequently
made: by whom and with what consequences? How are all these
phenomena related to Korea's economic development?

Common to the case studies were not only a set of questions
to be answered but also a vocabulary. It is this vocabulary to
which attention will first be directed. Of the terms used, the

broadest is the word adoption, which will signify for us all that takes place, between the time the matter of a technology is first broached and the time when it has been mastered by Korea. Adoption implies, as transfer does not, that events are being considered from the vantage-point of the developing country. Such a vantage-point was almost forced upon us, because our research was done in a developing, not a developed country, drawing upon the information available there; but it is also voluntary, because it is the developing country's interest that we had at heart. Transfer as a word is neutral, whereas we are prejudiced on the behalf of the recipient.

We will define all the terms below, but refer first to Figures 2.1 and 2.2 in which the majority are displayed. The two figures are complementary; both start with the same event (industrial planning) and both portray the same sequence of events. The difference between the two figures is that Figure 2.1 focuses on the activities that take place, whereas Figure 2.2 focuses on the major decisions that follow each activity. Thus the first activity in the sequence, 'Planning and Investigation', leads to the choices of what technology is to be employed, what products are to be manufactured, what scale of operation is to be selected and to what structure the producing industry is to conform. The reason for splitting activities from decisions or choices is that some of the terms to be defined refer chiefly to the activities that are undertaken within the developing country while other terms refer chiefly to the decisions that are made. To take as an illustration the term that has been used already, adoption, it is meant to cover the sequence of decisions or choices from the first activity to the last, inclusive; it therefore appears in Figure 2.2.

The definitions are:

(1) Adoption: The entire sequence of decisions made within the developing country determining how, when, where and with what consequences an imported technology is to be employed. The term is employed in a manner similar to the adoption of a child, in which the child is selected by the husband and wife, legal requirements are fulfilled specifying the rights and duties of all three, and the child is subsequently raised by its new parents. The course of adoption ends when the child becomes self-sufficient.

(2) Transfer: Once foreign suppliers of the technology are

Figure 2.1: Flow diagram illustrating activities in process of incorporating foreign technology

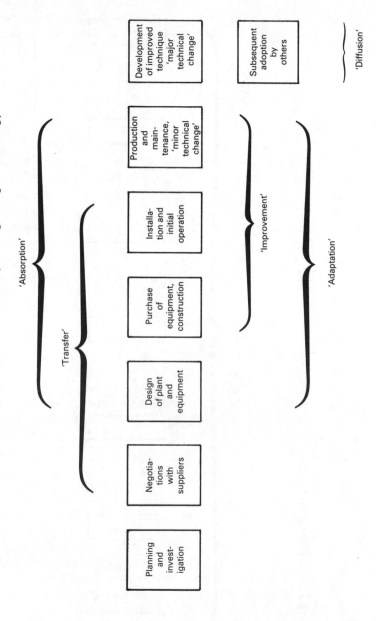

Figure 2.2: Flow diagram illustrating major decisions

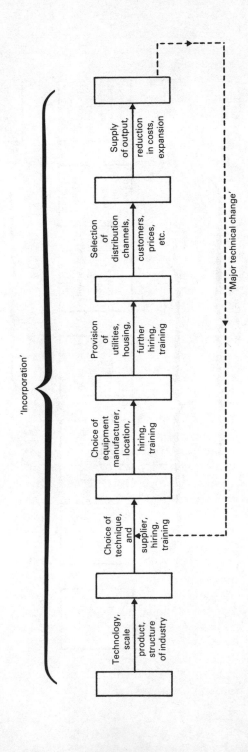

8

approached, the transfer is said to begin. Transfer is complete when the importing country has carried out all the activities necessary to commence production.

(3) Technology: A distinction will be made between techniques of production and technology. Technology is defined as the general knowledge or information that permits some tasks to be accomplished, some service rendered, or some products manufactured.

(4) Technique: Technique is defined as the knowledge necessary to design and operate the specific plant and equipment used in production.

(5) Technical Change: By technical change is meant any change in the technique of production of given commodities by specific plants, designed to reduce unit production costs or improve product quality.

(6,7) Direct and Indirect Technical Change: The former permits the production of given output levels at lower total costs and thereby reduced unit costs, and the latter permits the production of higher output levels from substantially unchanged plant facilities and complementary units.

(8,9) Major and Minor Technical Change: As in Hollander (1965), technical change is defined as 'major' if its development is considered 'difficult' to accomplish by men skilled in the pertinent arts before the development programme, while it is considered 'minor' if its development is judged to be relatively easy.

(10) Absorption: By absorption of technical know-how is meant the process by which imported technical knowledge is learned and embedded into local systems, in ways which allow it to be used in its original state and improved upon.

(11) Diffusion: Diffusion relates to international or inter-firm spread of production techniques or disembodied technical knowledge.

(12) Assimilation: Assimilation relates to a state of integration between an imported technique and its environment, such as integration of the production system with local supplies of inputs.

(13) Adaptation: Adaptation is considered to be technical change applied to imported techniques. This adaptation process can occur either during the process of transfer or

9

following its initial use. If it occurs after initial use, it is called improvement.

(14) Improvement: This is defined as better (marginal) performance of the firm in any of the activities of construction, installation, start-up, operation and maintenance of new and existing capital goods.

(15) Accumulation: This means that improved technology is absorbed and stored as types of physical and human capital in a plant.

THE CONCEPT OF THE COURSE OF ADOPTION AND DIFFUSION

Returning to Figure 2.1, it can be seen that no single term covers all the activities from beginning to end. This is not surprising, for the variety of activities is vast, extending over long periods of time and drawing upon many different individuals and organisations. Yet it would seem to be useful to have some way of consolidating all the activities in the sequence. The concept that will act as the unifying force is that of the 'course', in this case the course that, when followed, leads to the adoption and diffusion of the technology. The association is with the race course, over which a race is held, or an obstacle course. The course is so broad as to be all-encompassing; it extends through time, taking several years or even a few decades, to come to completion; it extends across space, from the point of import into the rest of the country; it extends through institutions, public and private, profit and non-profit, economic and political; and it extends from individual to individual, involving some at the very beginning, some later, some at the end, but hardly any single person throughout.

It is thus the course that has continuity and not any of its elements — temporal, geographical, institutional, human. It is the course that can be observed throughout. The scene shifts, actors emerge and exit, objectives and attitudes change, different events command attention, different outcomes result; it is only the course that is constantly present. To focus on a particular period of time is to miss important events that preceded or followed that period; to focus on one part of the country is to miss what occurred elsewhere; to focus on one institution or one set of individuals is to miss the contributions of others equally influential; even to focus on the technology itself is to miss the alterations that are obtained through adaptation, and possibly subsequent innovation. But to focus on the course of adoption and diffusion, the process of bringing the foreign technology into the body economic, is to include everything within the scope of one's inquiry.

Continuous courses are characterised by what happens regularly and in sequence at each point in a distinct series. Seven steps can be identified in the course of adopting an imported technology. Briefly stated, they are: determining the needs; surveying the alternative technologies and the alternative suppliers; choosing a particular combination of technology and supplier; absorbing the techniques in their first application in the importing country; disseminating the techniques throughout the economy; improving upon them; and developing new and superior techniques through research and development in the importing country itself.

From the definition of the 'course' it can readily be seen that it will extend over a long period of time. Each of the seven steps will consume appreciable resources, applied over weeks, months, even years. Planning takes time; choosing takes time; negotiating takes time; constructing takes time; operating takes time; and so on. Moreover, from the definition of the course it can readily be seen that different institutions and different individuals may make and carry out the decisions at different steps. In economic theory it is the entrepreneur who undertakes all these tasks; but in reality it may be one government ministry that plans, and another that chooses the technology and the supplier, and a third that negotiates, and a private firm that constructs the equipment embodying the technology, and another private firm that operates it, etc. Finally, from the definition of the course it can readily be imagined that it may not be run to completion. Because of a failure at one step, or because it is not seen to be in anyone's interest, the progression may be halted. Examples of arrested courses, particularly during the step of absorption, are all too common in the developing countries. Less common, although equally possible in principle, are examples of repeated courses, in which first one and then successive technologies are adopted into the importing country's economy. Such repetition seems likely to arise frequently in Korea's future.

That at least some courses of adoption and diffusion are

being carried to completion in Korea can be seen from observing changes in the direction of flow of resources. Typically, resources — technical knowledge, engineers, managers, capital equipment, specialised raw materials and spares — flow into the developing country during the initial period; money may flow in too, if the financing occurs abroad. As the developing country begins to adopt the imported technology, some of these flows may cease and may even reverse. Money will flow out in the form of licence fees, interest on borrowed funds, purchases of the specialised raw materials, salaries of the expatriate engineers and managers. The importing of the final products now manufactured in the new plants will cease, and the products manufactured in the new plants may even be exported themselves. With still further experience the developing country may start to supply to countries less developed than itself the very resources that it first imported; it may export technical knowledge, engineers, managers, capital equipment, specialised raw materials and spares of its own. It might be said that only when the direction of flow of resources has reversed can the developing country be considered to have followed the course through to completion. Certainly when the course of adoption and diffusion is arrested, the direction of flows of resources will be frozen: changes in the direction of flow of resources can therefore be a useful indicator of the success over the course.

MEASURES OF SUCCESS

As an indicator, change in the direction of the flow of resources is crude, being neither quantitative nor detailed; other indicators are needed which are more precise and more sensitive. Moreover, it would be surprising if a single measure were available for such a complex set of activities as those which comprise the course of adopting and diffusing a foreign technique: rather, one would expect to find many measures, some of which would apply to no more than a single step on the course, others of which might apply to two or three steps.

So far as the first three steps on the course are concerned — determining needs, examining alternative techniques and suppliers, and making a choice among them — the only quantitative measure that is feasible is the number of alternatives available. Measures of the precise terms on which alternatives are available will be difficult to assemble, since the only supplier whose terms are specified will be the one that is finally chosen.

The fourth step on the course — the absorption of the imported technology in its first application in industry — can be measured reasonably well. Four measures, two general and two limited, offer themselves. The general measures are easy in their construction, although not necessarily simple in their interpretation; they are the speed with which each of the activities involved in absorbing a technology is carried out and the percentage of the individuals carrying out each of the activities who are citizens of the importing country. The difficulty in interpreting these measures arises because an activity may be terminated prematurely or a foreigner replaced too soon, with a subsequent loss in efficiency or increase in cost. The opposite could be observed too, namely an activity extended too long in time or a foreigner held in his post longer than necessary, although these last phenomena would not be expected to occur often. So long as the activities are carried out effectively, and so long as the citizens of the importing country perform their duties adequately, the measures of speed of accomplishment and replacement of expatriates provide revealing measures of the degree of absorption.

The two limited measures of absorption both apply to the production of output only. To be sure, production of output is the rationale for the import of a technology, but it is only part of one step, albeit a long one, in the course of adoption. These two measures of absorption are the actual rate of output relative to the design rate and the cost of production. Since it is dimensionless, the rate of capacity utilisation is effective for comparisons across industries within a single country as well as across countries for a single industry.

Cost of production is a measure without these comparable features, and yet, for a single technology, it is probably the most revealing one to be conceived. Moreover, from it can be obtained, as by-products, partial measures of efficiency of use of each factor of production, i.e. productivities. The difficulties in the derivation of a measure of cost are chiefly informational.

Considering measures of diffusion, the most common and elegant — the sequential pattern, through time, of adoptions by firms in the industry — is not appropriate for any of our studies excepting possibly that of the textile industry. The other industries are all monopolised, so the first firm to incorporate the technique is the only one. To find measures of diffusion we must look backward to the suppliers of inputs for the operating firm or forward to the customers. Where suppliers of inputs are concerned, perhaps the most significant for the developing countries are the capital-goods manufacturers; the higher (in value terms) the fraction of the plant and equipment that local capital-goods manufacturers supply, the further has the technology diffused. But the same sort of measure could be applied to suppliers of other inputs — materials or energy, for example. If the base of the measure of diffusion is the total cost of all the inputs, then a more nearly complete measure of diffusion to suppliers would be the fraction of total cost of inputs supplied by domestic firms.

No such quantitative measure exists for diffusion to customers; where this phenomenon is concerned we will have to resort to description, from general observations on the flow of technical knowledge to users of the product, to universities and technical schools, and to government. This descriptive material will occupy parts of the four case studies on the absorption and diffusion of imported technology, one each in the petrochemical, textile industries, machinery and iron and steel.

The final measure worthy of mention is not quantitative but qualitative — the objectives of the participants. Technologies themselves, being impersonal, have no objectives, but all the individuals who evaluate and choose and employ and improve them have objectives of their own. As their objectives differ, so will their behaviour. Assuming rationality, the former can be inferred from the latter, perhaps with greater accuracy than objectives can be determined directly by questioning. But if the two sorts of information — one from inferences, the other from questions — are consistent, an accurate knowledge of objectives can have considerable explanatory power.

Particularly revealing would be the presence of conflict of objectives. It is not that all the participants' objectives can be expected to be in harmony but that in their attempts to secure their own aims they must oppose others in their attempts, and that in this opposition the course of absorption and diffusion may be hindered, interrupted or perverted. A conflict of objectives is unlikely to be desirable from the point of view of the successful completion of the course, but it is desirable from the point of view of gathering information on its progress.

In enumerating those indicators of the success with which the course of absorbing a foreign technology is followed we are presuming that all the data exist. But information is not readily at hand, and the search for it consumed much of the time spent in the study. Many different sources of data had to be utilised; many different persons approached; many different institutions involved. If there is any conclusion to be drawn from the inquiry it is certain to be that no single source is consistently better than any other source; no single individual more revealing than any other individual; no single institution more accessible, more replete with data, than any other institution. Of course, multiple sources are necessary if one is to be able to check the consistency of one's data; but even more importantly, multiple sources are indispensable if one is to find answers for all one's questions, if one is to fill in all the numbers in one's statistical series, if one is to determine the behaviour of all the participants on the course.

In the acquisition of data we were extremely fortunate. With the exception of the finer details of a technical nature, chiefly to do with equipment design and operating conditions for proprietary techniques, almost every other piece of information has been made available. Alternatives were defined, negotiating stances described, legal agreements revealed, objectives admitted, costs reported, responsibilities allocated; these sorts of information were at our disposal. Three factors seem nicely to explain the general availability of data; the first was the care with which the gathering of data was organised. In particular, permission was sought, from the relevant government ministries and private firms, to obtain all the information needed.

The second factor was the willingness of all the respondents, official and private, to answer questions and provide data. The honesty and candor of all the participants, inside government and outside, Korean and foreign, were greatly appreciated by the investigators. Perhaps because they were pleased by their accomplishments and proud of their roles, those who secured the adoption of the imported technology into the Korean economy were happy to share their experiences with us.

The third reason for the openness of the participants to inquiry seems to be a combination of curiosity as to the general course of adoption and diffusion of imported techniques and of interest in the results of our study. The curiosity and interest surpassed courtesy; the responses to our inquiries appeared to be quite genuine and full.

THEORY RELATING TO ADOPTION

We hoped that casting our net wide, over many individuals in many institutions, would enable us to gather enough data to comprehend all the activities included in the course of adoption and diffusion; thereby we hoped to avoid gaps in the description of events and in the evidence with which to confront our explicit hypotheses. But there are certain other hypotheses that are implicit and we should admit to these too. Perhaps the most important presupposition is that of the desirability of steady progress. To be successful, we suppose that the course of adoption and diffusion should move smoothly and rapidly to its completion. Such movement, swift and final, is presumed to be the ideal, against which actual progressions are to be compared. We did not ask questions such as: Would an erratic process, with starts, stops and shocks, produce a better result? Would it be better for the country if the course were to terminate short of completion? Would the failure to adopt one technology lead to subsequent technologies being more satisfactorily adopted? To the contrary, we presumed that the course of adoption and diffusion should, ideally, be steady and complete.

Another presupposition is that of comparability, or, more precisely, a lack of incomparability. Incomparability is not inherent in the quantitative measures employed; they are either dimensionless (e.g. a fraction of domestic engineers working on each stage) or time rates of change (e.g. a percentage reduction in average cost of production per year). Yet, incomparability can arise because of the intrusion of outside factors, beyond the control of those persons engaged in absorbing the imported technology. Such factors are scarcity of raw materials, deficiency of demand for outputs, shortage of spares. While not the fault of those whose responsibility it is to adopt the technology, those shortages may well delay or even prevent the course of adoption and diffusion from arrival to completion. Any comparison of, say, the speeds of absorption of two different technologies within a single country would be invalid if one technology were employed in a firm which suffered no shortages and the other technology in a firm which suffered shortages which it could not alleviate through its own efforts.

Another factor, which leads to incomparability between countries engaged in the same industry, or even between firms engaged in the same industry within a single country, is a different choice of technology. Imagine two countries at equivalent levels of development, one of which chooses an advanced and sophisticated technology and the other of which chooses an intermediate technology. The reasons for the different choices may be 'economic', in the sense that relative input prices differ; or they may be 'political', in the sense that one set of people find it in their own interests to choose an 'uneconomic' technology, say, the sophisticated one: whatever the reason, the country that has imported the sophisticated technology is likely to find it more difficult to absorb than it would have found the intermediate technology. The measures of the speed and efficiency of absorption will therefore indicate a lack of success, but it is not in the course of absorption that the lack of success arises but in the initial choice. The country might have been able to absorb the intermediate technology quite readily, had it been given the opportunity. Of course, it would be best analytically to limit comparisons to those cases in which technologies were chosen on 'economic' grounds, but such cases are difficult to isolate with assurance and are, for all too many countries, quite scarce. We were fortunate in the case of Korea that, with possibly one exception, all the technological choices we observed appeared to be made strictly on economic grounds.

Comparability can exist at two levels; at the level of external events, as presumed in the preceding paragraphs, and at the level of the processes that generate the events. The description of underlying processes, when carried out with a high degree of abstraction, is called theorising. Theorising in economics also involves defining the variables and parameters with precision and relating them, one to another, in a logically correct manner. Once formulated, theory can then be a guide to inquiry.

What theory is available to guide an inquiry into the adoption of sophisticated techniques in the economy of a developing country? The answer must be, unfortunately for our purposes, very little. And what theory there is is not well designed for our use. Reasons for theoretical inadequacy are not hard to find; the adoption of a foreign technique is a complex and extended activity, and the important variables do not lend themselves readily to precise definition and measurement. The following theory, or theories, may therefore seem fragmentary and inappropriate, but they are the best that are available.

The most nearly comprehensive theory, or non-theory, of the

course of adopting a technology is the neo-classical micro-economic theory of the firm, devised by Walras, Marshall, Hicks, Samuelson and their many followers. In its simplest version, the neo-classical theory of the firm assumes that knowledge is acquired instantaneously and without cost. Moreover, knowledge is defined so broadly as to include all the abilities and skills needed to assimilate an imported technology into the local environment. The local environment is represented in the theory solely by a different set of relative factor prices. By these assumptions any difficulties are effectively dispensed with, and the course of absorption offers no challenge at all.

Recent work in the theory of the firm relaxes the assumption of costless and timeless acquisition of knowledge, in recognition of the fact that resources are consumed in the process. The work, summarised and advanced in the survey by Kamien and Schwartz (1982), still assumes that the enterprise creating and adopting the new technology is a monolithic body responding perfectly to its single-minded owner/manager, and so neglects such factors encountered in developing countries as physical bottlenecks, government controls and regulations, conflicting objectives, unco-ordinated behaviour, risk and ignorance. Since these are the very factors that we are focusing on here, in other words since these are our variables not our parameters, we find the neo-classical microeconomic theory of the firm vacuous.

Putting neo-classical theory aside, the investigator seeking guidance is left with a rogue theory, usually called 'learning-by-doing'. The phenomenon was recognised by production engineers, observing that the labour cost per unit in the assembly of a single type of aircraft fell as the number of units increased. Work by economists began with that of Hirsch (1956) and Enos (1958); the term 'learning-by-doing' was invented, and utilised in the context of a macroeconomic model, by Arrow (1962). Subsequent work is summarised in Rosenberg (1976).

Applied to the production of a single commodity, endlessly repeated, the theory of 'learning-by-doing' states that the direct cost of manufacturing a unit of the good will decline as the experience gained increases. Experience is measured by the accumulated sum of all units previously manufactured; mathematically the relationship appears as

$$c_i = \alpha \sum_{x=0}^{i} x^{-\mu} \tag{1}$$

where c_i = average direct cost of producing the ith unit of
good x;

α = a scale parameter;

μ = a parameter, whose value lies in the range
$0 < \mu < 1$.

There is one thing to notice about this theory; it is mechanistic, saying nothing about how learning takes place. Learning proceeds automatically and costlessly with production. Although the assumption of costless learning is convenient for the development of the theory and for its econometric testing, it is by no means realistic, as economists such as Katz (1978) have argued and as our own case studies demonstrate.

In the case studies we will discover that learning takes many different forms, which should be separated one from another. To do so will require that equation (1) above be placed in an explicit time scale and that the output-dependent relationship be decomposed into as many terms as there are recognisable forms of learning.

In equation (1) the index i advances through time. Knowing the time path of output x(t), i and c_i can also be written as functions of time i(t) and $c_i(t)$. Let us define β as the average rate of decrease of direct cost attributable to all forms of learning. This new variable β is related to cumulative output x(t) via $c_i(t)$:

$$\beta = 1 - \left[1 - \frac{c_i(t)}{\alpha} \right]^{-t} = 1 - \left[1 - \left(\sum_{x=0}^{i(t)} x(t) \right)^{-\mu} \right]^{-t} \tag{2}$$

Imagine that there are n forms of learning: the contribution of all will be β. Given separability, the individual β_j — average rates of cost reduction — can be combined additively,

$$\beta = \beta_1 + \beta_2 + \dots \beta_j + \dots \beta_n \tag{3}$$

We will now identify forms of learning and try to relate them systematically to equation (2). The first, β_1, will be assigned to the cost reduction attributable to the exploitation of static economies of scale in successively larger plants. That a firm in a

19

developing country should initially install a small plant, so as to reduce the risks in adopting a new technology, is sensible: once the technology has been absorbed in the small plant, the accumulated experience can be applied to successively larger plants. If the firm collects and reveals its costs plant by plant, no difficulty arises, since the scale of neither has been altered. It is only if the firm aggregates its cost data across plants, presenting a single, average cost figure for each time period, that allowance for different scale plants must be made. Typically, firms reveal aggregate data only, augmented with the dates when new plants were constructed and these plants' design capacities.

Consider the design capacity of plants, producing a commodity sufficiently homogeneous as to be reported on a multi-plant basis, as $\hat{q}_k$, $k = 1, 2 \ldots m$, where $\hat{q}_k$ is the rate of output of the kth plant, so many physical units (say, metric tons) per year. Provided that the plant is operated exactly at design capacity throughout its life of t years, $\hat{q}_k$ is equal to cumulative output x in equation (1), divided by t:

$$\hat{q}_k = \frac{x^k}{t} \tag{3}$$

where k is placed as a superscript, so as to distinguish the kth plant from, in equation (1), the ith unit of output whose average cost is c_i.

Besides $\hat{q}_k$, the annual rate of output at design capacity, we shall need to define four other variables:

$\hat{C}_k$ = total expected cost of production in the kth plant at the design rate;

$\hat{c}_k$ = average expected cost of production in the kth plant at the design rate, often called 'standard cost',

$$\hat{c}_k = \frac{\hat{C}_k}{\hat{q}_k} \, ;$$

$\hat{c}$ = average expected cost per unit, a weighted average over all m plants,

$$\hat{c} = \frac{1}{\sum\limits_{k=1}^{m} \hat{q}_k} \left(\sum\limits_{k=1}^{m} q_k \, \hat{c}_k \right) \tag{4}$$

$\delta =$ the parameter representing static economies of scale, $0 < \delta \leq 1$.

Static economies of scale in the operation of different sized plants, say plants 1 and 2, are usually represented by the expression:

$$\frac{\hat{C}_2}{\hat{C}_1} = \left(\frac{\hat{q}_2}{\hat{q}_1}\right)^{\delta} \tag{5}$$

the smaller is the value of δ, the larger are the economies of scale. Specific values of δ, drawn mainly from engineering studies, are in the range of 0.6 to 0.9 for the production processes analysed in our case studies (Yotopoulos and Nugent, 1976, Table 9.1, pp. 152, 153).

It remains to relate the expression for the relative (total) costs of operating different sized plants, equation (5), to β_1, the average rate of reduction in cost from exploiting economies of scale in successively larger plants. Let the index k, in $\hat{q}_k$ and $\hat{C}_k$, run chronologically from the first plant constructed (k = 1) to subsequent ones; and let the same subscript apply to the time when the plant begins operation; e.g. the first plant with design capacity $\hat{q}_1$ begins operation at t_1. Assuming that any 'learning' that takes place in the operation of plant 1 between the date it is brought into operation, t_1, and the date the second plant is brought into operation, t_2, is also assimilated into design and operation of the second plant, the relation between the total operating costs of the first and second plants, both producing at design capacity, will be reflected exactly in equation (5). The difference between average costs of the two plants, at t_2, will be $\hat{c}_1(t_2) - \hat{c}(t_2)$, all of which is attributed to the addition of the second, larger-scale plant. Spread over the interval between the initial operation of the first and second plants $(t_2 - t_1)$, the contribution from economies of scale, β_1, averages

$$\beta_1(t_2) = \frac{1}{(t_2 - t_1)} \left(\frac{\hat{c}_1(t_2) - \hat{c}(t_2)}{\hat{c}_1(t_1)}\right) \tag{6}$$

where β_1 is measured at t_2. The total rate of cost reduction β, at t_2 will be

21

$$\beta(t_2) = \frac{1}{(t_2 - t_1)} \left(\frac{\hat{c}_1(t_1) - \hat{c}(t_2)}{\hat{c}_1(t_1)} \right) \tag{7}$$

and the difference between $\beta(t_2)$ and $\beta_1(t_2)$ will be the contribution of the other forms of learning.

Now imagine that both plants are operated until a further date t (t $>$ t_2), and that additional 'learning' of forms β_2, β_3 ... β_n takes place. The overall annual rate of reduction in average cost over the entire interval from the initial operation of the first plant, t_1, to t is defined as β, and the contribution of economies of scale is indicated by equation (6), with t substituted for t_2 in the left-hand side and for t_2 in the term $(t_2 - t_1)$ in the denominator of the right-hand side. Substituting total costs, $\hat{C}_k$, for average costs, $\hat{c}_k$, in equation (6), and then design capacities $\hat{q}_k$ for total costs, from equation (5), we can obtain the value for β_1, over the entire interval to t:

$$\beta_1(t) = \frac{1}{(t - t_1)} \frac{\hat{C}_1(t_2)}{\hat{C}_1(t_1)} \left\{ 1 - \frac{\hat{q}^1}{(\hat{q}_1 + \hat{q}_2)} \left[1 + \left(\frac{\hat{q}_2}{\hat{q}_1} \right)^{\delta} \right] \right\} \tag{8}$$

Examining equation (8) we observe that the expression is appropriate for a sequence of two plants; similar but increasingly more complicated expressions will apply for sequences of three, four or m plants. In all expressions there will appear the total cost of the first plant to be brought into operation, at its initial date, $\hat{C}_1(t_1)$, and at the dates of initial operation of subsequent plants, $\hat{C}_1(t_2)$, $\hat{C}_1(t_3)$ ... $\hat{C}_1(t_m)$. Also appearing in the expression for an arbitrary k plant will be total costs for the $(k - 1)$ plants previously constructed, at each date up to and including t_k. Finally, the design capacities of all plants and their dates of initial operation will be needed. These data — total costs at different dates, design capacities and dates of initial operation — are generally available, so β_1 can be calculated.

Because of the necessary inclusion of values of total cost, any calculated value of β_1 is not independent of the overall measure of cost reduction β. Such interdependence is not encountered in these additional forms of 'learning' we will attempt to measure, namely those attributable to saving on raw and processed materials (β_2), saving of energy (β_3), savings through the localisation of supply, particularly the supply of capital equipment (β_4) and quality improvements (β_5). There are, however, two final forms of 'learning' that are not independent of the previous form, learning that results in a reduction in the cost of labour (β_6) and learning that results in an ability to operate equipment in excess of design capacity, thereby reducing the average cost of capital (β_7). In the chemical process industries, the number of operating (as distinct from maintenance, clerical and managerial) personnel is usually fixed at the time of initial operation, according to the specification of the firm's insurers. 'Learning' only reduces labour costs in the other functions of maintenance, purchasing and marketing, and administration: the reduction in operating labour costs comes about through increases in the scale of operation, already considered, at least in part, in β_1, and to be considered below in β_7. In the mechanical process industries this interdependence between the requirements for operating labour and scale does not arise to such a great extent, and can be neglected without admitting too much inaccuracy.

The last form of 'learning', already labelled β_7 and not independent of β_1, is the ability to operate equipment in excess of its initial ceiling or design capacity. Sometimes this phenomenon is called dynamic economics of scale, so as to distinguish it from the static economies inherent in larger sized equipment, but the dividing line between the two is not clear. In making a distinction between cost reductions attributable to building a succession of larger-scale plants (our β_1) and cost reductions attributable to operating any single plant at a scale in excess of that for which it was designed (our β_7), and in measuring these separately, we are following the habit of engineers, while recognising, as do engineers and economists, that the separation is arbitrary. Occasionally a plant is 'over-designed', in which case β_1, for the sequence including that plant, would be understated and β_7 overstated; occasionally a plant, perhaps one incorporating an innovation, has a bottleneck that takes some time and effort to eliminate, in which case β_1 is overstated and β_7 understated.

This enumeration of forms of learning, together with our ways of measuring them, does not exhaust the possible economies that a swift and steady absorption of technology may generate. The treatment of absorption is further complicated by changes in the technique occurring on its transfer from the developed to the importing, underdeveloped country. For many reasons, the most familiar of which is the desire to exploit differences in relative input prices, the technique may be adapted before or during its transfer. There is a literature on adaptation prior to transfer, more, it must be admitted, on the need to generate techniques that are appropriate to the under-developed countries than on the experience of doing so. On adaptation during transfer, there is some case material, interest-ing in its own right. Work prior to 1974 is reviewed in Jenkins (1974); more recent evidence is provided in Stewart (1978) and Moxon (1979); but the results have not led to the formulation of a theory of the adaptation of techniques for developing coun-tries, nor to any ability on our part to measure its significance.

In the absence of an adequate theory relating to absorption some economists have focused on concepts and issues (Nelson, 1981). Those closest to us, mentioned in the first two sections of this chapter, are Westphal, Kim and Dahlman (1984). Drawing on Dahlman's and Westphal's earlier work, they provide a functional classification, as distinct from our chrono-logical classification in Figure 2.1, of the course of adoption and diffusion. Their functional classification is in terms of the activities of production, innovation and investment, the first having to do with operating productive facilities (our 'initial operation' and 'production'), the second with scanning improvements and carrying out expansion (our 'minor technical change' and a *second* wave or course of adoption) and the third with developing new technologies (our 'major technical change'). They call the abilities of a firm in a developing country to perform these three functions, one by one, its 'capability': 'capability' to follow subsequent courses of adoption is implied in our concept of success in a previous course. In detail, the (sub)functions that Westphal, Kim and Dahlman identify (see their Table 1, p. 7) are almost identical to the activities that we consider, so that there would be no signifi-cant difference in any investigation conducted by them and our case studies; differences would arise only in summarising results.

Other distinctions that persons enquiring into the transfer of technology to Korea have found fruitful are those between transfers stimulated by the users of the products produced as a result of the transfer and transfers initiated by the firm that adopts the technology (Kim, Lin-Su and Young-Bae Kim, forthcoming); and those between transfers involving, for the importing country, radically new technologies and those involv-ing standard technologies, measured along the dimensions of product and manufacturing process (Utterback and Kim, Lin-Su forthcoming). In our cases the reader will find an awareness of these distinctions.

THEORY RELATING TO DIFFUSION

Considering the diffusion of technology, the investigator finds more theory at his disposal. Where the diffusion of a technique within an industry comprised of many producers is concerned, the theory is eclectic, stemming from theories of the communication of infectious diseases. In epidemic theory, contact between infectious and susceptible persons leads to the latter acquiring a disease: the graph of the proportion of the population afflicted versus time takes on an 'S-shaped' or sigmoid pattern, rising first at an increasing rate, and then at a falling rate, towards some asymptote (Bailey, 1957).

The economic theory of the diffusion of a technique within a multi-firm industry implies a similar pattern of acceptances. The theory was first tested by Mansfield (1971) and Griliches (1971); theirs and subsequent studies have revealed a conformity to the general pattern of diffusion, with variations in the speed with which diffusion occurs and the fraction of the total number of firms that ultimately adopts the technique. With the exception of agriculture (Simmonds 1979), all these studies refer to the diffusion of techniques within the economies of the developed countries. There is no reason, however, to assume that the theory is not applicable to the developing countries, even though there is as yet no evidence to support it.

Serious criticisms of the theory of diffusion in its application to developing countries arise not from the lack of evidence but from the paucity of firms in most of their industries and from the need to spread knowledge of the technology throughout their economies. The theory may not be applicable because there are no similar firms for a technique to diffuse to; it may not be adequate because what diffusion is wanted is to firms in other industries, to government, to educational institutions and to the public at large. To be sure, these institutions do not use the technique in production; but they do use its product, or control its supply, or train its operators, or judge its usefulness. And a general theory of diffusion throughout an economy does not exist.

PREVIOUS CASE STUDIES OF ADOPTION AND DIFFUSION

If there were many studies of the adoption of sophisticated technologies in developing countries, this inquiry of ours would not
be necessary; but the literature is scanty. Most of the studies
that we have read were directed towards the adoption and
diffusion of new techniques in developed countries. We will
conclude this chapter with a listing of those that we drew upon
for ideas, so as to acknowledge our debt to others.

In many of the studies of the adoption of technology the term
is used in the same broad sense that we have defined, i.e. in the
sense of the acquisition of an entire body of knowledge
necessary to fulfil a specific task, usually the production of a
commodity. If the commodity is, say, diesel engines, then the
technology encompasses the knowledge required to comprehend the manufacturing technique; to design and construct the
plant and equipment that permit the technique to be employed;
to bring the plant into operation; to maintain efficient production; to train all the personnel involved; to make improvements
in the existing operations; and, possibly, to advance to superior
techniques. Such a broad definition of technology is the one
used by most individuals actively engaged in its transfer
(Veldhuis, 1979; Ramaer, 1979) and by those who have studied
its diffusion (Tilton, 1971; Nabseth and Ray, 1974; and Davies,
1979).

We are aware of only three case studies drawn from other
developing countries in which the technology as a whole is the
subject of enquiry; one has to do with cement (Doyle, 1965),
one with the refining of petroleum (Turner, 1977), and one with
the milling of flour (Gouverneur, 1971). Unfortunately, each is
taken from a different developing country — Indonesia, Nigeria
and Zaire respectively — so it is not possible to eliminate
geographical variability.

For Korea itself the World Bank has initiated studies of the
absorption of technology, studies which are contemporaneous
with and complement ours. Coverage in the World Bank's work
is broader, so that generalisations across industries are easier;
but almost necessarily, there is less technological detail. The
work is summarised in Westphal, Kim and Dahlman (1984); the
individual studies are described in Amsden and Kim, Lin-Su
(1982), and Kim, Lin-Su (1982).

We will refer to the World Bank's studies in our concluding

chapter. The intervening chapters begin (Chapter 3) with a resumé of the growth of the Korean economy over the last generation, first in general terms and second in terms of each of the industries — petrochemicals, textiles, machinery and iron and steel — from which our cases arose. In between the macroeconomic and the industrial material of Chapter 3 will be found a summary of the Korean government's policies towards the import of foreign technology and some overall measures of their magnitude and effects.

With Chapter 4 the case studies begin — petrochemicals, synthetic fibres (5), machinery (6) and iron and steel (7). Chapter 8 is a brief description of the experience of the Japanese in these industries, for it is from Japan that Korea has most frequently imported its technology. Chapter 9 concludes our study; there we collect the results of our cases, compare them with the results of others, and draw the implications for the developing countries as a whole.

3

Economic and Technological Background

For the case studies reported in Chapters 4 to 7 firms were selected from four industries: petrochemicals, textiles, machinery, and iron and steel. In this chapter some economic and technological background to those four industries is provided. The relation between the firms studied, on the one hand, and their industries, on the other, varies; in the case of iron and steel, the firm is coincidental with the modern portion of the industry. In the cases of petrochemicals and machinery, the firms are typical of those in their industries, whereas in the final case of textiles, the firm selected represented only the small portion which is vertically integrated, from the production of artificial fibre through the weaving and finishing of fabrics.

In furthering the industrialisation of Korea, the government is forging links between industries. Among our sample, the iron and steel industry now provides the major raw material to machinery producers, whose output in turn provides capital goods for the other three. Petrochemicals are intermediate goods providing the inputs to artificial fibre production. Textiles generate foreign exchange, which finances the import of capital goods, technology and raw materials for the other three.

The synchronisation of growth of Korean industries, as well as the forging of links between them, is beyond the scope of our inquiry. For studies of the planning and policy-making that have directed the growth of the industrial economy of Korea we refer readers to the works of foreign authors such as Adelman, ed. (1969), Adelman and Robinson (1978), Cole and Lyman (1971), Jones and Sa-Kong (1980) and Michell (1984), as well as various publications of the Korean Economic Planning Board, the Korean Development Institute (KDI), the Korean

Development Bank (KDB), the Korean Institute of Science and Technology (KIST), now the Korean Advanced Institute of Science and Technology (KAIST), and the Bank of Korea (BOK). We will draw upon the most recent of these organisations' publications for information on Korea's industrial performance in the last few years, since our concern has been primarily with the 20-year interval period encompassed by the Second through the Fifth Five-year Plans, 1967-86, during which the technologies that we studied have been chosen and absorbed.

Before we describe the background to the four industries we will look at the overall growth of the Korean economy and at its reliance upon foreign technology. This overview is chiefly statistical and uncritical; for greater penetration the reader is referred to the sources already cited.

GROWTH OF THE KOREAN ECONOMY

Since the beginning of the 1960s the economic life of Korea has undergone astonishing change. War-devastated only 30 years ago, Korea has metamorphosed into a modern industrial country, with an economy that ranks approximately eighteenth in the world in terms of its gross national product, and much higher still in terms of its rate of growth.

In 1962 the Republic of Korea promulgated its first economic development plan projecting rapid economic growth; five subsequent plans have been equally ambitious. Achievements have been impressive: since 1962 real GNP has already, as of 1985, risen seven times; by 1991, according to the figures in the first row of Table 3.1, it will have risen tenfold. The rate of growth of GNP, in constant prices, has exceeded 8 per cent on the average; GNP per capita has increased from US$477 in 1962 to $2,003 in 1985, and is expected to increase to $2,910 (all in constant US dollars at 1980 prices) at the end of the Sixth Five-year-Plan. Over the 20 years 1967-86 with which we are particularly concerned in this study of technological input, the rates of growth peaked during the interval of the Third Five-year Plan, suffered a decline during the world's recession of 1980-3, and recovered thereafter.

At least two important factors have contributed to the rapid growth of the economy, namely soaring exports and vigorous

Table 3.1: Macroeconomic indicators of the growth of the Korean economy, 1962-91

	Absolute Figures						
	1962	1966	1971	1976	1981	1986[a]	1991[a]
Gross National Product (millions of US dollars in 1980 prices)	12,607	18,060	28,717	36,509	61,010	93,300	130,000
Population (000 persons)	26,513	29,436	32,883	35,860	38,723	41,839	44,690
GNP per capita (US dollars in 1980 prices	477	613	873	1,297	1,575	2,331	2,910
	Rates of growth						
	1962-6	1967-71	1972-6	1976-81	1982-6[a]	1978-91[a]	
Gross National Product	7.8	9.7	10.1	5.6	7.6	7.0	
Population	2.7	2.2	1.7	1.55	1.55	1.30	
GNP per capita	5.0	7.3	8.2	4.0	5.9	5.6	

[a]planned.
Sources: 1962-81; Governments of the Republic of Korea, *The Fifth Five-Year Economic and Social Development Plan 1982-1986*, Seoul, 1982; and ibid., 1986-91; 'Report Presented to Consultative Meeting on Macroeconomic Policy for the Formulation of the Sixth Five Year Plan', Seoul: Economic Planning Board, 13 July 1985.

investment. Exports of commodities, in real terms, increased at an average rate of 23.2 per cent annually during the decade of most rapid growth, 1970-80. Throughout the years of the Fifth Plan 1981-6 an annual growth rate of exports of approximately 8.9 per cent will be attained; throughout the Sixth Plan one of 9.0 per cent is being projected. Only about 3.5 per cent of GNP was exported in 1962; by 1986 the percentage will have risen to 29, and by 1991 to 38 per cent.

From the point of view of a study of the import of modern technologies, most of which are applied to the production of intermediate rather than final goods, the growth of exports is a less significant factor than is the growth of investment. The modern technology is embodied in capital goods whose purchase and installation comprise investment; and many of the intermediate goods produced as a consequence of the investment are themselves allocated to further investment. It is therefore worth looking at the recent course of Korean investment in some detail.

Gross investment in 1962 and in the terminal year of each of the Five-year plans is shown, in constant prices, in Table 3.2. Breakdowns of investment into its components and into the sources of its finance are shown in Tables 3.3 and 3.4 respectively. The first fact to be observed is the relatively low rate of investment, as a fraction of GNP, during the 1960s. Throughout the decade, capital requirements of industry were kept minimal, as Korea allocated its resources to those of relatively low capital intensity. Education received a relatively large share of total investment, with effects that we shall observe in the case studies in Chapters 4 through 7.

In the Second, Third and Fourth Five-year Plans it was social overhead capital upon which increased emphasis was placed; in the Fifth it was housing; and in the Sixth, for which only the figure for aggregate investment is available, it will be manufacturing, particularly the machinery industries which produce capital goods. But more significant than shifts in the composition of investment, as revealed in Table 3.2, is its rapid overall growth. Throughout, gross investment has grown, and is planned to grow, more rapidly than GNP, roughly half as fast again. In the decade of the 1970s, when GNP was growing at an average annual rate of 8.0 per cent, fixed investment was growing at an annual average rate of 12.7 per cent, according to figures from the Economic Planning Board. In the five years of the Fifth Plan, the growth rates were expected to be 7.3 per cent and 10.2 per cent respectively; and over the equivalent period of the Sixth Plan, 7.0 per cent and 8.0 per cent respectively.

Table 3.2: Gross national product and its major components, selected years, 1962-91 (in billion won, at 1975 constant market prices)

	1962	1966	1971	1976	1981	1986	1991
Gross investment	295	824	1,955	3,112	4,892	6,800	9,950
Consumption	3,086	3,846	6,043	8,669	11,371	15,740	20,600
Exports	121	315	1,143	3,932	7,204	13,240	15,700
Imports	424	717	2,229	4,583	7,968	13,180	15,050
Statistical discrepancy	−31	58	38	203	−131	−	−
GNP	3,071	4,378	6,962	11,276	14,724	22,600	31,200

Sources: 1962-81; The Bank of Korea, *National Income in Korea* 1, Seoul: 1982. 1986, 1991; converted from data presented in the Report cited in footnote to Table 3.1, at the rate of 1,000 won = US$ 4.15.

Table 3.3: Composition of investment by sector during the First through Fifth Five-year Plans (percentages at current market prices)

	1962-6	1967-71	1972-6	1977[a]-81	1982[a]-6
Agriculture, forestry & fishery	11.4	7.1	9.3	10.4	8.7
Mining	1.1	} 24.2	0.9	1.6	0.7
Manufacturing	26.8		22.3	26.7	22.5
light			(8.6)	(9.5)	(7.4)
chemical					(4.9)
metal			(13.7)	(17.2)	(2.3)
machinery					(8.4)
Social overhead capital	31.6	} 35.8	41.4	} 40.7	34.1
electricity	(7.2)		(6.9)		(6.5)
comm. & transport	(22.9)		(18.9)		(23.5)
others	(1.5)		(15.8)		(4.1)
Other services	29.1	32.7	17.3	20.6	34.0
housing	(11.2)		(13.9)	(13.9)	(20.0)
education	} (17.9)		(2.5)	(3.9)	(5.0)
others			(0.9)	(2.8)	(9.0)
	100.0	100.0	100.0	100.0	100.0

[a]Planned.
Source: Government of Korea, Economic Planning Board, 1978.

Over the 30 years from 1962 to 1991, the ratio of gross investment to GNP will have risen from 0.10 to 0.32.

Looking at Table 3.4 we can observe the steady substitution of domestic for foreign savings in the financing of investment. During the five years of the First Plan, Korea had to raise half of its investment capital abroad; that fraction has fallen to one twelfth in the period of the current Plan (1982-6). Domestic savings are even expected to continue to grow faster than investment throughout the period of the next plan, 1987-91, enabling Korea to begin to reduce the amount of foreign loans outstanding. Borrowing abroad permitted rapid industrialisation in the early years. Accompanying the rapid industrialisation was a rapid rise in incomes; consumption patterns have been shown to change, however, so savings have accumulated. Thus, when a nation like Korea grows faster than its tastes change, it can initially afford to become indebted abroad.

Table 3.4: Sources of finance for investment, 1962-91 (at current market prices)

	1962-6		1967-71		1972-6		1977-81		1982-6	1987-91
	billion won	%	billion won	%	billion won	%	billion won	%	%	%
Gross investment	578	100.0	2,896	100.0	11,266	100.0	48,694	100.0	100.0	100.0
Domestic savings	267	46.2	1,759	60.7	8,643	76.7	38,704	79.5	91.7	101.3
private	226	39.2	1,126	38.9	6,909	61.3	29,025	59.6	n.a.	n.a.
government	40	7.0	632	21.8	1,735	15.4	9,678	19.9	n.a.	n.a
Foreign savings	281	48.6	1,129	39.0	2,665	23.7	10,083	20.7	8.3	−1.3
Statistical discrepancy	27	4.7	10	0.3	−42	−0.4	−93	−0.2	—	—

Source: Government of Korea, Economic Planning Board.

THE ESTABLISHMENT OF THE HEAVY AND CHEMICALS INDUSTRIES

As has already been noted, during the periods of the First and Second Five-year Plans, Korea built up substantial productive and export capacities in relatively labour-intensive light industries, such as textiles, wigs, rubber footwear and toys. Entering these activities relatively late in their product cycles, the Korean firms were none the less quick to apply the appropriate manufacturing techniques and to master the design and marketing skills needed for successful entry into international commerce.

But by the beginning of the 1970s the Korean government had realised that the country's interests might best be served by integrating backwards into heavy industry. The time seemed propitious: in 1971 Japan announced a new policy which was to reorientate the economy, away from 'pollution-prone' and 'natural-resource-consuming' heavy and chemical industries to 'clean' and 'brain-intensive' industries. On the international front, Japan was to stress a greater reliance than before on exports which would compete in quality, variety and sophisticated design, rather than in price.

Sensing that this was a trend which would be followed by many of the developed countries, Korea began to attract Japan's fading industries such as metal castings, bicycles, sewing machines, ceramics, leather products and the like. Furthermore, in 1972, at the start of the Third Five-year Plan, the Korean government decided to make the chemical process industries the focus of investment activity. Chemicals, petrochemicals and iron and steel were entered into. New to the country, the manufacture of these commodities required resources that were scarce in Korea, particularly foreign capital and technology. To acquire these resources on the very large scale that capital-intensive industries require, the government had to systematise entry into these industries and to shape an environment within which they could flourish. The first of these efforts resulted in guidelines to aspiring firms: first, suppliers of technology and of foreign loans would be selected in a competitive manner; second, projects funded by foreign loans should be internationally competitive in scale, and prices of their products must be in the neighbourhood of international prices; third, in order to assure sound financial structures, entrepreneurs undertaking heavy and chemical projects would be expected to provide capital for at least 40 per cent of the total investment. This was to be facilitated by improvement of the development financing systems, fostering the capital market and stronger savings promotion campaigns. Foreign capital was to be limited, in principle, to no more than 60 per cent of the total investment. Foreign funds were to be utilised primarily for the acquisition of capital goods and advanced technology not locally available, rather than as equity. Fourth, although priority was to be given to loans on favourable terms, *direct* foreign investments were to be encouraged, especially when they would help to secure dependable sources of raw materials, expand markets for products or provide advanced technology. In this case, however, the foreign share was expected, in principle, not to exceed 50 per cent; and fifth and finally, only the most modern techniques, those representing the current 'state of the art' in the developed countries, were to be chosen.

Various incentives were offered to Korean and foreign firms willing to invest in the new industries. A National Investment Fund was established whose purpose was to offer loans at less than market rates for the purchase of plant and equipment and even for the provision of working capital. These loans were extended for periods of longer than five years.

Tax privileges under the Foreign Capital Inducement Act and other tax laws were granted. Income and corporation taxes on enterprises with foreign capital were exempt, or were reduced in proportion to the percentage of the total equity which foreign investors held. In the event of capital expansion, both income and corporation taxes were also exempt or reduced in proportion to the foreign share. Such exemptions or reductions were to hold for five years from the initial reckoning date prescribed in the Income Tax Law and the Corporation Tax Law respectively, and to be extended at half the rate for the ensuing three years. Enterprises with foreign capital were also exempted from acquisition taxes from the date of registration, and from property taxes from the initial reckoning date prescribed in the respective tax laws. Even before the registration of an enterprise with foreign capital, it might be exempted from acquisition and property taxes on the property acquired for the original business purpose of the enterprise.

Creating an hospitable environment for the development of the heavy and chemical industries involved the Korean government in substantial investment in supporting facilities. Industrial sites were selected upon governmental initiative. In order to support construction of the selected industrial sites, the Industrial Site Development Promotion Law was enacted in 1973. The Gumi Electronics Industry Complex, the Changwon Machine Industry Base, the Yeocheon Chemical Industry Base and several others were constructed by the Industrial Sites Development Corporation and/or the Water Resource Development Corporation, both governmental organisations being established under the law. For these industrial complexes the government provided the infrastructure, such as harbour facilities, water supply systems, roads and so on.

THE ACQUISITION OF TECHNOLOGY

Under the four successive Five-year Development Plans 1962-81, foreign technology has been imported in company with foreign capital. Four laws govern the import of foreign technology into Korea: the Foreign Capital Inducement Law (1966), the Foreign Exchange Control Law, the Law Concerning Establishment of Free Export Districts and the Science and Technology Promotion Law. The Foreign Capital Inducement Law is the major policy instrument with respect to attracting both foreign capital and foreign technology. This law stipulates the criteria for screening technologies to be imported, and establishes priorities and procedures for their import. The various financial and administrative inducements given to suppliers of desirable foreign techniques are also based on this law. Preference ratings are assigned in the following order:

1. technology with high potential to expand export markets;
2. technology for manufacturing components and developing new processes for the capital goods industry;
3. technology which would be costly to develop domestically in time and expense; and
4. technology whose spill-over has the potential for cost reductions and productivity increases.

If a contract concerning the import of technology lacks any of the above provisions, it should be augmented by guarantees of the quality of the product by the supplier of the technology, and

36

for the provision of any improvements in the technology developed by the supplier during the contract period. The guidelines also limit payments for imported technology generally to 3 per cent of the net sales of the resulting product and the contract period for such payments to three years, except in cases where the payment takes the form of a lump sum. Finally, the guidelines require the deletion of any clause that denies the importer of the technology rights to acquire other products or technologies sold in competition to those of the supplier or that prevents the importer of the technology from exporting to foreign countries in which the supplier does not exercise exclusive selling rights. The application of these guidelines will be observed in each of the four case studies in the subsequent chapters.

Since April 1979, the regulations governing the import of foreign technology into Korea have been relaxed. Before, the Korean government's role was active; it took part in any negotiations involving large expenditures and it vetted all agreements for lesser sums. By 1979 the government had recognised that most large Korean firms had accumulated experience in screening the proposals of prospective suppliers and conducting negotiations with them. Moreover, the government had found it difficult to keep up with the pace at which new contracts were being submitted to it for approval; in the 15 years from 1962 to 1976 the government had to approve a total of 752 agreements; in the next three years it had to approve as many again (see Table 3.5). By the dual devices of raising the ceiling on the value of contracts needing approval and exempting an increasing number of industries from the regulations, the government has kept the approval scheme to manageable proportions.

How has Korea acquired 'Western' technologies? At what cost? What have been the nature and scope of the technologies imported? From where? These are questions that will be answered in detail in each of the case studies, but it might be useful to see what data are available for the Korean economy overall.

The first point is that technology is not a phenomenon that lends itself to measurement: we will not find aggregate statistics on technology imports. What we will find are statistics on items — e.g. numbers of contracts containing clauses related to the provision of technology, imports of capital goods in which tech-

Table 3.5: Number of technology contracts approved by the Korean government, by industry, 1962-84

Year Industry	1962-6	1967-71	1972-6	1977	1978	1979	1980	1981	1982	1983	1984	Total
Agriculture & horticulture	0	6	–	0	1	2	1	1	3	5	5	24
Food	2	6	7	0	1	9	5	15	21	20	24	110
Pulp & paper products	0	4	3	3	2	0	0	2	2	0	1	17
Fabrics, woven	5	2	10	2	2	1	4	4	4	3	2	39
Chemical fibres	2	5	14	1	6	12	3	6	23	27	29	128
Cement	1	11	9	3	10	7	9	5	9	6	10	80
Oil refining & chemicals	5	59	85	25	42	54	36	38	44	50	64	502
Pharmaceuticals	2	17	8	1	4	0	5	17	12	6	20	92
Metals	1	28	45	17	24	26	19	19	24	22	21	246
Electrical & electronics	5	65	84	32	51	42	47	33	60	80	77	576
Machinery	6	58	116	56	115	102	59	70	62	82	123	849
Ship-building	0	1	10	6	12	3	5	19	14	21	17	108
Communication	3	13	10	0	4	8	6	3	12	7	0	66
Electric power	0	2	7	8	11	6	4	8	8	4	4	62
Construction	1	3	4	3	4	2	8	4	6	9	7	51
Others	0	5	22	11	7	14	11	3	4	18	28	123
Total	33	285	434	168	296	288	222	247	308	360	432	3,073

Source: Government of Korea, Ministry of Science and Technology, 'Technology Imports Annual', 1984.

nologies are embedded, and investment and income flows to and from abroad — which are indicators of technology imports. Let us commence by addressing the first of the questions posed: how does Korea acquire 'Western' technologies? A comparison of imports of technology into the five newly-industrialised countries of Argentina, Brazil, India, Mexico and Korea carried out by the World Bank and reported in Westphal, Kim, Lin-Su and Dahlman (1984, Table 3, p. 26) reveals that Korea's outstanding characteristic is the large fraction of its total gross domestic investment represented by imported capital goods. In the interval from 1977 through 1979, over a quarter (27.2 per cent) of Korea's investment was comprised of imported capital goods, whereas the next highest figure (11.8 per cent) was that of Mexico. To interpret these statistics we will draw upon our own observations that, unlike the three Latin American countries in the sample, Korea has not relied upon direct foreign investment as a source of foreign technologies. Korea has hired technology but has not hired production; Korea has welcomed foreign techniques but has not encouraged foreign ownership. Together with the modern capital goods that Korea has imported in such large quantities has come the know-how to operate them; but in the main Korea has purchased both the capital goods and the know-how, rather than letting foreign firms possess them.

To support this generalisation we can draw upon some additional data provided by Westphal, Kim, Lin-Su and Dahlman (1984, Table 2, p. 24). During the period 1962-81 the total amount of foreign investment in assets embodying technology new to Korea was, in current prices, US$ 1,249 million. Over the same period the Koreans paid royalties on licences for new technology equal to US$ 565 million. If one assumes that all royalty payments were on a current basis, at the rate of 5 per cent of sales revenues, and that foreign investment in modern technologies was undertaken at a capital : output (revenue) ratio of 4:1 and with 50 per cent local participation, the average annual revenues attributable to technologies acquired through investment would have been $625 million and those attributable to technologies acquired through licences would have been $11,300 million. This works out to $18 of revenue generated by Korean firms utilising foreign (licensed) technology for each dollar generated by foreign firms operating in Korea under their own technology. (A check against this crude comparison can be made by utilising the figure for the total value-added 1962-81 in the production of goods utilising imported technology, reported by Westphal, Kim, Lin-Su and Dahlman as $156,000 million, in constant 1975 prices. Dividing this figure by 20, the number of years in the period 1962-81, one obtains an annual average value-added of $7,900 million. Since value-added in production is less than sales revenues, excluding as it does the value of purchased components, the total annual figure for value-added of $7,800 million does not seem out of line with the total annual figure for revenues, $625 million plus $11,300 million or $11,925 million.)

Since our thesis — that Korea imports foreign technology chiefly by means of licensing — is sustained by the evidence, we shall proceed to examine the sources, destinations and cost. Table 3.6 provides a summary of the sources and applications of technologies obtained over the 20 years 1962-81 through agreements with foreign suppliers. Nearly two-thirds of the agreements were approved in the last five years, during the Fourth Plan. Payments to foreigners for technology, mainly royalties on production but also including service, administrative, legal, travel and accommodation charges, are bunched even more towards the most recent years: data from the Economic Planning Board reveal that in the period of the First Five-year Plan, 1962-6, payments were $0.8 million; in the Second, $16.3 million; in the Third, $96.5 million; and in the Fourth, $451.9 million. Yearly figures for 1982 ($115.7 million), 1983 ($149.5 million) and 1984 ($213.2 million), the first three years of the Fifth Plan, show that payments are accelerating, and no remission is expected during the period of the Sixth Five-year Plan 1986-91.

From Table 3.6 one observes that Japan has been the leading supplier of foreign technology, Japanese firms being the signatories on 55 per cent of the total number of contracts approved by the Korean government. The United States is the second most important supplier, and Western European countries minor contributors. The machinery industry in Korea has initiated the largest number of contracts, 28 per cent of the total; with the electrical and electronics, and the oil and chemical industries, accounting for 19 per cent and 16 per cent respectively.

As to the content of the contracts providing for the import of technology, the bulk of them are concerned with know-how.

Table 3.6: Cumulative number of technology contracts approved by the Korean government, by country of supply, 1962-84

Industry	USA	Japan	West Germany	UK	France	Others	Total Numbers	Per cent of Total
Agriculture and horticulture	9	14	0	0	0	1	24	0.78
Food	34	48	1	4	4	9	110	3.58
Pulp & paper products	8	7	1	0	0	1	17	0.55
Fabrics, woven	18	11	2	1	1	6	39	1.27
Chemical fibres	27	57	5	3	24	12	128	4.17
Cement	12	53	4	5	3	3	80	2.60
Oil refining & chemicals	122	297	17	23	14	34	502	16.34
Pharmaceuticals	27	33	12	6	2	12	92	2.99
Metals	41	155	7	14	6	23	246	8.01
Electrical & electronics	151	355	21	4	8	37	576	18.74
Machinery	140	528	62	39	17	63	849	27.63
Ship-building	16	19	12	7	9	45	108	3.51
Communication	19	31	4	0	0	12	66	2.15
Electric power	36	14	4	0	2	6	62	2.02
Construction	19	16	0	4	1	11	51	1.66
Others	29	57	10	1	5	21	123	4.00
Total	708	1,700	162	111	96	296	3,073	100.00

Source: Government of Korea, Ministry of Science and Technology, 'Technology Imports Annual', 1984.

Scrutinising 1,720 contracts authorised between 1962 and 1980, the Economic Planning Board discovered that 50.2 per cent covered the provision of know-how only, and another 23.8 per cent licences and the know-how necessary to exploit them. Of the remaining contracts, 21.2 per cent granted licences only and 4.0 per cent permitted the use of trade-marks. In a subsequent scrutiny covering 603 contracts authorised in the three years 1981-3, the Korea Industrial Research Institute (KIRI), the umbrella association covering all corporate research institutes, found roughly similar percentages of 48.4 per cent, 37.2 per cent, 5.8 per cent and 8.6 per cent respectively. As to the form that the know-how took, of the 516 contracts in KIRI's sample calling for the provision of know-how (either alone or together with licences), 20 (3.8 per cent of the 516) provided it solely in the form of blueprints and designs, 24 (4.7 per cent in the form of visits from foreign consultants, and the remainder (472 or 91.5 per cent) in the composite forms of blueprints, operating manuals, consultation, training and supervision. Just as advanced technology has been acquired by Korea chiefly through the device of contracts with foreign suppliers, so most of those contracts have been broadly written so as to assure the provision of all the necessary knowledge, in its many modes.

The demand for foreign technology, in whatever form, reflects in part a recognition on the part of the Korean government and Korean firms that capital can be more easily raised for technically advanced projects. Foreign capital, particularly, is more readily available to those Korean firms which adopt the technology that is generating profits to producers in developed countries. Lenders appear to attribute lower risks to absorbing the most advanced technology than to developing a less-advanced but more readily absorbed technology, or even an already existing, obsolete technology.

The demand for foreign technology in Korea also may reflect a lack of confidence in domestic capacity for research and development. It appears on occasion that even simple techniques, well within the capability of Korean firms, are acquired from abroad. Perhaps the reason is to enhance public acceptance of the final products; perhaps to establish links with foreign suppliers; perhaps to gain experience in negotating with foreign firms and in securing approval from government ministries. This matter will be pursued in the case studies, but a few general answers can be attempted.

THE ADEQUACY OF RESEARCH AND DEVELOPMENT

Of the possible reasons for the import of technology, the only one that can be investigated on an aggregate basis with the data available is that of inadequate R & D. Even then most of the comparisons are with developed countries, from which Korea would be expected to emerge badly. The first bloc of figures in Table 3.7 makes this comparison, from which it is seen that Korea's total investment in R & D, as a fraction of GNP, runs between a third and a half that of the four major developed countries. The second bloc of figures in Table 3.7 reveals that this gap is expected to be almost completely eliminated by 1991, at the end of the Sixth Five-year Plan. Then it will be the

Table 3.7: Expenditures on research and development in some developed and developing countries

Country	Year	Total R&D Expenditure		Public R&D Expenditure	
		Relative to Korea in 1982 (Korea = 1)	As a % of GNP	Relative to Korea in 1982 (Korea = 1)	As a % of the government's total budget
USA	1982	93	2.5	142	4.9
Japan	1982	39	2.2	23	2.9
France	1980	38	1.8	30	6.2
West Germany	1981	44	2.7	19	4.8
Korea	1982	1	0.9	1	2.0
Korea	1984	2.0	1.5	n.a.	2.0
Korea	1986 (planned)	2.8	2.0	n.a.	n.a.
Korea	1991 (planned)	5.0	2.5	n.a.	n.a.
Korea	1978	0.5	0.6	n.a.	2.6
Argentina	1978	n.a.	−0.4	n.a.	n.a.
Brazil	1978	n.a.	0.6	n.a.	n.a.
India	1978	n.a.	0.6	n.a.	n.a.
Korea	1973	n.a.	0.4	n.a.	2.3
Argentina	1973	n.a.	0.3	n.a.	n.a.
Brazil	1973	n.a.	0.4	n.a.	n.a.
India	1973	n.a.	0.4	n.a.	n.a.
Mexico	1973	n.a.	0.2	n.a.	n.a.

Sources: Data for Korea and the developed countries; Government of Korea, Ministry of Science and Technology (MOST), *Annal on Science and Technology*, Seoul, 1979; and 'Report to the President by the Minister of Science and Technology', Report no. 84-2-1, Seoul: November 1984; data for developing countries; Westphal, Kim, Lin-Su and Dahlman (1984), Table 3, p. 26.

smaller size of the Korean economy, relative to those of the developed countries, that will restrict its expenditures in R & D.

When the basis of comparison is other developing countries, Korea may have become superior only after the recession of 1980-1, when both GNP and the fraction devoted to R & D resumed their rapid rise; even then we cannot be certain that those other developing countries listed in Table 3.7 have not raised their standards too.

Shifting our attention to more detailed figures, the ratios of expenditures on R & D to total revenues of Korean industries indicate that Korean firms currently spend from a third to a quarter as much as do firms in developed countries. The discrepancy is least for Japan, most for West Germany. As might be expected there is considerable variability industry-by-industry, Korean chemical firms incurring a much smaller ratio than their foreign counterparts and Korean general machinery firms a nearly equal ratio. Even more notable is the variation between different industries within Korea, electrical (and electronic) firms spending five-and-a-half times as much on R & D, per won of sales, as chemical firms.

Incomes of research workers in Korea are less than those in the developed countries, as are most of the other prices of resources necessary to undertake R & D. Additional data from KIRI provide estimates of national expenditure, in US dollars per research worker per year, for the three developed countries in Table 3.8, plus France and England; the results are, in descending order, $230,000 per year for West Germany (1979), $184,000 for France (1979), $89,000 for the USA (1979), $79,000 for Japan (1982) and $27,300 for the UK (1978) versus $24,300 for Korea (1983). The comparison in which Korea comes out in the best light is that of the fraction of the population engaged in R & D. Per 10,000 citizens, the figures for the developed countries listed in the same order and during the same years as above are 18, 14, 28, 28 and 15, versus eight for Korea. On this last basis, as on the first (namely, the fraction of GNP allocated to R & D, Table 3.7), the figure for Korea is currently about one-half to one-third that of the developed countries and, relative to theirs, is increasing rapidly. Some five years earlier, the newly industrialised countries in Westphal, Kim, Lin-Su and Dahlman's sample (1984, Table B, p. 26) recorded per 10,000 citizens, three scientists and engineers in R & D in Argentina (1978), two in Brazil (1978),

44

Table 3.8: Ratio of R&D expenditures to total sales of industrial firms in USA, Japan, West Germany and Korea, late 1970s and early 1980s

Late 1970s	USA (1975)	Japan (1970)	West Germany (1975)	Korea (1978)
Total manufacturing	3.1	1.6	3.3	0.75
Chemical industry	3.6	2.4	3.3	0.50
Electric machinery	7.1	3.7	6.7	1.34
Precision machinery	5.3	2.4	4.5	0.94
General machinery	4.1	1.6	3.1	0.94
Automobiles	3.5	2.2	2.9	0.94
Aeroplanes	13.8	—	44.0	—
Early 1980s	USA (1980)	Japan (1982)	West Germany (1979)	Korea (1983)
Total manufacturing	3.1	2.15	3.2	0.80
Chemical industry	3.5	3.05	4.4	0.56
Electric machinery	6.5	4.52	7.2	3.01
Precision machinery	6.0	3.97	4.7	1.28
General machinery	5.6	2.34	3.0	2.00
Automobiles	5.0	3.02	3.1	1.48
Aeroplanes	11.6	—	30.3	—

Source: Korea Industrial Research Institute (KIRI), 1985.

0.5 in India (1976), and 0.1 in Mexico (1974), versus four in Korea (also 1978), similar to the ranking in Table 3.7.

The preceding tables provide measures of the use and costs of technical resources by Korean R & D establishments, but say nothing about the outputs that these inputs provide. Of course, it is notoriously difficult to attribute specific outputs to such generalised inputs as R & D, but it is still worthwhile attempting the task. Three partial measures are available of the contribution of R & D to the output of Korean industries; the first of these gives the numbers of patents registered in Korea, in various years between 1960 and 1983, by both Koreans and foreigners: over the 23 years the number granted to foreigners has increased fairly steadily from 45 in 1960 to 2,203 in 1983, whereas those granted to Koreans have fluctuated between a low of 104 in 1977 to a high of 258 in 1979 without any noticeable trend (Government of Korea, Ministry of Science and Technology, *Science and Technology Annual*, Seoul: 1984). The second measure focuses not on quantity of output of R & D but on the quality of the products that are

45

manufactured in Korea with its assistance. In an inquiry into product quality conducted by the Korea Industrial Research Institute and published in *The Eleventh Study on Trends in Industrial Technology Development* (Seoul: KIRI, May 1985), KIRI asked the managers of the institutes it represents to categorise the products of their industries according to their international competitiveness. The distribution of answers along the product's dimensions of quality, design, durability, precision and practicability were remarkably similar — approximately 10 per cent of the products were classified as being at the highest level in the world, approximately 50 per cent as being at the same level as those of the developed countries, and approximately 40 per cent as being at the same level as those of the rest of the world. The final category, below the level of those of the rest of the world, contained very few observations, too few to be statistically significant.

The third partial measure of the contribution of R & D to Korea's development is that derived from econometric analyses of the sources of a country's economic growth, applying the methodology of E.F. Denison (Denison and Chung, 1976). The results for Korea are given in Table 3.9: a comparison with the USA and Japan reveals that Korea's growth has stemmed proportionally more from increases in labour supply and proportionally less from advances in technology. The relative contribution of technological advance to growth in Korea, *vis-à-vis* the two developed countries, corresponds closely to the

Table 3.9: Contributions of technological advance and other factors to the growth of GNP in the USA, Japan and Korea

Source of Growth	USA (1948-69) %	Japan (1953-72) %	Korea (1963-82) %
Labour	22.0	17.1	35.8
Capital	19.8	23.8	21.4
Economies of scale	10.5	22.0	18.0
Technological advance	29.8	22.4	11.8
Miscellaneous	17.7	14.7	13.0
Total	100.0	100.0	100.0

Sources: USA and Japan; Denison and Chung (1976). Korea; Government of Korea, Economic Planning Board, 'Report Presented to Consultative Meeting on Industrial Structure and Strategy of Technological Development for the Formulation of the Sixth Five Year Plan', Seoul: 12 July 1985 (in Korean).

relative fraction of its resources devoted to research and development (from Table 3.7).

This completes our presentation of data on the extent to which research and development are conducted in Korea. We will return to this topic in our concluding chapter, when we can augment this general material with results from our case studies.

Before we present our four case studies we wish to describe more generally the industries within which the firms selected for investigation operate. The order of description here will follow the order of the chapters; first petrochemicals, second textiles, third machinery and finally, iron and steel. The order is arbitrary; had we been proceeding in terms of chronology, or of the complexity of the technology, or of the degree of success in choosing and absorbing it, we might have followed a different order.

BACKGROUND OF THE PETROCHEMICAL INDUSTRY

Korea has chosen the petrochemical industry as one of the major industries in the promotion of its industrialisation. The petrochemical industry is a typical industry intensive in its use of capital, natural resources and technology, and may be disadvantageous to a country like Korea, which lacks all three. However, petrochemical products such as plastics, fibres, rubber and various chemicals are vital inputs to the fabricating industries from which so much of Korea's exports are derived, and so Korean planners considered it strategic for overall industrial development.

The petrochemical industry may be divided into three stages, in which the preceding supplies input to the succeeding: stage I, by which such basic materials as ethylene, propylene, benzene and butadiene are produced by distilling or cracking petroleum; stage II, by which such intermediate materials as low-density polyethylene (LDPE), high-density polyethylene (HDPE), polypropylene (PP), acrilonitrile monomer and caprolactum are produced by polymerising or cracking the basic materials; and stage III, by which the intermediate materials are processed into synthetic resins, synthetic fibres, synthetic rubber and other petrochemical products.

After the first oil refinery (the Korean Oil Corporation) was established as a joint venture by the Korean government and the Gulf Oil Company in 1964, the Korean government invited an American consulting firm, Arthur D. Little Co., and the Fluor Corporation to make marketing and engineering feasibility studies for a petrochemical industry in Korea. The first reports, submitted in 1966, indicated only a moderate increase in the demand for petrochemical products in the early 1970s and concluded that the domestic market was far too small to support plants capable of producing at low unit costs, relative to plants abroad.

However, the Korean government had made different forecasts, yielding higher estimates of demand for petrochemicals, high enough to make new plants economically feasible. These demand estimates suggested that a petrochemical complex changing 66,000 metric tons per year of ethylene would be appropriate. To exploit economies of large-scale production, the Korean government chose an even more ambitious programme for inclusion in the Second Five-year Economic Development Plan (1967-71), one which resulted in the petrochemical complex changing 150,000 MT/Y of ethylene and taking on the schematic form shown in Figure 3.1.

Korea's petrochemical industry is heavily dependent on foreign capital. All but one of the petrochemical plants in Figure 3.1 were built as joint ventures between a Korean firm and a major petrochemical company in the US or in Japan. The pattern was that the foreign firm invested half of the equity capital and provided the technology, whereas the local partner, usually established as a government firm, provided the other half of the equity capital, the site and most of the personnel. The bulk of funds necessary for the construction of the plants were secured from foreign investors in the form of long-term loans. All but one of the plants were designed by the foreign investor, utilising a modern process that had been well proven abroad. The choice of the technology was tied in with the choice of the foreign investor.

It took almost two years to complete the financial arrangements with foreign investors and international banks. During this period demand grew, justifying the ambitious programme. In 1970 the Korean government issued a Law for the Promotion of the Petrochemical Industry, which offered five years of full tax holiday. This incentive was supplemented by a guaranteed return on the invested capital. In 1975 the second petro-

Figure 3.1: Flow sheet for the Ulsan Petrochemical Complex

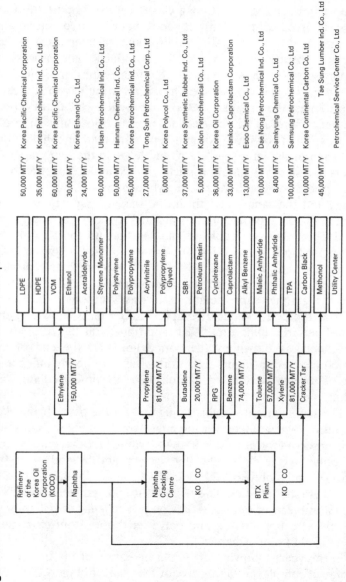

LDPE	50,000 MT/Y	Korea Pacific Chemical Corporation
HDPE	35,000 MT/Y	Korea Petrochemical Ind. Co., Ltd
VCM	60,000 MT/Y	Korea Pacific Chemical Corporation
Ethanol	30,000 MT/Y	Korea Ethanol Co., Ltd
Acetaldehyde	24,000 MT/Y	
Styrene Monomer	60,000 MT/Y	Ulsan Petrochemical Ind. Co., Ltd
Polystyrene	50,000 MT/Y	Hannam Chemical Ind. Co.
Polypropylene	45,000 MT/Y	Korea Petrochemical Ind. Co., Ltd
Acrylnitrile	27,000 MT/Y	Tong Suh Petrochemical Corp., Ltd
Polypropylene Glyeol	5,000 MT/Y	Korea Polyol Co., Ltd
SBR	37,000 MT/Y	Korea Synthetic Rubber Ind. Co., Ltd
Petroleum Resin	5,000 MT/Y	Kolon Petrochemical Co., Ltd
Cyclolrexane	36,000 MT/Y	Korea Oil Corporation
Caprolactam	33,000 MT/Y	Hankook Caprolactam Corporation
Alkyl Benzene	13,000 MT/Y	Esoo Chemical Co., Ltd
Maleic Anhydride	10,000 MT/Y	Dae Nong Petrochemical Ind. Co., Ltd
Phthalic Anhydride	8,400 MT/Y	Samkyung Chemical Co., Ltd
TPA	100,000 MT/Y	Samsung Petrochemical Co., Ltd
Carbon Black	10,000 MT/Y	Korea Continental Carbon Co. Ltd
Methonol	45,000 MT/Y	Tae Sung Lumber Ind. Co., Ltd
Utility Center		Petrochemical Service Center Co., Ltd

Source: *10 Year History of Petrochemical Industry in Korea, 1967-1976,* Seoul: Korea Petrochemical Industry Association, 1977, Figure 3.1, p. 104.

chemical complex at Yeocheon was authorised without these special incentives.

What stimulated the establishment of the petrochemical industry in Korea was the expansion in demand for intermediate and basic materials brought about by the expansion of production of final goods. It is thus a classic case of import substitution; of chemicals for identical goods manufactured abroad and incorporated into domestic production at a later stage — i.e. import substitution of intermediate products. The process of import substitution is revealed in the four graphs of Figure 3.2. The graphs form two pairs, each pair referring to a single class of products; the first pair to those petrochemicals that become synthetic fibres, and the second pair to those that become plastics. The two graphs forming a pair are read in conjunction, and each of the letters — 'a', 'b' and 'c' — in the two graphs — refers to a single chain of products. For example, the letter 'b' in the uppermost graph refers to nylon, a product of the third stage, and the same letter 'b' in the second graph refers to its intermediate, caprolactam, a product of the second stage. Looking at the top graph we can see that up to 1963 all the nylon used in Korea was imported as nylon itself; between 1963 (top graph) and 1977 (second graph) the intermediate caprolactam was imported and polymerised into nylon; and after 1967 (second graph), caprolactam itself was synthesised in Korea (first at the petrochemical complex in Ulsan, as shown by the solid line; and then, after 1981, additionally at the complex in Yeocheon, as shown by the dotted line). By the end of the period covered in Figure 3.2, Korea was very nearly independent of foreign sources of caprolactam, the intermediate, and nylon, the fibre.

The same pattern — substituting first for the petrochemical of the third stage and later for the intermediate of the second stage — is observed for polyester fibre ('a' in the first two graphs) and for polyethylene ('a' in the third graph, and 'a' and 'b' in the fourth), and polyvinyl-chloride (PVC — 'c' in the third and fourth graphs) plastics. The two plastics polyethylene and PVC are the subjects of our case study on petrochemicals (Chapter 4) and the two fibres nylon and polyester those of our case study on artificial fibres (Chapter 5).

In the years following the initial operation of the first petrochemical complex at Ulsan, five of the plants in Figure 3.1 were expanded; the polystyrene plant from 50,000 metric tons per

Figure 3.2: Rate of dependence on imports of petrochemical products, 1961-81

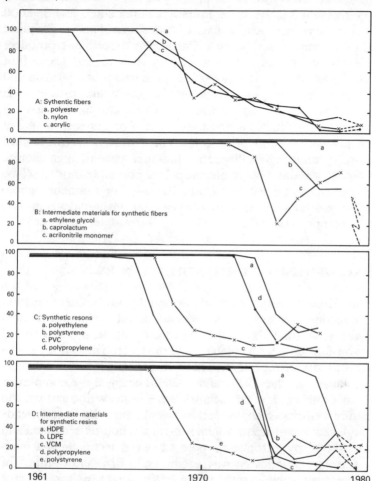

Source: Data from Korea's Synthetic Resins Association and Petrochemical Industry Association.

year to 100,000; the polypropylene plant from 45,000 to 80,000; the acrilonitrile plant from 27,000 to 77,000; the synthetic butadiene rubber (SBR) plant from 37,000 to 50,000; and the phthalic anhydride plant from 8,400 to 23,400. In addition, a new plant was built by Korea Synthetic Fibre Co. producing 70,000 metric tons per year of ortho-xylene and 30,000 metric tons per year of para-xylene.

The second petrochemical complex at Yeocheon, which began operation in 1981, produces a more limited range of products on a larger scale. From a naphtha cracker of 350,000 metric tons per year capacity, the Korea Pacific Chemical Corporation (now Hanyang Chemical Corporation) produces 100,000 metric tons per year of polyethylene, and 150,000 of VCM, as well as the first-stage products EDC (at 286,000 metric tons per year) chlorine (210,000) and caustic soda (231,000). The Keum Ho Chemical Corp. also has a first-stage plant making 42,000 metric tons per year of cumene, 30,000 of phenol and 18,000 of acetone. The Ho Nam Petrochemical Corp. produces 70,000 metric tons per year of high density polyethylene, 80,000 of polypropylene and 80,000 of ED/EG. Korea Synthetic Rubber Corp. has another synthetic rubber plant of 50,000 metric tons per year; and Hyundae a caprolactam plant of 100,000.

BACKGROUND OF THE TEXTILE INDUSTRY

The Korean textile industry entered into modern factory production systems in the second decade of the twentieth century. At that time cotton products, silk yarn and silk and rayon fabrics were available in the market. The output of the textile industry represented 12 to 16 per cent of all manufacturing output in the 1920s and 1930s. During the Korean War, most of the industrial facilities were destroyed, but by 1956 natural fabrics such as cotton, wool and silk were already produced in sufficient volume to satisfy domestic demand. In the 1960s, by introducing more advanced technology, a man-made fabric industry was established, first substituting for imports and subsequently, in the 1970s, producing for export.

Over the 20 years with which we are most concerned, the textile industry has exhibited high but fluctuating sales of growth of inputs, outputs and exports, as well, as we shall see in Chapter 5, of technical change. During the 1960s and 1970s, when the Korean economy was growing in real terms at approximately 9 per cent per annum (see Table 3.1), the textile industry's output was growing at approximately twice that rate. Until 1970, the growth of the textile industry was in parallel with that of manufacturing as a whole, and represented between 25 and 29 per cent of the total value-added; but in the 1970s, when the

52

government's attention turned to heavy industry, the rate of growth of the textile industry fell behind that of all manufacturing. By the early 1980s, the textile industry's portion of total value-added in manufacturing had dropped below 20 per cent, and its rate of growth to two-thirds that of all manufacturing.

This relative decline of Korea's textile industry should not be allowed to detract from its contribution to the earning of foreign exchange, one of Korea's scarcest resources. Throughout the 1960s and 1970s, exports of textile fibres and products averaged about 35 per cent of the total value of exports of industrial products. From a peak in 1972 of 45 per cent of the total, textile exports have fallen fairly steadily to 31 per cent in 1980, and approximately 26 per cent in 1984 and 1985.

Of equal substance in the background of the textile industry is the gradual substitution of synthetic for natural fibres. At the beginning of the period covered by our study, natural fibres constituted over 90 per cent of the total inputs by value to the textile industry; by 1965 the percentage had fallen to 80, and by 1970 to 60. Between 1971 and 1972 the proportion of natural fibres in the total switched from more than to less than half; in recent years it seems to have stabilised at just over 10 per cent. In 20 years, therefore, the balance swung completely from almost complete reliance upon natural fibres to almost complete reliance on synthetic.

In the preceding section on the background of the petro-chemical industry, we saw how Korea had displaced imports with domestic production. The growth of Korea's capacity to produce synthetic fibres is indicated in Table 3.10, in which separate figures are given for each of the major fibres — nylon, polyester, acrylic, polypropylene, viscose and acetate. The increases are impressive, particularly in nylon and polyester, the two fibres whose history is the subject of Chapter 5, and acrylic fibre.

Although numerous firms utilise artificial fibres in their production of textiles, few polymerise or synthesise the fibres themselves. Polypropylene, viscose and acetate fibres are produced by one firm each, and acrylic fibres by two. In the polymerisation of caprolactam to nylon and its subsequent spinning there are three firms — Kolon Industries, Tong Yang (Nylon) Company and Kohap Ltd — and in the polymerisation and spinning of polyester eight firms — the three nylon produ-

Table 3.10: Growth of production capacity of synthetic fibres, various years, 1962-85 (capacity[a], metric tons per day)

Fibre	1962	1964	1969	1974	1978	1985
Nylon	—	4	30	116	209	386
Polyester	—	—	26	291	461	600
Acrylic	—	—	39	159	276	459
Polypropylene	—	—	10	28	26	10
Viscose	—	—	15	32	32	109
Acetate	—	—	8	8	16	23
Total	—	4	128	634	1,030	1,587

[a]includes filament, staple and tow.
Source: 1962-78: *Handbook of chemical textures*, 1974 and 1979; 1985: Korea Fibres Association, *The chemical fibre*, June 1985.

cers, plus Dae Han Synthetic Fibre Co., Sunkyong Fibres Ltd, Sam Yang Co., Cheil Synthetic Textiles Co. and Jeil Synthetic Fibres Co. Of these companies, Kolon was the first to begin production of nylon (in 1963) and polyester (in 1971); Tong Yang followed closely, producing nylon in 1964; and the remainder entered several years later. In 1985 the shares of the firms in total nylon production capacity were Kolon (30 per cent), Tong Kang (50 per cent) and Kohap (20 per cent); and in polyester capacity Kolon (11.7 per cent), Tong Yang (11.3 per cent), Kohap (4.0 per cent), Dae Han (11.2 per cent), Sunkyong (25.4 per cent), Sam Yang (20.6 per cent), Cheil (15.1 per cent) and Jeil (0.5 per cent).

The final observation relates to the prices of synthetic fibres. In absolute terms the price of nylon has risen somewhat since polymerisation began in 1963, the index being 100 in that year, rising to 142 in 1965, falling to 77.5 in 1971, and rising again gradually over the interval to the present to approximately 200; polyester prices have shown the same behaviour. In real terms, deflated for the increase in the general price level, the prices of artificial fibres have fallen substantially. The wholesale price index for all commodities, again on the basis of 1963 = 100, stood in 1985 at approximately 1,450; whereas the prices of all commodities have risen 14 times in the intervening 22 years, those of artificial fibres have risen only two to three times. Relative to the price of other commodities, artificial fibres in Korea cost today only one-fifth to one-seventh what they did when production began. The international competitiveness of Korea's textile industry has been assisted by regular and sizeable reductions in the cost of what is now the major raw material.

BACKGROUND OF THE MACHINERY INDUSTRY

Compared to the petrochemical and artificial fibre industries, the machinery industry is exceedingly complex. The various names — 'machinery', 'metal-working', 'mechanical industry' — with their overlapping definitions are sufficient indication of the heterogeneity of processes and products. Fortunately the structure of Korea's machinery industry has already been carefully examined by the World Bank's team of Amsden and Westphal, Kim and Dahlman, whose work has been referred to earlier in this chapter.

For our purposes, it is only the part of the machinery industry involved in the manufacture of diesel engines, and particularly those of medium and large size, that is relevant. For these, the industrial structure was set by the Korean government in the common form of a private-firm monopoly, the firm that we examine in Chapter 6. In the Second Five-year Plan, 1967-71, the government had designated the machinery industry, together with steel and petrochemicals, as strategic to the country's industrialisation. Within the confines of the plan, and with the Ministry of Commerce and Industry as the implementing agency, the private firm was authorised to construct and operate a diesel engine plant, sufficient in scale to satisfy total domestic demand. Although it has never been verified, domestic demand was apparently defined to include not only the demand for diesel engines mounted in commercial vehicles — trucks and buses — but also a demand by the military forces for portable generators of electric power and, possibly, armoured cars and tanks.

Whatever the range of uses upon which the demand for medium and heavy engines was based, the estimates, and consequently the scale of the diesel engine plant, turned out to be excessively high: the plant has never been stretched to produce at its full capacity. The failure to utilise capacity cannot be assigned to the firm, which has mastered the production processes, nor to the Ministry of Commerce and Industry, which has ensured that competing imported engines are excluded from the country. Some blame can be attached to technical change, specifically to the attachment of turbochargers to smaller-size diesel engines, increasing their power output and enabling them to be substituted for medium-sized engines; but the major cause must be the original over-estimation of demand.

It is not just the demand for diesel engines that has not fully materialised but the demand for most of the products of the machinery industry. Although the Korean government has instituted various programmes since the Secnd Five-year Plan, most importantly the measures under the Heavy and Chemical Industrialisation Policy of January 1973, excess capacity in machine-building has persisted. Acknowledging this, and recognising that potential output is being lost, the government has chosen the machinery industry as its focus in the Sixth Five-year Plan, 1987-91.

BACKGROUND OF THE IRON AND STEEL INDUSTRY

The iron and steel industry, which supplies basic materials for the heavy and chemical industries, as well as for manufacturers, is regarded by the Koreans as one of the key industries in the Korean economy. They express it as being the stepping-stone in the establishment of a self-sufficient reproduction system. For this reason, the iron and steel industry was chosen as one case study. Furthermore, a study of the absorption and diffusion of the technology for iron and steel manufacture has implications for the rest of the Korean economy, as the industry is characterised by machinery and equipment which is very intensive in capital and which operates at an extremely large scale.

The iron and steel industry is composed of the following three processes, carried out in sequence: iron-making, steel-making and rolling. Historically iron-making technology was the first developed, followed by that of steel-making and rolling. The modern iron and steel industry has integrated the processes, combining them within a single plant.

Until 1973, the industry in Korea lacked iron-making capacity completely. Iron, in the forms of pig iron and scrap, had to be imported; subsequently it was converted into steel in open hearth and electric furnaces of relatively modern technology but small scale, and processed further in old-fashioned, non-continuous rolling mills. The products — steel sheets, bars, rods, wire and pipe — were uneven in quality and low in volume. In 1970 construction began on the first integrated iron and steel plant at Pohang, a small port on Korea's south-east coast. A public undertaking, it was established as Pohang Iron and Steel Ltd, but has familiarly been called POSCO which abbreviation we shall henceforth use. POSCO's initial capacity was 1,032,000 tons of crude steel per year, and was increased to 2,600,000 tons in May 1976: a survey of Korea's iron and steel industry in the following year, 1977, reported in Table 3.11, reveals its already dominant position. Second and third expansions, completed in 1978 and 1981 respectively, reasserted POSCO's dominance.

Since 1973, when POSCO's first blast furnace was topped, domestic demand for steel products has been met almost

Table 3.11: Capacity of steel facilities in Korea as of December 1977 (capacity in thousand tons)

Process		Number of companies	Capacity	Names of major companies
Iron-making	Iron-making	2	2,640	POSCO (2,515)
	Ferro-alloys	5	87	Sam Chok Industrial Co. (35.8)
Steel-making	Linz Donan converters	2	2,635	POSCO (2,600)
	Electric furnaces	14	1,880	Dong Kuk Steel Mill Co. (602)
	Open hearth furnaces	1	120	Inchon Iron & Steel Mill Co. (120)
	Total	17	4,635	
Continuous casting		5	2,140	POSCO (670); Dong Kuk Steel Mill Co. (570)
Rolling	Slabbing mill	1	1,651	POSCO
	Bar steels	83	2,694	Dong Kuk Steel Mill Co. (592) Inchon Iron & Steel Mill Co. (641)
	Sheets	7	3,017	POSCO (1,787); Union Steel Mfg Co. (720)
	Plates	3	486	POSCO (336)
	Others	7	140	—
	Total	101	7,988	

Source: POSCO.

entirely by domestic production. In 1977, for example, Korea supplied over 80 per cent of the country's demand for steel bars, sheets, strips and tubes out of domestic output; only rods and plate (60 per cent of each produced domestically) and nails (31 per cent) were produced in insufficient volumes. By 1979, when the second expansion became effective, Korea sharply increased its exports of pig iron and crude steel products. Throughout the 1980s exports of iron and steel have contributed approximately 10 per cent, by value, of Korea's total commodity exports.

From a dependence upon imported intermediates in the 1960s Korea has switched to a dependence upon imported raw materials. Of the major inputs to the industry — iron ore, bituminous coal, limestone and scrap — only limestone is available domestically in the quantity needed. Domestic supply of scrap fills about one-third of the need, while that of iron ore and coal fills less than one-tenth. Increasingly the acquisition of adequate supplies of raw materials on a long-term basis is occupying the attention of the nation.

4

Case Study: The Petrochemical Industry

INTRODUCTION

The first of the case studies of the adoption and absorption of imported technology has to do with the petrochemical industry. Chosen because of its reputation for being extremely capital-intensive and for employing a very sophisticated technology, the petrochemical industry in Korea has, none the less, exhibited an extraordinarily rapid rate of absorption of foreign techniques. As will be seen, the chief reasons for the rapid absorption arise within Korea itself, out of the inclination of the people, their educational system and their form of government.

In outline, this chapter will first deal very briefly with the sources of the information on the adoption and absorption of petrochemical techniques. After this, there will be a short section on the organisation of the Korean petrochemical industry, focusing on the effects that different forms of organisation exert upon the choice of technique and upon its subsequent absorption and diffusion: the issues raised will be illustrated by the experience of one petrochemical company. This same company will provide the data for the next two sections describing the technologies that have been imported, their absorption and the improvements that were subsequently made upon them. Following these lengthy sections will be a shorter one describing the diffusion of the imported technologies, and then another one, shorter still, mentioning some elements that are believed to be unique to Korea. Finally, there will be a conclusion in which the results are gathered together.

SOURCES OF INFORMATION

As described in Chapter 2 on methodology, our approach has been to study one company in depth and as many others as time and resources permitted superficially. The company chosen for detailed study was Hanyang Chemical Corporation, a wholly Korean-owned firm. Hanyang currently produces two major petrochemicals — polyethylene (or Polythene) and vinyl chloride monomer (VCM) — and will add other products in the future.

The information from Hanyang was supplemented by data gathered from other firms, both Korean and international, and from the authors' general knowledge. The source of most of the information on Hanyang was the company's employees; whenever other sources were drawn upon they will be cited: the source of information on other companies will also be cited whenever it seems necessary.

ESTABLISHMENT OF THE KOREAN PETROCHEMICAL INDUSTRY

The story of imported technology in the Korean petrochemical industry starts in 1960 with the establishment of the first modern chemical plant, the Chungju Fertiliser Company. Aided by the US Agency for International Development and staffed by most of Korea's university-trained chemical engineers, Chungju formed the nucleus of the modern chemical industry. Next, in 1967, came the first oil refinery, operated by the Korea Oil Corporation (KOCO) at Ulsan in south-eastern Korea.

Assured of a steady and reasonably cheap supply of raw materials, the government proceeded to insert a petrochemical 'core' in the Second Five-year Economic Development Plan. This 'core' emerged from a preliminary study commissioned by the US Agency for International Development and conducted by an American firm of management and engineering consultants, Arthur D. Little Inc.,[1] which had identified the products for which there were sufficient demands within Korea, estimated their costs of manufacture at different rates of output, and recommended minimal plant sizes for their production. The technological assumptions underlying the report were that the petrochemical plants should embody the current 'state of the art', without any attempt to incorporate substantial innovations; and that the processing facilities should all be located at an integrated complex adjacent to the petroleum refinery, so as to minimise the cost of transporting intermediates and provide a common source of inputs such as utilities and maintenance.

From alternative figures provided by Arthur D. Little (ibid., Tables II and III, pp. 254 and 255) it was apparent that there were substantial economies of scale in petrochemical manufacture; taking the two petrochemicals that Hanyang now produces, the comparison was as indicated in Table 4.1. To exploit these economies of large-scale production, the Korean government chose a more ambitious programme for inclusion in the Second Five-year Economic Development Plan, one which resulted in the petrochemical complex taking on the schematic form displayed in Chapter 3, Figure 3.1. (The two products — low-density polyethylene [LDPE] and VCM were assigned to Hanyang's predecessor, the Korean Pacific Chemical Corporation, whose origin and subsequent history will be discussed below.)

Having chosen the size, location and products for its petrochemical industry, the Korean government next decided who was to undertake manufacture and what technology they were to employ. In the petrochemical industry, as in the chemical industry from which many of its processes and know-how descend, these are closely inter-related matters. Frequently a manufacturing firm develops and employs its own technology. The basic characteristics of its chief chemical process are often patented, but the 'know-how' is always carefully guarded, so that potential competitors are denied its use. Sometimes the owner of a technique will license it to other firms, particularly if the technique is employed to produce a product long in use

Table 4.1: Comparison of unit costs of producing polyethylene and VCM at two different scales of operation, as of 1967

Product	Smaller scale		Larger scale	
	Capacity (MT/yr)	Unit cost (d/Kg)	Capacity (MT/yr)	Unit cost (d/Kg)
Polyethylene (low density)	20,000	38.4	60,000	28.8
Vinyl chloride monomer (VCM)	22,300	17.2	40,000	15.0

(Stobaugh, 1971, particularly p. 28); sometimes the owner will demand a proprietary interest in the venture. So, for the Korean government, selecting a technology was connected to selecting a foreign firm, and vice versa. Moreover, since all the current processes in the petrochemical industry were, in 1967, and are today extremely sophisticated technically, the universe of firms from which potential collaborators could be selected was comprised wholly of American, Western European and Japanese companies.

In the petrochemical industry, plants are also highly capital intensive.[2] Since, in 1967, Korea was severely constrained in its programme of industrialisation by a shortage of foreign capital, the government's selection was even more limited by the need to raise capital abroad. The choice of who was to undertake manufacture and what technology they were to employ was inseparable from who was to provide at least some of the capital. In the case of the petrochemical industry, the Korean government felt it could not initially afford complete national ownership: it was constrained to accepting participation by foreign firms.

When it became known that Korea intended to establish a petrochemical complex, foreign firms began to apply for permission to participate. Three — Union Carbide Company, Gulf Oil Co. and Dow Chemical Co. — offered to manufacture polyethylene; and four — Gulf Oil Co., Dow Chemical Co., Skelly Oil Co. and Union Oil Co. of California — VCM.[3] Rather than choosing from among this short list, the government decided to approach all the firms which owned polyethylene and VCM manufacturing processes, expanding their alternatives in the case of low-density polyethylene to 13[4] and in the case of VCM to six;[5] such information was gleaned from annual reports of plants under construction, together with their licensor, in the trade journal *Hydrocarbon processing*. The firms were asked to submit processing schemes and financing proposals, on the basis of sharing the equity ownership of the joint venture 50-50 with the Korean government. The Korean government put stress on the foreign firm's ability to raise capital, not only its own share of the equity but also the amount as debt, since the latter would constitute the major portion of the total capital investment.[6] From among the 13 firms competing for permission to manufacture polyethylene and the six to manufacture VCM, the Dow Chemical Co. was chosen, and as a consequence of that choice it was Dow's technology that was chosen.

While Dow was being chosen as the foreign partner in the joint venture, detailed negotiations continued over the financial and technological conditions of its contract. Representing the Korean government was the Chungju Fertiliser Company, which was then producing fertiliser in the country's two urea plants. Being the only modern chemical plant in the nation and employing the bulk of the nation's chemical engineers, the Chungju Fertiliser Co. was the only organisation which was capable of appreciating the technological complexities of the negotiations and of defending Korea's interests. Chungju also represented the government in the negotiations with other foreign companies participating in the Ulsan petrochemical complex and, under its subsequent name Korea General Chemical Corporation, in some of the negotiations preceding the establishment of the second petrochemical complex at Yeocheon.

So far as the results of the negotiations with Dow were concerned, the major clauses relating to the transfer of Dow's technology taken from the agreement signed by Dow Chemical N.V. and Chungju Fertiliser Corporation dated 8 November 1968, were as follows:

(1) The processes for the manufacture of LDPE and VCM were to be those employed in Dow's plant in Freeport, Texas;

(2) Dow was to grant an exclusive licence for their use in Korea to the joint venture, subject to the payment of a royalty and certain fees for technical assistance;

(3) In exchange, the joint venture was to receive all Dow's 'know-how', 'know-how' being defined as '... all inventions, trade secrets, technical information, data, shop practices, plans, drawings, blueprints, specifications and methods possessed by Dow on or prior to November 8, 1968 ...' The only limitation on the existing 'know-how' was that it should apply to plants of the capacity of those to be constructed at Ulsan: Dow did, at this time, operate considerably larger-scale plants as well.

(4) The joint venture would also receive in exchange all information on improvements made by Dow, and by its licencees: and would inform Dow of all improvements it made in the

course of carrying out its operations at Ulsan, and permit Dow to incorporate such improvements in any of its subsequent licences. The interchange of information on improvements was limited to those affecting the existing processes; if Dow decided that the improvements were so substantial as to represent, separately or in combination, a new process, or if their implementation cost more than US $200,000 to install, it could refuse to supply the information free of charge.

(5) Dow was to employ and train Korean engineers in numbers and to such an extent that they could completely and independently employ the technology: that is, that they could design the basic plant; design and procure its individual pieces of equipment; supervise the construction; test, start-up, operate and maintain the equipment; and carry out those activities that would lead to process and product improvements.

(6) Until the Korean engineers absorbed the technology, Dow would continue to provide engineers from among its own employees. Dow's minimum contribution was listed in terms of the number of men and their responsibilities. (The extent to which this has been necessary in, first, the Ulsan plant and, second, the Yeocheon plant, is described later.)

(7) All engineers, Korean and expatriate, would maintain the 'know-how' secret.

(8) It was anticipated that the plant would be operated as intensively as possible, supplying the Korean market. If domestic market demand was not sufficient to justify full capacity operation alone, however, rather than cut back on output the joint venture would sell the excess first to Dow, or, if Dow did not want it, in world markets at a price not below, or at terms not more favourable, than Dow itself conceded.

(9) Again to the greatest extent possible, domestically produced inputs would be substituted for imported inputs. (There will be more on this subject in the section on the diffusion of the technology.)

Such were the major clauses in the agreement in 1968 governing the establishment of the Ulsan plant. The terms in the agreement seven years later governing the establishment of the Yeocheon plant were identical with one exception: the design engineering services for the different LDPE process were not to be revealed by Dow to the Koreans. The reason for this exclusion was that the tubular process utilised in the Yeocheon plant did not belong to Dow itself but was licensed by that company from the German firm A.G. Für Olefin-polymerization (AGFO), which prohibited Dow from revealing its proprietary knowledge.

The importance of these clauses in affecting the rates of absorption and diffusion of the imported technology will be brought out in the concluding section to this chapter; in the next section the actual absorption of the technology will be discussed.

THE ABSORPTION OF IMPORTED TECHNOLOGY

First we will describe the initial absorption of technology at the Ulsan plant. The negotiations between the Korean government and Dow Chemical completed, the joint venture, then called the Korea Pacific Chemical Corporation (KPCC), could proceed, within the limits set by their agreement. Product type, plant location and capacity having been decided before the negotiations took place, and the processes to be employed and the contributions to be sought from Korean engineers having been decided in the course of the negotiations, little else of principle remained. Already, among its recommendation two years before, Arthur D. Little Inc. had included one that the processes adopted should represent the best current practice in the developed countries, and this recommendation had been adopted by the Korean government. Dow Chemical concurred, so it was not surprising that the processes chosen should be those employed by Dow elsewhere. These processes, one for low-density polyethylene and the other for VCM, are presented in Figures 4.1 and 4.2 respectively. They are typical petro-chemical processes — continuous; needing little attention when operating smoothly but great skill in starting-up, shutting-down, maintaining and compensating for unpredictable shocks; embodying much prior research, development and operating experience; and requiring great investment in capital and rela-tively little in labour, all of that technically trained and adept. Competing processes vary little, and hardly at all in their economic aspects. The possibilities of replacing those inputs

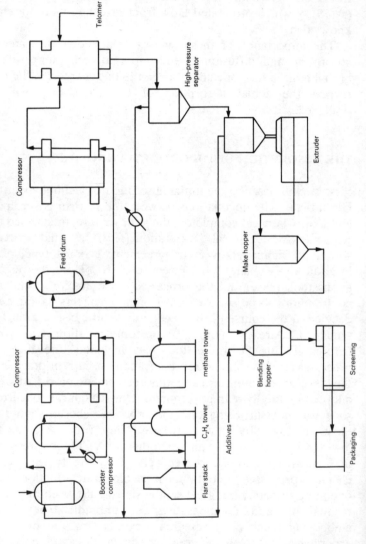

Figure 4.1: Flow sheet for the polyethylene manufacturing process

Figure 4.2: Flow sheet for the VCM manufacturing process

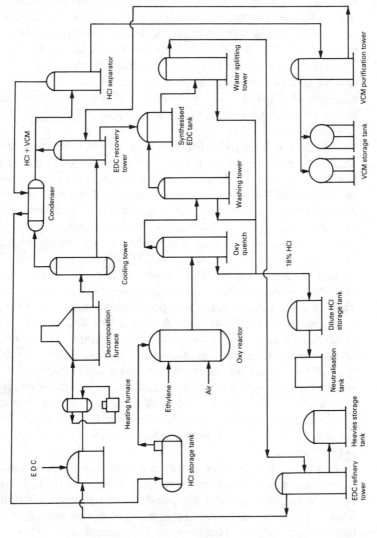

which are relatively scarce in the developing countries, particularly capital and technically proficient managers, with abundant inputs, particularly unskilled labour, seem to be negligible: the processing scheme and mode of operation in Hanyang's plant were identical to those in Dow's plants in the United States. The only observable differences were: (1) that the maintenance department of Hanyang was larger than its American counterpart, because independent maintenance contracting firms are only now, as of the time of writing, being established in Korea, and because refurbishing of worn-out parts is more profitable in Korea; and (2) that a larger inventory of spare parts was kept, because of delays in processing orders and receiving delivery from abroad.

If there was little room for manoeuvre in the choice of technique, there was more in the contributions to be sought from Korean engineers. The major contribution would be expected to come from those engineers employed by Hanyang, contributions ranging from supervision of conventional operations, the least demanding, to the conduct of research and development on new processes, the most demanding. As a matter of legal obligation, so as to preserve AGFO's monopoly over the tubular process for LDPE in the Yeocheon plant, Dow excluded Koreans from gaining knowledge of the crucial variables, those governing the polymerisation of ethylene at high pressures in a long tube. As a matter of economy, Dow maintained a single Technical Centre in Freeport, Texas, where all technical information generated in the design and operation of Dow's processes was collated. Engineers in the plants of Dow and in those in which it was engaged in joint ventures received monthly reports from the Centre summarising all new information acquired, and sent to it all they learned from their own activities; but only employees of Dow Chemical were employed at the Centre.

Again as a matter of economy, so as to secure advantages of large scale, research and development was, until 1978, carried out only in Dow's laboratories, and only by its own personnel. This policy has since been reversed. Upon the urging of the Korean government, Hanyang in 1978 decided to establish a research, development and technical service department to initiate work in these spheres.

Apart from these restricted areas, Korean engineers from Hanyang were expected to absorb the remaining petrochemical technology as rapidly as possible. As defined in the chapter on methodology, a technology consists of all knowledge utilised in, and stemming from, the design of a process, the design and procurement of the equipment that incorporates the process, the construction of the plant, the testing and start-up of the equipment, and its steady operation and improvement. The research and development that leads to a new, superior process might also be included, as being no different in nature, only in degree, from process or product improvement. Given these definitions, the participation of Korean engineers employed by Hanyang in its first petrochemical plant at Ulsan is summarised in the first column of Table 4.2. For comparison, the contribution of expatriate, chiefly American, engineers seconded by Dow Chemical is summarised in the second column.

Thus, by the end of, say, the first year of operation of the Ulsan plant, by which time only two expatriate engineers remained, the Korean engineers could be said to have absorbed those portions of the imported technology relating to the start-up, operation and maintenance of the petrochemical process, and to have made some small progress in absorbing the knowledge required for the prior stages of equipment design and procurement, and plant construction. Basic process design had not been encountered; nor, of course, had research and development. Finally, the ability to carry out improvements was being acquired.

The evidence for the rapid absorption of the operating stage of the imported technology is very strong. It comes from the production records of the Ulsan plant and reveals the quick attainment of a rate of output of polyethylene and the steady approach of the rate of VCM to the 'design capacity' of the processes, where 'design capacity' has the meaning and, consequently, the ambiguity assigned in the chapter on methodology. Monthly production figures for each product over the first two years of operation are given in Table 4.3, and yearly figures for subsequent years. Within one month for polyethylene and two months for VCM, rates of output nearly equal to design capacity had been achieved; in the following months, design capacity of polyethylene was exceeded.

Since March 1973, production at Ulsan has continued at high levels, consistently exceeding the initial design capacity in the polyethylene plant and, since 1976, in the VCM. The reasons for shortfalls are indicated at the foot of Table 4.3: only two —

Table 4.2: Participation of Korean and non-Korean engineers in various aspects of the imported petrochemical technology

Aspects of the technology	Number of engineers participating			
	In the first plant at Ulsan, 1970-7		In the second plant at Yeocheon, 1975-9	
	Korean	Non-Korean	Korean	Non-Korean
Basic design of plant (at Dow Technical Centre, Freeport, Texas)	0	6	4	4 (including project manager)
Application for foreign loans (in London)	0	3	1	2
Detailed design and procurement of equipment				
(a) core of process	0	1	0	1
(b) remainder	0	4	2	2
Construction				
(a) civil, plus housing	2	2 (inc. manager)	2	2 (inc. manager)
(b) underground piping and warehouse	several	1 (inc. manager)	many	1 (inc. manager)
(c) foundations, roads, office	several	1 (inc. manager)	4	1 (inc. manager)
(d) structure and erection	2	2 (inc. manager)	2	2 (inc. manager)
(e) commissioning	18	4 (inc. manager)	18	4 (inc. manager)
Start-up	18	9 (inc. 5 specialists)	18	9 (inc. 5 specialists)
Operation	42 (18 on days; remainder on shift)	4 (2 for about a year; 2 for 4 years)	42 (18 on days; remainder on shift)	4 (3 for 6 months to a year; one longer as liaison)
Maintenance	5	0[a]	5	0
Training	6 (in plant operations)	—	1 (in design and construction)	—
Research and development	0	all	several (at KPCC's research centre)	remainder

[a]There was to have been one expatriate maintenance manager, but, due to a strike in Dow's plants in the USA, the Korean maintenance leader took his place.

Source: Hanyang.

Table 4.3: Output of polyethylene and VCM from Hanyang's Ulsan plant, 1973-85

Month	Low density polyethylene (metric tons per month)		VCM (metric tons per month)	
	1973	1974	1973	1974
January	3,943	6,245	2,650	3,800[d]
February	5,245	4,462[a]	4,292	5,098
March	5,780	5,475	5,585	5,837
April	4,664	6,222	4,615	5,384
May	480[d]	6,628	5,028	5,498
June	2,826[d]	4,575[b]	4,588	4,764[b]
July	5,523	4,446[b]	5,986	5,048
August	5,768	6,372	5,440	5,684
September	5,817	6,262	3,398[a]	4,754[d]
October	5,721	6,410	5,008	3,639[c]
November	5,837	6,386	4,823	1,476[a]
December	4,784	6,311	4,778	4,259

Year	(metric tons)	(metric tons)
'Design capacity'	50,000	60,000
1973	56,431	56,185
1974	69,799	55,263
1975	60,945	57,309
1976	63,767	60,680
1977	65,460	61,804
1978	71,925	65,344
1979	67,902	60,008
1980	63,391[c]	48,869[c]
1981	57,332[c]	56,401[c]
1982	48,863[c]	51,695[c]
1983	57,806	59,440
1984	67,282	59,936
1985 (6 months)	29,330	26,858

[a]Annual shutdown for maintenance.
[b]Shortage of raw material from naphtha cracker.
[c]Insufficient market for output.
[d]Trouble with equipment.

an explosion in the polyethylene plant in May 1973, and the equipment failures in the VCM plant in January and September 1974 — can be assigned to the category of operating problems; the others were beyond the control of the plant's operators.

Equivalent data on the absorption of the imported technology at the Yeocheon plant are presented in the last two columns of Table 4.2, and in Table 4.4. Before any comparison is made, four major differences between the technologies at Ulsan and at Yeocheon must be remembered: first, the Yeocheon plant utilises a different process for the manufacture

Table 4.4: Output of polyethylene and VCM from Hanyang's Yeocheon plant, 1980-4

Month	LDPE (MT) 1980	VCM (MT) 1980
January	7,661	150
February	4,268	3,108
March	6,947	2,635
April	5,302	10,205
May	2,498	9,949
June	1,378	7,469
July	4,236	8,373
August	4,256	12,331
September	4,810	11,233
October	9,397	7,009
November	11,285	12,359
December	12,834	9,240
Year	(MT)	(MT)
'Design capacity'	100,000	150,000
1980	74,832[a]	94,061[a]
1981	63,332[a]	114,542[a]
1982	61,660[a]	106,906[a]
1983	90,216	119,864
1984	115,482	130,054

[a]Low volume due to insufficient market.

of polyethylene; second, the Yeocheon plant contains an ethylene dichloride (EDC) production unit of design capacity 286,000 metric tons per year, in which ethylene and chlorine are combined, whereas the Ulsan plant has none, having previously imported its EDC directly from Dow; third, all the units at the Yeocheon plant are larger in scale than those at Ulsan and fourth, the Yeocheon plant began operation six years after Ulsan. Hence, much of the experience gained in the construction, operation and improvement of the Ulsan plant was relevant to the Yeocheon plant. Moreover, most of the engineers in whom this experience resided were available for employment at the new plant; in fact, 21 were assigned to it.

In the light of these similarities and differences, a comparison can be made between the numbers of Korean engineers employed at the two plants in the development of the technology. The chief result derived from comparing the first two columns of Table 4.2 with the last two is that the Korean engineers employed by Hanyang entered into the deployment at an earlier stage — in the basic design — at the Yeocheon plant.

The detailed equipment design and procurement also saw their participation. Thereafter the differences between the two schemes become minor, with the exception of the shorter reliance upon Dow's engineers at the time of the initial operation and the fewer Korean engineers requiring training in Dow's American facilities. Under any definition, the absorption of the technology at Yeocheon was more thorough than at Ulsan, but several years had elapsed between the establishment of the two plants.

If a comparison between the employment of Korean engineers at the Ulsan and Yeocheon plants is valid, that between the speed with which output equal to design capacity was reached is questionable. Because the first three years of the latter plant's operation, 1980, 1981 and 1982 were marked by a recession in Korea as well as in world markets, there was not sufficient demand for the output of both plants; it was not until the year following the recession, 1983, that Hanyang was under any pressure to extract all the possible output from the Yeocheon plant. Excluding the three recession years suggests that the Yeocheon plant could have produced polyethylene at full capacity in two years, versus one year at Ulsan. Full capacity production of VCM had still not been reached at Yeocheon by 1984, after two untrammelled years, but then it had taken four years to achieve full capacity output at Ulsan. No conclusion about the relative rates of absorption can be drawn.

Were a third plant to follow on the first two, it could be designed, constructed and operated entirely by Koreans, so the authors were repeatedly told by their Korean informants. Not only did the Korean engineers believe that they had, as early as 1979, mastered all the technology underlying the Ulsan plant, but also they had the self-confidence necessary to consider undertaking such a task. The authors do not know if this confidence was shared by Dow's engineers, but on the basis of the evidence they were inclined to accept the Koreans' claim. To all intents and purposes, they would accept the thesis that today, 17 years after the initial agreement, Korean engineers have fully absorbed the technology that was transferred to them.

The ability to carry out improvements on an existing process requires, naturally, a prior knowledge of the process being currently carried out, the pieces of equipment that constitute it, and the mode of operation; it also requires both a fundamental knowledge of the principles of chemical engineering and a willingness, even an eagerness, to change. There is good evidence, from the information concerning the education, experience and talents of Korean engineers, to support the thesis that they have mastered the fundamental knowledge of their subject. The evidence regarding their ability to change is, however, conflicting: on the one hand, the remarks of expatriate engineers who have worked with them suggest that they lack the urge to change and the skill at improvisation, the tendency to 'fiddle', that stimulates improvement; on the other hand, there is evidence, from improvements actually obtained over the twelve years the Ulsan plant and the five years the Yeocheon plant have been in operation, to suggest that they do not lack this useful characteristic. The evidence of achievements is worth presenting in detail, so that some tentative conclusions can be drawn concerning the adaptability of Korean engineers and managers in the petrochemical industry.

IMPROVEMENT OF THE IMPORTED TECHNIQUES

Over the twelve-year period of successful operation of the Ulsan plant, there have been numerous cases of technological improvements, in which Korean engineers directly engaged in production have played the key role. Various incentive systems have been implemented to encourage their activities. Together, these events have made significant contributions to reductions in cost. Since the technology involved is extremely sophisticated, it is not to be expected that the engineers would accomplish a major technological change (or a change in the 'core' technology); all the technological changes accomplished in the plant have been related to peripheral equipment and complementary activities.

Many of the changes and improvements were motivated and propelled by the increases in oil prices that came late in 1973. This event led the company to launch the 'Raw Materials Savings Movement' and the 'Energy Conservation Movement'. These movements have been integrated as parts of the 'Saemaeul Movement', which is a government-sponsored, nationwide activity encouraging the whole nation to be more productive and constructive through maintaining new attitudes. Other areas of emphasis at Ulsan have been safety and loss prevention, anti-pollution and quality control.

In the following pages the improvements in technology at the Ulsan plant during the period 1971-7 are classified by their apparent motivation: raw materials savings and energy conservation. The more important improvements under each category will be described and evaluated in terms of their contribution to lower costs. Following this, a similar analysis will be conducted for the Yeocheon plant.

RAW MATERIALS SAVINGS AT THE ULSAN PLANT

Since the major raw materials are all petroleum derivatives, the impact of oil price rises in 1973 was great. The company immediately organised the Safety and Loss Prevention Council, which encouraged employees to propose ideas on technological improvements and provided full supports to implement the ideas. Excellent performances have been rewarded.

Recovery of ethylene at Ulsan's LDPE plant

When major parts of the LDPE plant, such as compressors, heat exchangers, the recycle system of the pressurised gas and the refinery system of recycled gas, were to be repaired or replaced, the original practice was to shut down the whole plant, to blow off the ethylene gas remaining in the process lines and equipment, and finally to burn off the gas in the incinerator. In 1974 the process was revised to recover the ethylene gas for reuse as raw material. As a result, the ratio for ethylene input weight to polyethylene output weight was steadily reduced from 1.543 in 1973 to 1.011 in 1978 (see Table 4.5). The net effect was a cost reduction of $600,000 per year in terms of 1976 prices; this was equivalent to a reduction in total manufacturing costs of 1.25 per cent.

Process change in the compressor system

The LDPE plant at Ulsan consists of two process lines in parallel. When the primary compressor was out of order, not only it and the hyper-compressors but also the polymerisation reactors had to be shut down. Subsequently a substantial volume of ethylene was wasted in the course of shutdown and start-up.

Early in 1974 the pipelines for ethylene were reconstructed in such a way that, when the primary compressor in one line was

75

Table 4.5: Productivity of raw materials in the Ulsan plant, 1973-84

Year	Polyethylene production index (tons of ethylene input per ton of LDPE output)	VCM production indices	
		(tons of ethylene input per ton of VCM output)	(tons of EDC input per ton of VCM output)
1973	1.054	0.242	0.900
1974	1.030	0.237	0.885
1975	1.035	0.229	0.869
1976	1.024	0.231	0.867
1977	1.020	0.230	0.875
1978	1.011	0.227	0.886[a]
1979	1.022	0.223	0.904
1980	1.027	0.221	0.923
1981	1.021	0.222	0.884
1982	1.017	0.223	0.891
1983	1.015	0.224	0.869
1984	1.013	0.222	0.892

[a] Increase due to replacement of catalyst.

out of order, the ethylene supply line was automatically connected to the primary compressor in the other process line. This arrangement enabled both the hyper-compressor and the reactor to continue their operations without interruption. Savings on ethylene amounted to $55,000 per year or approximately 0.11 per cent of total manufacturing costs.

Recovery of waste ethylene dichloride (EDC)

At Ulsan, until the EDC plant at Yeocheon came on steam in 1980, Hanyang imported all the EDC needed as input to the VCM plant from the USA. Since the imported EDC contained water and other light components as impurities, it was refined through two distillation towers. In this part of the process, a small amount of EDC is dissolved in water and drawn off.

The original practice was to dispose of the EDC-dissolved water as waste water. A recovery system for the EDC was designed and installed in the middle of 1974. Thereafter, the EDC-dissolved water was treated to recover the EDC and reuse it as raw material. This arrangement removed the cause of water pollution and contributed not only to reducing costs but also to savings on foreign currency. The amount saved was $350,000 per year, in 1976 prices, or 0.75 per cent of total manufacturing costs.

Loss prevention of additives

When LDPE of film grade (Grade No. 301 and Grade No. 303-02) is produced, some additives are added to the reaction mixture. The original design apparently required adding an excess amount. This excess, when oxidised by contact with air, became yellowish, discolouring the LDPE.

New facilities were installed to regulate the amount of additives and to protect the additives from exposure to air. Consequently, the loss of additives was minimised, the blending time reduced and the product quality increased. The contribution to reduction in costs amounted to $30,000 per year, in 1976 prices, or 0.06 per cent of total manufacturing costs.

Energy conservation at the Ulsan plant

As energy consumption in the plant is considerable, amounting to approximately 9 per cent of direct operating costs, the rise in the cost of fuel late in 1973 affected the cost of operations seriously. In November 1973, the company established a programme for energy conservation. Since then the programme has been in practice through the activities of the 'Energy Conservation Council'.

Typical data for energy consumption are given in Table 4.6. Steam and electricity are supplied by the Petrochemical Service Centre (PCSC) in the Ulsan complex, while naphtha is purchased from the petroleum refinery operated by Korea Oil Corporation. The PCSC supplies only high-pressure steam (HPS) at 16.5 Kg/cm^2. The medium-pressure steam (MPS) and the low-pressure steam (LPS) are obtained by depressurising the high-pressure steam. A portion of the condensate recovered is reused in the process and the remainder is returned to the PCSC.

Table 4.6: Energy consumption at the Ulsan plant, 1977

Source	Unit	Quantity	Cost
Steam (16.5 Kg/cm^2)	MT	120,000	$1,307,600
Electricity	KWH	76×10^6	$1,996,400
Naphtha	Bbl	11,000	$ 941,000
Condensate	MT	70,000	$ 14,530
Total			$4,259,530

Recovery of low-pressure steam (LPS) from high-pressure condensate (HPC)

According to the original design, the condensate from low-, medium- and high-pressure steams (to be called LPC, MPC and HPC, respectively, in the following) were all to be drawn into the storage drum (D-16 in the flow sheeet, Figure 4.3) through a common pipeline. Since, however, the LPC and MPC could not pass through the steam trap due to the high pressure in D-16, troubles were frequently encountered and, in addition, steam loss occurred through the condensate line.

A preliminary modification was made which involved draining the LPC and the MPC directly to the ground and generating LPS from the high-pressure condensate collected in D-16. The LPS was then vented out of the drum. This arrangement, however, caused a decrease in the condensate recovery efficiency and an increase in the heat loss due to the steam vent.

Finally in 1976, the HPC line was separated from the line for LPC and MPC. The former was then connected to the drum D-11, where it would generate LPS and LPC. The LPS produced here is now supplied to LPS process vessels while LPC and MPC are reused in the plant or returned to PCSC. In physical units, the savings in steam were 8,622 MT/year; the cost of the repair work was $3,200; and the reduction in cost, after allowing 20 per cent for depreciation and interest, was $93,360/year. As a percentage of total manufacturing costs in 1976 this saving represented 0.20.

Development of new product grades

The LDPE plant produces polyethylene of four different classes, characterised by their melt index and density. These are used for different purposes and are represented by their grade no.; i.e. 301 (heavy-duty film grade), 303 (thin-film grade), 722 (injection molding grade) and 960 (extrusion coating grade).

The original design specified operating the polymerisation reactor at low temperature and high pressure for products 303 and 960, but with low reaction temperature the product yields were poor. In 1974, a series of test runs was carried out at higher temperatures and lower pressures. The new products were confirmed to have nearly the same characteristics as the original ones, yet the power consumption and the steam consumption were reduced by virtue of the low pressure and the improved production yield, respectively. The new products

Figure 4.3: Flow sheet for the low-pressure steam recovery system

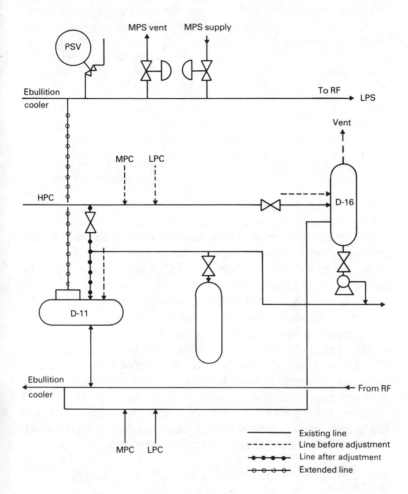

were designated by grade numbers 303-02 and 960-02, respectively, and are compared in Table 4.7.

Modification in the condensate line

In the VCM plant, the original design was to recover the HPC to produce LPS in the LPS generator. There, the HPC was heated by an additional supply of HPS. Since, however, the HPC from the reboilers of the distillation towers was drawn off at a relatively low temperature, it might have caused hammering

Table 4.7: Yields of polyethylene at the Ulsan plant under original and revised operating conditions

Polyethylene grade no.	Operating conditions			
	Original		Revised	
	303	960	303-02	960-02
Pressure (atm)	1,200	1,400	1,200	1,200
Yield	0.150	0.166	0.173	0.175
Savings on steam		4,100 MT/year $44,000/year		
Savings on electricity		69,331 KWH/year $1,800/year		
Reduction in cost		$45,800/year (0.10 per cent of total manufacturing costs)		

in the LPS generator; instead it was sent to the LPC line. It then followed that the lowered liquid-level of the LPS generator had to be controlled by supplying the LPC, which in turn had to be heated up by using the HPS.

It was noticed in 1974 that the temperature of HPC from the reboilers tended to increase if a certain period passed after the reboilers were cleaned. The optimum temperature was then determined, so that the HPC from the reboilers could be sent to the LPS generator without the phenomenon of hammering. This arrangement made it possible to cut off the LPC supply to the LPS generator and consequently to save the HPS. The savings on steam were 1.900 MT/year; the repair costs were $250; and the reduction in costs achieved was $20,650/year, approximately 0.04 per cent of total manufacturing costs.

Use of low-pressure steam (LPS) in ethylene dichloride (EDC) distillation tower

The EDC distillation tower in the VCM plant normally used HPS for its reboiler. Since the LPS generator was supplying the LPS in excess, especially in summer, the steam supply for the reboiler was replaced by excess LPS during the three summer months. The savings on steam were 1,382 MT/year; the repair costs were $210; and the reduction in cost was $15,000/year, or 0.03 per cent of total manufacturing costs.

Steam savings in the EDC purification system

In the oxi-reactor of the VCM plant, ethylene dichloride (EDC) is synthesised from ethylene, oxygen and by-product hydrogen chloride. Before being recycled to the decomposition furnace, the EDC is treated in two separate distillation towers (T-116 and T-120 in Figure 4.4) to remove successively the lighter and heavier components. These units consume more than one half of the total steam required in the VCM plant.

Investigations were carried out for the purpose of reducing the reflux rates and thereby the steam consumption in the reboilers. After 1974, it was possible to achieve substantial reductions of the reflux rates in both towers without sacrificing the purification requirements, as indicated in Table 4.8.

Steam savings in EDC separator

The product stream from the decomposition furnace is treated in a distillation tower to separate the unreacted EDC from VCM and hydrogen chloride. Here also the reflux rate was adjusted successfully to a lower value; i.e. from 2,558.4 Kg/H to 2,184 Kg/H (a 14.6 per cent reduction). The savings on steam were 485.5 MT/year and the reduction cost was $5,300/year, one-hundredth of a per cent of total costs.

The by-passing of one distillation tower in normal operation

In the final stage of the VCM plant, the vinyl chloride monomer is treated in two separate distillation towers, in which hydrogen chloride and lighter components are removed successively. In the second half of 1974, operating conditions for the first of the two distillation towers were improved systematically so that all the lighter components could be satisfactorily removed there. Consequently, the second tower in the sequence could be by-passed in normal operation. Since then the steam consumption in the second tower has been entirely saved. The savings on steam were 4,490 MT/year; the expense of constructing the by-pass line was $170; and the reduction in cost was $48,900/year, or 0.10 per cent of total manufacturing costs.

Improvement in operating conditions for the VCM purification tower

The VCM from the distillation tower in the preceding case is again treated in the next distillation tower, T-260, to remove the heavier components. The waste heat of the unreacted EDC is

Figure 4.4: Flow sheet around the distillation towers in Ulsan's EDC purification system

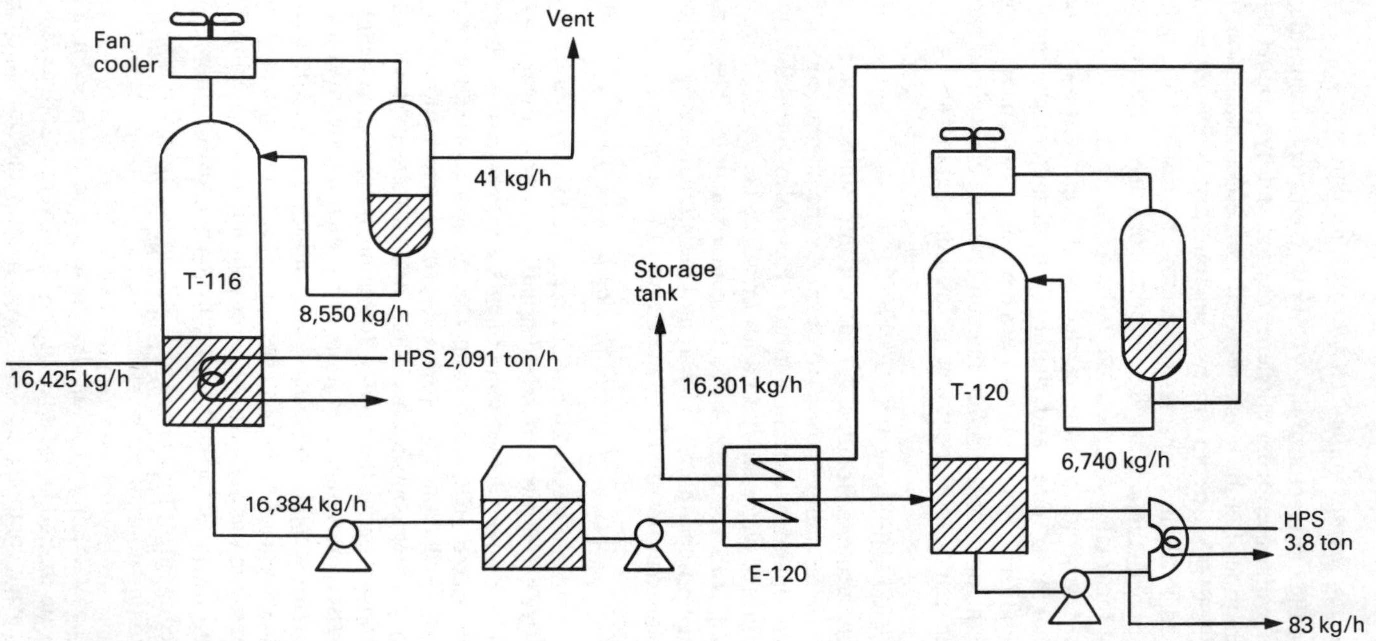

HPS 3.8 ton

83 kg/h

6,740 kg/h

T-120

16,301 kg/h

E-120

Storage tank

Vent

41 kg/h

HPS 2,091 ton/h

8,550 kg/h

16,384 kg/h

T-116

Fan cooler

16,425 kg/h

Table 4.8: Improvements in reflux rates at the distillation towers in Ulsan's EDC purification system

Distillation tower		T-116	T-120	Total
Reflux rate	Original	16,425	9,622.4	
	Adjusted	8,550	6,740	
Kg/H	% reduction	48	30	
Steam saved, MT/year		10,486	3,841	
Reduction in cost $/year		114,200	41,800	156,000 (0.32 per cent of total manufacturing costs)

recovered by a heat exchanger and used as the heat source for a subsequent tower, T-260. There is also a reboiler to supplement the heat requirement.

After the performance of the previous stage was improved, the optimum condition for the reflux rate of tower T-260 was studied, so as eventually to reduce the reflux rate from 12,925 Kg/H to 8,897 Kg/H (31.2 per cent reduction) while maintaining product quality. By virtue of this adjustment, the supplementary reboiler was eliminated from operation. The savings on steam were 4,668 MT/year and the reduction in cost $50,800/year, or 0.10 per cent of total manufacturing costs.

Improvements in the tarpot system

In the tarpot system (see Figure 4.5), chlorine is added to the unreacted EDC mixture to convert the heavier components to saturated chloride compounds (reactions occur in tower D-330), which are then removed in the distillation tower (T-330). The EDC mixture is subsequently treated in the tower (T-340) to remove the remaining chlorine. The purified EDC stream is drawn into the storage tank while a partial fraction is recycled to the tower T-330.

Studies were carried out to find the optimum reflux rate for the tower T-330, as well as to determine the minimum steam requirement for the tower T-340, in the light of the fact that the boiling point of chlorine is −34°C. The reflux rate to T-330 was successfully reduced from 1,188.3 Kg/H to 466 Kg/H (a 61 per cent reduction). The steam supply to T-340 was adjusted from 306.8 Kg/H to 59 Kg/H (an 81 per cent reduction) and yet the requirement of chlorine removal was satisfied. The savings on steam were, for T-116, 961.5 MT/year, and for T-120, 1,962.5 MT/year; the reductions in cost were, for T-116, $10,500/year, and for T-120 $21,400/year, a sum of $31,900/year (0.06 per cent of total manufacturing costs).

There have been additional cases of minor technological improvements, accompanied by energy savings. All of the minor cases, plus the eight major ones already identified, have contributed to reducing the 'energy unit ratio', which is defined as the ratio of the total amount of energy consumed (Kcal) to the total weight of product (Kg). The overall effects of the energy conservation movement from its initiation in 1973 till mid-1976 are summarised in Table 4.9.

In comparison, contemporary 'energy unit ratios' for the LDPE plants of Asahi Dow in Japan and the US Dow were reported as 1,498 Kcal/Kg and 2,071 Kcal/Kg, respectively. These values are 19.6 per cent and 65.3 per cent higher, respectively, than the 1,253 Kcal/Kg of the Ulsan plant of KPCC. The contemporary 'energy unit ratio' for the VCM plant of Toyo Soda in Japan was reported to be 3,194 Kcal/Kg,

Table 4.9: Improvements in the energy unit ratio at the Ulsan plant, 1973-6 (in 1976 prices)

		Period	'Design value'	1973 (before improvements)	1974.7- 1975.6	1975.7- 1976.6
LDPE plant	Energy unit ratio (Kcal/Kg)	Production (MT/year)	50,000	56,431	71,762	74,846
		Steam	1,444	623	537	546
		Electricity	1,767	927	771	740
		Condensate	−113	−20	−29	−33
		Total	3,098	1,530	1,279	1,253
		% reduction (vis-à-vis 1973)		−	16.4	18.1
		Reduction in cost ($/year)		−	436,300	516,300
VCM plant	Energy unit ratio (Kcal/Kg)	Production (MT/year)	60,000	56,185	49,126	64,250
		Steam	2,579	1,282	940	726
		Electricity	455	232	229	216
		Naphtha	3,025	2,035	2,057	2,013
		Condensate	−202	−44	−51	−43
		Total	5,857	3,505	3,175	2,912
		% reduction (vis-à-vis 1973)		−	9.4	16.9
		Reduction in cost ($/year)		−	246,600	570,700
Total reduction in cost ($/year) (as a percentage of 1973 manufacturing costs)				−	682,900 1.41	1,087,000 2.25

which is 9.7 per cent higher than 2,912 Kcal/Kg of the Ulsan plant of Hanyang.

The total energy savings for the one-year period between July 1975 and June 1976 amounted to $1,087,000. The standard yearly cost of production in 1976 was $48,363,000. This implies that improvements in energy conservation reduced production costs by 2.25 per cent; this is equivalent to 25 per cent of the total energy consumed.

Raw material and energy savings after the inauguration of the Yeocheon plant

The savings in raw materials and energy at the Yeocheon plant of Hanyang itself have not been so dramatic as those at the Ulsan plant, as Table 4.10 indicates. It is only the consumption of EDC, per unit of output of VCM, that has fallen noticeably, and that fall is more a consequence of the approach to full capacity operation (see Table 4.4) than it is to improvements in process design and control.

The emphasis at Yeocheon has been on economising in energy consumption, a natural response to the second oil price rise in 1980-1. The previous threefold increase, in 1973, to the basic cost of energy for petrochemical manufacture had already provoked a change in the design of Yeocheon's plant, so as to permit a greater recovery of heat. Had it been built to the standards of the Ulsan plant, the VCM plant at Yeocheon would have recovered 50,000 BTU per hour; with the altered design, involving an increase in the heat exchanged between outgoing and incoming streams, 90,000 BTU per hour were recovered. In

Table 4.10: Productivity of raw materials in the Yeocheon plant, 1980-4

Year	Polyethylene production index (tons of ethylene input per ton of LDPE output)	VCM production indices (tons of ethylene input per ton of VCM output)	(tons of EDC input per ton of VCM output)
1980	1.001	0.220	0.970
1981	0.995	0.232	0.909
1982	0.988	0.225	0.879
1983	0.993	0.221	0.903[a]
1984	0.998	0.220	0.888

[a]Increase due to replacement of catalyst.

85

order to effect this saving in energy, Dow and Hanyang's designers together increased the heat transfer between the exit gases and entering steam in furnace flues and substituted methyl chloride for fuel oil as a heat transfer medium. Minor improvements in operation at Yeocheon were also made between 1980, when operation began, and 1985.

The major savings derived from the operation of the Yeocheon plant accrued not at Yeocheon but at Ulsan. Exploiting the knowledge they had gained in redesigning the VCM plant at Yeocheon, Hanyang's engineers turned their attention to increasing the recovery of heat at Ulsan. The flues of the furnaces, the quenching zone, the thermal oxidiser and one more distillation tower were all candidates. In the years 1983-4 the company undertook capital expenditures modifying the furnaces and incinerators so as to secure all these potential savings: in 1984 there was a consequential saving of 2,606 tons of fuel oil, worth some US $500,000 or approximately 0.20 per cent of total costs.

The results of the energy savings at Ulsan between 1977, when the previous analysis ends, and 1984 are revealed in Table 4.11 ('unit ratio' in the table signifies consumption of steam or electricity per unit of product output). We observe that it was steam whose consumption was so reduced, by nearly half overall. In spite of the improvements at Ulsan, however, the newer plant at Yeocheon, initially designed so as to economise on energy, reveals itself to be superior on this count.

Table 4.11: Average energy consumption in Ulsan and Yeocheon plants, 1977 and 1984

LDPE plant		Ulsan 1977		Ulsan 1984		Yeocheon 1984	
Source	Unit	Quantity	Unit ratio	Quantity	Unit ratio	Quantity	Unit ratio
Steam	MT	47,491	0.810	33,344	0.496	30,657	0.265
Elec.	KWH	49,739	0.848	58,233	0.866	126,004	1.091
VCM plant							
Steam	MT	58,723	1.068	26,782	0.462	17,054	0.131
Elec.	KWH	13,744	0.250	14,636	0.253	31,459	0.242
Fuel	KL	9,916	0.180	10,096	0.174	15,802	0.122

THE DEVELOPMENT OF NEW PROCESSES AND PRODUCTS

All the improvements described above have been directed towards producing more efficiently the existing products on the existing equipment; neither the types of products nor the overall processing schemes were altered. Within the last two years, however, three programmes have been initiated which will lead either to the construction of a new plant or to the conversion of existing equipment, so as to produce new products. New construction at Yeocheon will result in a much cheaper mode of producing a different form of polyethylene; conversion at Ulsan has, as of June 1985, resulted in the production of a 'purified' LDPE suitable for electrical insulation and will, by 1986, result in the production of a product entirely new to Hanyang, namely a co-polymer combining VCM and ethyl vinyl acetate (EVA). We will give a brief description of the changes at both sites and of the skills required to generate them, taking Yeocheon first and Ulsan second.

The new form of polyethylene to be produced at Yeocheon, starting in June 1986, is called 'linear' LDPE, abbreviated L-LDPE. Suitable for many uses to which ordinary LDPE is put (Hanyang estimates 30 per cent of their market for LDPE can be filled by L-LDPE), the 'linear' form is much cheaper to produce. The fundamental reason for the cheapness of the L-LDPE process is that the polymerisation step is carried out at a low pressure, rather than, as with LDPE, at a very high pressure. The substantial costs of compressing gases to very high pressures, and of constructing and maintaining the thick-walled vessels and piping necessary to contain the materials at these pressures, are avoided in processes operating at pressures somewhat above or equal to that of the earth's atmosphere.

The inherent cheapness of low-pressure processes is well known, but it has taken some 30 years to develop one for the manufacture of LDPE. By the time that Hanyang had decided to adopt the technique, there were six foreign firms — Dow Chemical, du Pont, British Petrochemical, Mitsubishi, Union Carbide and an Italian company — with proprietary processes for the production of the 'linear' form. As had been done at the time of the first petrochemical complex, so in 1982-3 Hanyang entered into negotiations with all potential suppliers, finally selecting an American firm, Union Carbide.

If the adoption procedure had not altered in the intervening fifteen years, the capabilities of Hanyang had, for the company itself was the negotiator, rather than, as earlier, the Korean government (the Korean government's role was merely to scrutinise the contract with Union Carbide and to authorise its signature), and the company undertook unassisted all the activities subsequent to the overall process design. (To acquire specific operating details, four engineers and eight operators were dispatched to Union Carbide's plant in Houston, Texas.) Moreover, the plant's scale, at 50,000 metric tons per year, rather than being smaller than some production lines that Union Carbide was already operating, has the highest design capacity of any single L-LDPE facility in the world. The process that the Korean firm is adopting is familiar, but the scale of operation is not. Finally, the most complex piece of equipment in the plant, the reactor, was designed by Hanyang and the Korean engineering firm Daewoo Heavy Industries (coincidentally the subject of the case study in Chapter 6) and constructed by the latter. Of all the equipment in the new L-LDPE plant, only a large compressor and the instrumentation were produced abroad. Of the US $25 million that was invested, over three-quarters was spent domestically.

At Ulsan, the one higher quality and the one new product will both emerge from existing equipment, albeit altered in function and improved in precision. LDPE is the product, the so-called 'wire and cable' type, whose quality has been improved for a portion of its total output. The urge to broaden the LDPE product line arose during the recession of 1980-1, when the sales volume of LDPE fell, leaving excess productive capacity. By compounding, Hanyang was able first to produce the tough plastic used as an outer shield to cables; by further purification it was able to produce the electrically inert plastic used to insulate the metallic core. Wire and cable resin was formerly imported to Korea, but with the addition to the LDPE processing scheme of additional compounding and separating or purifying stages, Hanyang will be able to displace imports completely, producing more cheaply and undercutting importers' prices. With an expected output of 16,500 metric tons per year, two-thirds of one of the two LDPE production lines at Ulsan will be devoted to the wire and cable type of LDPE.

It is the other LDPE production line which is to be converted, in its entirety, to the production of the new product, the co-polymer of VCM and EVA. The co-polymer had been in

Figure 4.5: Flow sheet for the tarpot system in the Ulsan plant

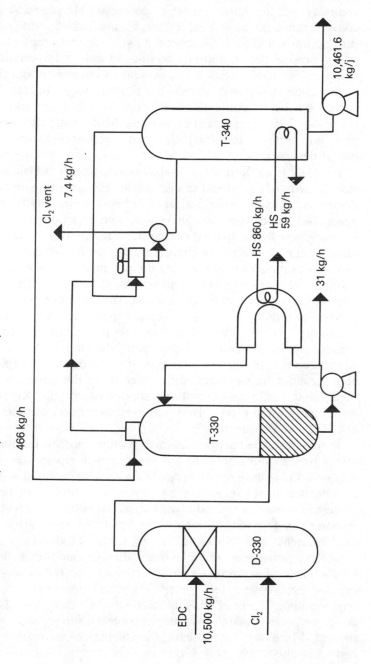

production at Dow Chemical before Dow and Hanyang parted company, so the latter knew its potential. The decision to convert the autoclave reactor (see Figure 4.1) to the new process was made in 1984, after the two companies separated, so the process design and engineering, as well as the physical modifications to the reactor and separation equipment and the construction of a vinyl acetate purification stage, had to be carried out by Hanyang alone. Production is to commence at the end of 1985, at a design capacity of 30,000 metric tons per year, and utilising imported ethyl vinyl acetate monomer as one of the raw materials.

It is clear from these three product developments at Hanyang that the tasks of equipment design, construction, starting up and operation, already performed at Yeocheon, were applied yet again. But there were new tasks too, whose performance by Hanyang was first displayed during the three product developments: namely, evaluating the desirability of introducing new products or processes; recognising the potential, in new uses, of existing pieces of equipment; and knowing how to redesign and convert that equipment to the new use. The latter two skills are part of the ability to design chemical processes, which had previously been conducted during the period of the joint venture by Dow Chemical's engineers; the first skill can be considered part of the overall design of any process (for profitability cannot be estimated without knowing the structure of costs) and had previously been conducted by the Korean government when it conceived of the petrochemical complexes at Ulsan and Yeocheon.

In summary, the move of the three product/process developments was an innovation in the sense that it represented an original combination of resources. What each represented was a combination novel to Korea, and what two out of the three represented was a novelty accomplished entirely with the resources in Hanyang's employ. By 1984, 16 years after its establishment and eleven after its initial production, the company's managers and engineers demonstrated that they were capable of carrying out all the activities involved in adopting and absorbing a technology. They had done more than improve upon a process already installed; they themselves had conducted the research and development leading to a new process. Moreover, in one case, that of the co-polymer, they had recognised that most pieces of capital equipment are of broader applicability than the specific process for which they are installed and that they can be converted to other uses: fortunate is the firm whose engineers can exploit all its equipments' potential.

THE DIFFUSION OF THE IMPORTED TECHNOLOGY

Having described the absorption of the imported technology within Hanyang it remains to describe its diffusion outside the importing firm. In order of increasing economic distance from Hanyang this means describing, first, diffusion of the technology to competing firms; second, to other firms in the petrochemical and chemical industries; third, to the suppliers of the petrochemical industry's inputs; and, finally, to the rest of the Korean economy.

Diffusion of the first sort has not yet occurred, for the simple reason that there is no competition within Korea. As the sole firm producing LDPE and VCM, Hanyang monopolises the employment of engineers for this activity; diffusion to competing firms is thus logically zero. But because diffusion to competing firms has not yet occurred, this does not mean that it will never occur. To the contrary, if there is to be a third petrochemical complex, it is likely that there will be an entrant, Lucky Petrochemical Company, a wholly Korean-owned firm, into the rank of polyethylene manufacturers. Then, diffusion of the LDPE technology might take place. One vehicle could be engineers currently employed by Hanyang, a few of whom might be tempted to move to Lucky Petrochemical Company with the prospect of promotion and higher salaries, although the agreement among Korean petrochemical manufacturers not to poach each other's employees would hinder this flow.

That diffusion is to be expected can be seen from the history of Chungju Fertiliser Company, which has supplied the nucleus of Korean engineers for the entire petrochemical industry. Of the five present and former Korean managers of the LDPE and VCM plants at Ulsan and Yeocheon, four were hired by Hanyang from Chungju as the core of the Ulsan technical staff. There is a similar history to Hankook Caprolactam Corporation, a wholly Korean-owned firm, which has lost experienced engineers both to subsequent entrants into caprolactam (the raw material for nylon) manufacture and to other petrochemical and chemical firms.

Hankook Caprolactam Corporation is the one deviant from the pattern of joint ventures in the Ulsan petrochemical complex. When it came to negotiations over possible joint ventures with foreign caprolactam manufacturers — du Pont, ICI, Union Carbide, etc. — the Korean government found that their demands were excessive. As a result, the Korean government decided to let Hankook take out a licence for caprolactam manufacture with a Dutch process design firm. Since then, two other Korean firms have also taken out licences with the same Dutch firm, one for manufacture at Yeocheon and the other at the proposed third complex. In Hankook's experience, engineers are most vulnerable to inducements from competing firms when they have accumulated about three years' service; by then they are eager for advancement and have acquired enough 'know-how' to make them valuable acquisitions. Lucky Petrochemical Company will doubtless find experienced engineers — and it is only at Hanyang that experience in LDPE production can be gained — expecting them to display much higher productivity, far surpassing the higher salaries they command, than their inexperienced colleagues.

Diffusion of the second sort — to other firms in the petrochemical and chemical industries — has hardly occurred at Hanyang. The turnover of engineers has been exceedingly low, as Table 4.12 indicates. All those with university education were engineers, but of the eight who left Hanyang, the five in 1976 went to Dow Korea, a wholly-owned subsidiary of Dow which was to manufacture chlorine and caustic soda at Yeocheon. Thus, out of some 70 engineers regularly

Table 4.12: Turnover of employees at the Ulsan plant, by level of education, 1973-7

| Year | Number leaving employment, by educational level | | | | |
	Primary school	Junior high school	High school	University	Total
1973	—	1	7	2	10
1974	2	1	5	—	8
1975	—	—	4	1	5
1976	—	—	3	5	8
1977	—	—	8	—	8

employed at Ulsan (the number has varied with the years, rising to 80 in the first year of operation (1973) and again (1977) when extra men were being trained for Yeocheon; and falling to 59 after their transfer (1979)), only three had left Hanyang's fold in the first five years of operation. Since the experience of other petrochemical companies has not been so uneventful, credit must be given to Hanyang for offering satisfaction to its engineering employees. To the authors it seemed that the explanatory factors were the expansion of Hanyang at Yeocheon, high salaries, exceptionally attractive housing provided in a private estate near Ulsan, and frequent contact with knowledgeable foreign engineers. If there has been little diffusion of technology to other firms in the petrochemical and chemical industries through changes in the employment of engineers, it was the result of the deliberate policy on the part of Hanyang to retain its men and the 'know-how' they have acquired.

Another company policy has deliberately encouraged diffusion; this policy is to disseminate information on the products it manufactures to its customers, by organising symposia on plastics and exhibitions for synthetic resins. The symposia have been co-sponsored by the Korean Institute of Chemical Engineers and the exhibitions by the Korea Petrochemical Industry Association. Information is summarised in Table 4.13. Both the symposia and the exhibitions appear to have been successful in view of not only the number of participants but also their response. The majority of participants were from the plastics industries, i.e. the users of LDPE and/or VCM. These participants have enjoyed the opportunity to associate themselves with researchers from universities and research institutes, learning in the process about recent trends in industrial development, new techniques of polymer-processing, new machinery, various applications of polymeric materials, etc. In return, the researchers from universities and research institutes have had the chance to recognise the technological problems which the industries were facing. Subsequently, a number of research projects have been supported by grants from industries and consulting opportunities have been gradually increasing for researchers.

Furthermore, in October 1976 after the first two symposia, people with interests in polymer science and engineering organised a professional society, separate from the Korean

Table 4.13: Symposia and exhibitions on petrochemical products, 1974-7

	Symposia on plastics				
	Dates				
	1974 2/21-22	1975 10/30-31	1976 11/23-24	1977 6/9-10	1977 11/10-11
Number of participants	450	400	500	300	450
Number of lecturers from:					
Government	0	1	1	1	0
Universities	4	0	1	4	2
Research institute	3	1	2	1	2
Industry	3	7	6	4	6
(Foreign)	(0)	(3)	(2)	(7)	(3)
Total	10	9	10	10	10
Hanyang's budget ($)	4,000	6,600	7,240	11,625	

	Exhibitions for synthetic resins		
	Dates		
	1976 11/22-12/1	1977 9/2-11	1979 4/17-30
Number of companies participated	63	59	45
(number foreign)	(2)	(7)	(15)
Hanyang's budget ($)	30,930	20,620	31,960

Institute of Chemical Engineers and the Korean Chemical Society. This society, the Polymer Society of Korea, has been growing rapidly, claiming 1,000 active members in 1979, publishing six issues of a journal each year, and holding various other activities. It has become one of the most active professional societies in Korea.

Less formal than the symposia and exhibitions have been renewed contacts stemming from earlier friendships between KPCC engineers and their colleagues in other companies and in the universities. The initiative has come primarily from the university professors, anxious to keep up with industrial developments, to follow the careers of their former students and to aid in finding stimulating employment for their present students. The diffusion of technology that follows from such activities is impossible to measure, difficult even to observe. All that can be done is to say that this channel does exist and to give one example that has arisen in the petrochemical industry.

The example concerns the disposition of a waste product from Hanyang's Ulsan plant. The VCM unit produces a heavy tar at the rate of 2,000 MT/year. Its composition is given in Table 4.14. Because of the toxicity of the tar, the original process was designed in such a way that the material should be incinerated.

Since 1974, the material had been processed by an independent company, in which the major component (1,1,2-trichloroethane; 'β-tri') was separated and sold as a solvent. The safety threshold limit value (TLV) for the β-tri is relatively low (80 ppm according to the American Conference of Governmental Industrial Hygienists) and thus the application is very limited.

It was also known that 1,1,2-trichloroethane and 1,1,2,2-tetrachloroethane could be used, after separation, as raw materials for the manufacture of freon. However, the volume of the components was not sufficient for this purpose and the separation is not simple. (This is probably the reason why the domestic freon plant, in operation since 1978, does not attempt to utilise the heavy tar material, but uses carbon tetrachloride as raw material.)

In 1975 and 1976, a research project was carried out in the Department of Chemical Engineering, Seoul National University, with financial support from the government and the U-In Chemical Company. This project was successful in establishing a process for the utilisation of the heavy tar material and was patented in Korea (Patent (Korea) 5513 (1977. 9. 28)). The process has been adopted by the U-In Chemical Co.: all the equipment except for the nickel alloy tube was designed and fabricated in Korea. Operation commenced in 1977. The U-In Chemical Co. buys the heavy tar from the Korea-Pacific Chemical Corp. for $40/MT; in addition, the company imports heavy tar from the Australia Dow Co. for $70/MT. The total capacity amounts to 3,000 MT of heavy tar per year.

The plant produces 1,1,1-trichloroethane ('α-tri') at a rate of

Table 4.14: Composition of heavy tar from Ulsan's VCM unit

Component	Composition by weight (%)
Ethylene dichloride (EDC)	5-15
1,1,2-trichloroethane ('β-tri')	40-55
1,1,2,2-tetrachloroethane	5-10
Other heavy products	25-35
Total	100

1,200 MT/year and trichloroethylene at a rate of 600 MT/year, receiving as market prices $800/MT and $700/MT, respectively. The heavier residue is collected and returned to Hanyang, which manufactures 2,000 MT of 18 per cent HC1 before incinerating.

The 'α-tri' is widely used as solvent because of its excellent properties. It is less toxic (the TLV is 350 ppm, in comparison to 80 ppm for β-tri), non-flammable and chemically stable. The rate of fat removal as well as the drying rate is relatively high, and the solvent can be applied for the following purposes: removing fats from all textile goods except for acetate; removing fats from various metals; cleaning electronic machines, fine instruments and watches; cleaning machinery, tools, gauges, etc.; and cleaning aircraft, automobiles, printing machines, etc.

Trichloroethylene, the second solvent manufactured, is not comparable to 1,1,1-trichloroethane, but it has better characteristics than 1,1,2-trichloroethane as a solvent. Both its rate of fat removal and the drying rate are better than 1,1,2-trichloroethane. It also has higher solubility. The TLV is 100 ppm, slightly higher than 1,1,2-trichloroethane. Trichloroethylene is also used to remove fats from metals and various machines, and also in lesser volumes as an anaesthetic, insecticide and steriliser.

The third sort of diffusion of imported technology is to the suppliers of inputs to the petrochemical industry. In this case there have been several minor examples involving diffusion of knowledge to raw material suppliers and one major example involving the replacement of imported capital equipment by equipment manufactured in Korea. The major example arose at both petrochemical complexes.

The Ulsan plant was imported on a 'turn-key' basis. Not only the technology itself but all the equipment and parts were imported. Although it was designed to utilise ethylene from the Korea Oil Corporation, it was necessary to import EDC and all other auxiliary raw materials. In April 1974, the company, in line with government directives, established a programme for the localisation of materials, equipment and parts; subsequently, a Localisation Council was organised. The programme has achieved some success in localising a few materials, a larger number of parts and some original equipment.

As its first act, the Council classified 10,493 plant items of material and parts into four categories:

Items that have to be imported (F)	4,749 items
Items that can be replaced by domestic products (L)	2,870 items
Items that can be fabricated within the company (SF)	874 items
Items that can be developed locally (IT)	2,000 items

Due to the high-pressure technology incorporated in LDPE manufacture, it was inevitable that the F-group occupied a large portion.

Next, the Council made a survey of the capabilities of local manufacturers, and assured them that they were to be given an opportunity to fulfil Hanyang's needs. The chief results of the localisation effort were:

(1) During the restoration work after the explosion in the LDPE plant in 1973, most of the damaged equipment and parts were replaced by domestic products, except for a few items that were required in the high-pressure processes. Local engineers successfully reconstructed the heat exchangers and fabricated aluminium hoppers.

(2) The following equipment, after being designed by the engineers of Hanyang, was fabricated and constructed by local manufacturers: an EDC storage tank (costing $120,000), dust collector ($16,000) and two heat exchangers ($39,200).

(3) When the incinerator was constructed in the VCM plant, at a cost of $1 million, 40 per cent of the parts by value were purchased from local manufacturers.

(4) Isopar-C is a solvent used for the catalyst in the LDPE polymerisation reactor. According to the original design, waste Isopar-C was to be recovered and burnt off in the incinerator. Since November 1973, however, the waste Isopar-C has been distilled and purified by an independent company. The regenerated Isopar-C is then returned to the plant and utilised. The regenerated volume amounts to nearly one half of the total volume required (some 500 MT/year). The reduction in cost in 1975 was $87,600, approximately 0.18 per cent of total manufacturing costs.

(5) A large volume of lubricating oil (16,000 gallons/year) is

used in various parts of the compressors. A recovery drum was installed for this oil in January 1974. The oil has then been regenerated by filtration process within the plant and reused. This arrangement has not only prevented the water pollution but has also contributed to a reduction in cost ($9,920 in 1975).

(6) Calcium carbonate ($CaCO_3$) is used as the anti-blocking agent for LDPE, at a rate of 58 MT/year. Since December 1973, the total volume has been replaced by domestic product to effect a cost saving of $150,000 per year, approximately 0.31 per cent of total manufacturing costs.

Accomplishments of the localisation movement in 1976 are given in Table 4.15, and those for the total period 1974-7 are summarised in Table 4.16. The benefit from substituting domestic for imported inputs was substantial, exceeding $1 million.

When the Korean government, via its agent Korea General Chemicals Corporation, began negotiations with Dow Chemical Company over Hanyang's proposed participation in the second

Table 4.15: Replacement of imported by domestic inputs at Ulsan, 1976 (costs in US dollars)

Input	Number of items	Imported cost	Local cost	Reduction in cost
Equipment[a]	2	$ 25,770	$ 9,420	$ 16,350
Construction[b]	1	304,930	183,310	121,620
Parts[c] Locally purchased (L)	415	77,160	64,090	13,070
Locally developed (IT)	13	4,850	3,170	1,680
Shop fabricated (SF)	47	6,180	3,800	2,380
Shop regenerated (S)	894	126,350	48,410	77,940
Sub-total	1,369	214,540	119,470	95,070
Raw materials[d]	3	302,580	116,980	185,600
Repair of equipment[e]	6	35,300	23,530	11,770
Total	1,381	$883,120	$452,710	$430,410

[a]Equipment: heat exchanger (E-171/172), filter (FL-320).
[b]Construction: incinerator construction work, excluding the items imported.
[c]Parts: major items only. Local purchase: pump casing (P-226), FL-filter, gate valve (V-40). Locally developed: FQ-60,62 diaphragm, pump sealing (P-6), fuse (2.5 amp). Shop fabricated: shaft packing, flexible hose (150 lb), flange for fire hose connection. Shop regenerated: safety valve, regulating valve, other valves.
[d]Raw materials: waste Isopar-C regeneration, lubricating oil regeneration, $CaCO_3$ replaced by local product.
[e]Repair of equipment: repair of sprinkler system around CP-262/263, repair of lubricating oil supply system for the compressors in the LDPE plant.

Table 4.16: Alternative costs of imported and domestic inputs, Ulsan, 1974-7 (costs in current US dollars)

Year	1974	1975	1976	1977	Total
Domestic inputs:					
Parts replaced by local products or locally regenerated	$48,000 (1,195 items)	$77,300 (939 items)	$123,590 (1,369 items)	$267,220 (2,123 items)	$516,110
Equipment fabricated locally	146,140 (5 items)	33,000 (2 items)	9,420 (2 items)	—	$188,560
Raw materials replaced by local products	94,600 (3 items)	122,000 (3 items)	117,000 (3 items)	101,110 (3 items)	$434,710
Total cost of domestic substitutes	$288,740	$232,300	$250,010	$368,330	$1,139,380
Imported inputs:					
Cost of equivalent inputs	$612,000	$721,000	$543,000	$647,000	$2,523,000
Savings in substituting domestic for imported inputs	$323,260	$488,700	$292,990	$278,670	$1,383,620

petrochemical complex at Yeocheon, one of its objectives was to have as much of the capital equipment as possible manufactured in Korea. To be sure, the equipment for the Ulsan plant has been wholly imported, but in the intervening years the capabilities of the Korean engineering industry had increased. Moreover, in replacing some foreign with locally-manufactured equipment after the plant explosion in 1973, KPCC had itself demonstrated that the skills of Korean equipment manufacturers could be exploited. The fraction of the total capital cost in the Yeocheon plant to be expended on locally-manufactured equipment became a bargaining point, with Hanyang arguing for a lower figure and the Korean government for a higher one. At the end of the negotiations the parties agreed on 16 per cent by value; in the event the actual figure has been 23 per cent.

To understand Hanyang's desire for a low figure, it is necessary to realise that Hanyang was motivated by a desire to equip its plant with precisely designed and carefully manufactured items obtained as cheaply and as quickly as possible. Complex equipment designed and built in Korea could suffer from either or both of the disadvantages of high cost and delay in delivery, because of inexperience or very low volume in manufacture, and low reliability because of, again, inexperience in manufacture or of low quality of unspecialised steel for construction material. Moreover, in most cases it is necessary for the engineer at Hanyang who has designed the equipment to spend some time, usually two to three days but occasionally longer, at the equipment manufacturer's factory, going over the design and fabrication. As a result of all these drawbacks, it is the least sophisticated equipment — storage vessels and tanks, piping, heat exchangers and pumps, all for low pressure and non-corrosive fluids — that have been locally manufactured.

Of the fourth and final extension of the technology — throughout the rest of the economy — nothing can be said; the authors did not observe any such extension but, given the complexity of the petrochemical technology, were not surprised.

SUMMARY AND CONCLUSIONS

The purposes of this last section are to summarise the findings of the enquiry and to suggest some reasons for them: these two matters will be considered together in what follows. The findings themselves can be stated, in an over-simplified manner, as: (1) the role of the Korean government has been crucial and beneficial; and (2) the rates of absorption and diffusion of the imported technology in the Korean petrochemical industry have been rapid.

The role of the Korean government

The Korean government affected the outcome initially by specifying output targets in successive Five-year Economic Development Plans, which in turn determined the scale and timing of investment. The scale of individual projects has been influenced by the government's penchant for large units; swayed by the argument that there exist substantial economies of scale in modern petrochemical plants, the Korean government has usually granted monopolies in the production of the targeted output when production is being undertaken in Korea for the first time, or in the increase in targeted output where expansion of existing production is being undertaken. Thereby the entire initial capacity is installed by one firm, and any increase in capacity between one plan and the next is also installed by one, occasionally the same, firm. Here government has had its first effect on the rate of absorption, absorption taking place at a faster pace in a single large firm than in many small ones.

The Korean government's next choice has been the difficult one of the degree of foreign ownership of the petrochemical plants — none, part or complete. Torn between conflicting desires of economising on scarce foreign capital on the one hand and retaining possession of productive assets for Korean citizens on the other, the government has chosen the middle course of 50–50 joint ventures, the only exceptions being the wholly domestically-owned Hankook Caprolactam Corporation's plant at Ulsan and Dow's (formerly) wholly-owned chlorine-alkali plant at Yeocheon. This precludes any choice of technique, for the foreign partners always employ the same technology in Korea that they have employed successfully at home, and it does mean divided interests, about which more will be said at the end of this chapter.

Picking a foreign participant means inevitably picking a technique, with its subsequent effect on the rates of absorption and diffusion; picking foreign participants in the petrochemical industry has meant picking capital-intensive processes of great technical sophistication, whose absorption and diffusion would be expected to be slow. But rather than denying the country any benefits of employing modern capital-intensive techniques, and the latest proven capital-intensive techniques at that, the Korean government has tried to compensate for the greater difficulties in the way of absorption by recourse to alleviating conditions imposed upon the foreign participants. In the case of Hanyang, the major conditions were fivefold: (1) that the foreign partner, Dow Chemical, would reveal all its own designs and 'know-how' to its Korean employees; (2) that the Korean engineers would be trained by Dow in the application of all the aspects of Dow's current technology — basic process design, detailed equipment design and procurement, construction, testing, start-up, operation and maintenance — and in the techniques employed in securing improvements to any petrochemical technology; (3) that the Korean engineers would participate in each of these activities as quickly as possible, and in sufficient numbers to replace Dow's expatriate engineers; (4) with some qualifications, that Dow would automatically inform Hanyang of improvements in the imported technology made by itself or any of its licensees; and (e) that Hanyang could object to the Korean government if it ('it' being the President and Executive Vice-President of the firm, both by agreement

Korean citizens) felt that Dow were not proceeding rapidly enough with the transfer.

Conditions such as these have been common to joint ventures in the Korean petrochemical industry and have even been imposed upon joint petrochemical ventures in other developing countries, but their enactment from country to country has been quite varied. In Korea they have, according to the authors' evidence, been speedily and effectively implemented: conditions have not been pious wishes but objectives systematically and conscientiously attained. And this brings up the last element in the role the Korean government has played in the creation of the petrochemical industry, the role of leader. Never has the government withdrawn its interest in the industry, never have ministers and planners and other civil servants slackened in their enthusiasm, in their determination, in their drive to secure maximum output and efficiency. It is not just that Hanyang and other petrochemical firms have felt that the Korean government stands in front of them urging them on, but that they have also feared the Korean government will accept nothing less than proficiency from them. Dedicated, hardworking, incorruptible as they are, Korean government officials expected identical behaviour from their private citizens. Adelman and Morris (1973) have presented evidence on an international scale that the degree of commitment of the government to the country's economic development is closely related to that country's overall performance; the Korean government's attitudes and behaviour, and the petrochemical industry's achievements, conform to this pattern.

Finally, the Korean government has tried to make generally available the resources necessary for Korean petrochemical firms to produce efficiently. Inputs, particularly the raw materials from petroleum, have been steadily provided in sufficient quantity to maintain production rates at full capacity. More importantly for the absorption of the technology, engineers have been educated at the universities and given initial experience in public firms (particularly the fertiliser producer, Korea General Chemical Company), and operators have been trained at the technical schools in sufficient numbers to staff the petrochemical firms completely with Koreans. As a simple indication of the care with which the government channels resources into technical education one can take enrolments in the country's top university, Seoul National University: of 3,315 places offered in 1979 for entering students, the College of Arts and Humanities accounted for 185, and the College of Social Sciences 250, whereas the College of Engineering admitted 795. Education in technical subjects is given highest priority by a government determined that its economy shall industrialise.

The absorption of the imported technology

In the establishment of the Korean petrochemical industry it was essentially the government's decisions that led to what type of technology should be imported and what means should be available to absorb it. But the outcome was still in some doubt: even with adequate numbers of talented engineers, the technology, novel and sophisticated, might have proved too exacting. What was the experience with absorption?

In two words, the absorption of petrochemical technology in Korea has been rapid and successful. As to the *speed* of absorption, two summary measures can be provided, one narrowly relating to the quickness with which the operating techniques were absorbed, and the other more broadly but less precisely relating to the quickness with which the entire technology was absorbed. As to the *success*, the overall reductions in cost provide an indicator.

Figure 4.6 illustrates the first summary measure for polyethylene and vinyl chloride monomer production at Hanyang's Ulsan plant in the years from its process design, commencing in 1970, through its start-up in January 1973, until the end of 1977. This interval of time is spread along the horizontal axis; on the vertical axis is the rate of output of the product, as a percentage of 'design capacity', as that term is defined in the chapter on methodology. For polyethylene, the graph of production through time shows that 'design capacity' output was surpassed after six months, and so long as sufficient demand for LDPE existed, did not fall below; for VCM, the graph shows a quick start-up and steadily rising production, but a failure to reach 'design capacity' until 1976, three years later. If the standard for full absorption is the rapid attainment of high and sustained rates of output, Hanyang can be said to have achieved it almost immediately; if the standard is the attainment of rates of output equal to or exceeding the capacity for which the plant was designed, Hanyang can be said to have achieved it

Figure 4.6: Graph of yearly rates of output of polyethylene and vinyl chloride monomer at the Ulsan plant, as percentages of 'design capacities', 1973-7

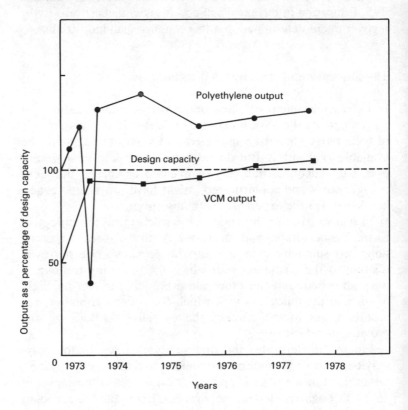

Source: See Table 4.3.

after approximately two years, as an average for the two products at Ulsan. The pattern at Yeocheon is similar, if one eliminates the three recession years of 1980, 1981 and 1982.

There is a distinction to be made between absorption by a firm and absorption by a nation. The latter is a more stringent concept, for a company can absorb a technology completely without using any engineers native to the country in which it is operating. To the extent that Hanyang absorbed the LDPE and VCM operating technology with Dow Chemical's engineers, the absorption cannot be said to be complete from Korea's point of view. Only when the entire process of incorporating a technology could be undertaken with Korean engineers in full command would the absorption be complete in national terms. To resolve this issue appeal to Figure 4.6 will not alone be sufficient; Figure 4.7 will also be necessary.

In Figure 4.7 the upper part of the horizontal axis relating to the experience of the plant at Ulsan extends over the same period, from 1970 through 1977, as did Figure 4.6. The lower part of the horizontal axis extends over an equally long period, October 1976 through October 1983, appropriate for the Yeocheon plant. The vertical scale differs from that of Figure 4.6, being the percentage of all the engineers engaged in absorbing and applying the technology who were *not* Korean. Thus a point at the top of the graph (equal to 100 per cent) would indicate wholly foreign participation in the absorption of the technique, and a point coinciding with the horizontal axis (equal to 0 per cent) would indicate wholly Korean participation.

The two plots in Figure 4.7 refer to the course of participation in the first of Hanyang's petrochemical plants at Ulsan and the second at Yeocheon. As would be expected, the second, occurring as it does about six years after the first and exploiting therefore what had already been learned, is never higher and is frequently lower, indicating earlier and more thorough participation by Korean engineers. The dramatic shift downwards occurred in the design and procurement stages of the technology; Korean engineers demonstrated that they had at least partially absorbed these difficult technical tasks.

Nevertheless, if one is strict in one's definition of absorption, only a horizontal graph of participation along the time axis, indicating 100 per cent participation by Korean engineers in all stages, would pass the test. It was not until 1984 that two projects were initiated to be entirely staffed by Koreans, one being the purification of LDPE to produce a type suitable for ,electrical insulation and the other being the production of the co-polymer of VCM and EVA.

Used in conjunction, Figures 4.6 and 4.7 indicate how quickly Korean engineers were capable on their own of sustaining a high rate of output (or full-capacity operation). The earliest date at which the expatriate engineers can be said to have been completely replaced in their role of operating the processes at Ulsan was October 1976; since the plant started up in January 1973, one can therefore say that the shortest period of time required for absorption of the operating technology was

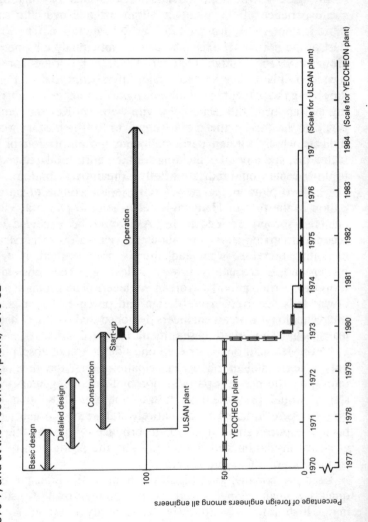

Figure 4.7: Graph of participation of foreign engineers in the stages of absorbing the imported technology at the Ulsan plant, 1970-7, and at the Yeocheon plant, 1975-82

three-and-two-thirds years. So the alternative measures of the minimum period of absorption of the operating technology are three months (by which time both Ulsan's LDPE and VCM units were operating at high rates of output) and 45 months (by which time the foreign engineers had been replaced); the minimum period for the absorption of the technology from process design through process and product improvement is twelve years (assuming that the electrical insulation and co-polymer projects are successfully carried out).

If the authors were to pick what they believe in their best judgement were the times that elapsed before the operating techniques and the technology were fully absorbed, they would pick one-half and twelve years respectively. The former choice is based on the Korean engineers' accomplishments in designing and procuring new equipment to replace that damaged in the explosion, and in bringing the LDPE unit back to full-capacity operation thereafter; the latter on accepting Korean engineers' claims to complete knowledge, on measuring their improvements in process operation, and on observing their ability to select and design production schemes for new products. These are quite rapid rates of absorption indeed.

Certain corroborating pieces of evidence are available to support these optimistic figures. Some comparative data on the performance of LDPE and VCM plants in other countries, as well as detailed data on process improvements, have been cited in the text; three others came to the attention of the authors. First of all, at the start-up of the Ulsan plant, Hanyang's engineers, American and Korean, were joined by five foreign specialists (in such fields as instrumentation, corrosion, etc.), who stayed on duty for three months. The common experience in Dow's joint ventures in other countries was for the start-up to be attended by six to eight specialists staying on duty for six months. Hanyang's start-up drew more upon Korean engineers than did Dow's plants in other countries.

The second corroborating piece of evidence concerns the efficiency of operation of the LDPE unit, again in comparison with those in other countries. Dow's process is also applied in plants in the USA, Canada, Holland, Spain, Hong Kong, Japan and Chile; compared to these on the bases of consumption of energy per unit of output and consumption of raw materials (chiefly ethylene) per unit of output, Hanyang's plant is today inferior to none and substantially superior to those in Canada,

Spain, Hong Kong and Chile.

The third corroborating piece of evidence came from another Korean petrochemical plant employing an imported technique. It, too, attained full-capacity operation and displaced its foreign engineers more rapidly than has been common in other countries using the same technique.

When reasons are sought for the rapid rate of absorption of petrochemical technology in Korea, the answers become largely subjective. To be sure, the necessary human resources have been available, as a result of government's foresight in stressing engineering education and training; to be sure, there have been carefully designed and rigorously implemented plans for the transfer of technological knowledge and experience from foreign to Korean engineers: and, to be sure, there was a large market in Korea eagerly demanding all the petrochemical products that could be produced. Nevertheless, the Korean government's impetus and the foreign companies' co-operation do not, even together, seem to be sufficient to explain the rapid absorption. Explanation can also be sought in the Korean character, particularly in the character of those Koreans drawn to engineering.

To expound on a nation's character is a hazardous activity, particularly when undertaken by economists. Yet to someone familiar with other developing countries, valuable national traits are evident in Korea's engineers — the desire to acquire modern technical knowledge, combined with mechanical aptitude; the courage to undertake unfamiliar activities; the lack of resentment at working intensely and regularly for long hours; a spirit of co-operation; a willingness to subordinate private interests to collective goals; a rough, combative energy; and an urgent pragmatism — all tend to enable them to absorb foreign ideas, foreign techniques. It was not that the authors failed to observe any impediments to the absorption of the imported technology: this is too negative a statement. It was that mastering the technology seemed to be the over-riding objective of the engineers they met, more important than increasing their salaries or cultivating their friendships or looking after their families or improving their status; and that this seemed perfectly within the Korean character.

Moving from the subject of the speed of absorption to its success, let us now summarise the financial indicators, in particular those stemming from direct and indirect technical change.

Table 4.17 provides the data at our disposal, which relate to the Ulsan plant over the first three years of its operation. Appearing separately in the table are the different inputs and outputs to and from the LDPE and VCM plants, and the extent to which technical change contributed to reducing their costs of production. The most substantial improvement came about through the increase in output obtained from the existing plants, permitting the overheads to be distributed over a greater volume. The reduction in average unit cost of production as a consequence of greater output was estimated to be almost 6 per cent, where the comparison is between unit costs in 1973 and in 1976; this is nearly two-thirds of the total reduction of almost 10 per cent. The other third came almost equally from savings on raw materials and energy.

An overall reduction in unit costs of nearly 10 per cent, secured over the course of four years' operation, averages out to an annual increase in the productivity of all the resources identified of approximately 2.4 per cent per year compounded. The chief resource not identified, and therefore not included in the calculations underlying Table 4.17, is labour. We were not able to determine by how much labour productivity had increased, although we would not expect it to contribute much more to the gains already displayed in the table, partly because labour's component in total costs of petrochemical production is low, and partly because most of the improvements in labour's performance are captured in the improvements in the inputs identified in the table. At most, the inclusion of direct and indirect technical change of labour would not propel the improvement in total productivity beyond 3 per cent per year. Such an annual percentage improvement in the operation of new and sophisticated techniques in their first installation in a developing country is a commendable achievement.

The diffusion of imported techniques

If the absorption of imported techniques in the Korean petrochemical industry seems to have been rapid and successful, the diffusion seems to have been less so. Diffusion to other manufacturing firms has not often occurred, for the simple reason that there has not been, and will not be before the completion of the third petrochemical complex, any general entry of competitors.

Table 4.17: Benefits of direct and indirect technical change accruing to Hanyang's Ulsan petrochemical plant from 1973 to 1976

			Annual savings over 1973 costs	Percentage reduction over four years, in average cost per unit of output
	Inputs	Means of achievement	Amounts (US$ in 1976 prices)	
Direct	Raw materials	Reduction in usage of ethylene for LDPE	$ 485,000	
		for VCM	167,000	
		Reduction in usage of EDC for VCM	350,000	
		Localisation of supply	185,600	
		Sub-total	1,187,000	1.71
	Energy	Various improvements in design and operation	1,087,000	1.57
	Capital	Localisation of supply	294,810	0.43
Indirect	Outputs Main products: LDPE and VCM	Expansion of output from existing plants LDPE 27.53% VCM 1.13% Average 19.62% (weighted)		5.92
	By-product	Increase in value	40,000	0.06
Total			approximately 6,700,000	9.69

Sources:
Raw materials; ethylene reduction, see Table 4.5. The value of ethylene was assumed to be $250 per metric ton. Product outputs were obtained from Table 4.3. EDC (ethylene dichloride) reduction, see text. Localisation of supply, see Table 4.16.
Energy; see Table 4.9, covering period July 1975-June 1976.
Capital; see Table 4.13, reductions in cost of equipment, construction, spare parts and maintenance.
Main products; for expansion of output above design capacity, see Table 4.3. The weights used in averaging the percentage expansions were by value of product, 0.70 for LDPE and 0.30 for VCM (see product prices for 1976 in *European chemical news*); for estimation of percentage reduction in average cost the following cost breakdown was used:

Percentage of Total Costs

	Feed stock and fuel	Capital	Other	Total
LDPE	45	40	15	100
VCM	47	26	27	100

(see Tomson, W.C., 'A positive attitude to new producers', address to the Society of Chemical Industry, The Hague, Netherlands, October 1979, quoted in D. Robinson, *Petrochemicals on the move: a study in industrial relocation*, MSc dissertation, Institute of Social Studies, The Hague, 1980). Total costs were obtained by adding to manufacturing costs of $48,363,000 an element representing overheads, chiefly capital. Overhead costs for the two processing schemes were 30.2 per cent of total costs, or $20,897,000; added to manufacturing costs these yielded total costs for 1976 of $69,260,000. By-product: sale of heavy tar, see text.

Where competition has arisen, as in the manufacture of caprolactam, engineers have moved in some numbers from the first firm in production to its successors. Where competition has not been created, as in the case of Hanyang's products LDPE and VCM, there has been hardly any turnover at all.

Yet it is chiefly by means of movement of engineers from one petrochemical firm to another, or to and from the chemical firms at large, that diffusion can take place in Korea. Engineering principles are freely communicated, but all the technological knowledge that is collected under the term of 'know-how', without which plant and equipment cannot be designed, constructed and operated, is not. 'Know-how' accompanies licensing agreements, but in their absence, moves only in the experience of engineers who change employment. If Korean engineers working in the petrochemical industry do not change employment, their 'know-how' will not be deployed.

That 'know-how' should be kept secret within the firm is not a Korean institution but one acquired, along with the technology, from the petrochemical industry of the developed world. When Korea imported petrochemical technology, it necessarily imported the manner of handling the technology; it would not have received the technology unless it had agreed to honour its privacy. Perhaps the Korean nation could get along without the secrecy surrounding 'know-how', but it could not have got along without the 'know-how' itself, and has had to accept the former to obtain the latter. In this manner the international scheme of confidentiality has been imposed on the Korean petrochemical industry, and has reduced the diffusion of the imported technology within it.

Diffusion outside the petrochemical industry has occurred to some extent, mainly in the dissemination of knowledge of equipment design and construction to capital goods manufacturers. That there has been a steady increase in the fraction of

111

locally-produced capital equipment incorporated in Korean petrochemical plants, and that this increase has been of advantage to the petrochemical firms has been demonstrated; but it is difficult to state how much further localisation of equipment can and should proceed. The direction and likely outcome of the programme of localisation remain mysterious, subject as much to unpredicted events (like the sudden need for equipment to replace that destroyed in the explosion at Ulsan) and to accidental encounters (like those between former engineering school classmates) as to deliberate undertakings.

Summarising what has been learned of the absorption and diffusion of imported technology in the petrochemical industry, the authors can say with some confidence that the rate of absorption has been rapid, and with considerable confidence that substantial improvements have been obtained in that part of the technology relating to the ancillary processes. The reasons for the rapid absorption stem from the Korean government's policies and actions, the foreign participants' planning and experience, and the attitudes and application of Korean engineers. The rate of diffusion of the imported technology appears to have been much less rapid, as was to be expected in a young industry, most of whose firms have been granted producing monopolies. The secrecy endemic to the petrochemical and chemical industries has helped to retard diffusion, whereas the government's and firms' programmes of equipment localisation have helped to accelerate it. Finally, the Korean government, in its many roles, has exerted a strong influence on the choice of the techniques that are to be imported and an equally strong influence on the speed and success with which those techniques are absorbed.

An epilogue needs to be written to the case study of the Hanyang petrochemical company. In 1982, squeezed between high prices for petroleum raw materials and reduced demand for petrochemical products, the world's chemical firms found themselves under financial pressure. The Dow Chemical Company's response was to dispose of its interests in most of its joint ventures, those in Japan, Saudi Arabia, Spain and Korea being four of them. At that time, Dow's investments in Korea consisted of its half share in the equity of the original Korea Pacific Chemical Corporation and its full share in the plant at Yeocheon producing chlorine and caustic soda, the former a raw material in the manufacture of EDC and hence in VCM.

These two properties made Dow Korea's largest foreign investor.

After negotiations with the Korean government, interspersed with appeals to the Korean courts, Dow transferred all its assets to the Korea Explosives Group, a medium-sized Korean enterprise keen to expand into chemicals. The latter established a separate company, Hanyang Chemical, to consolidate Dow's former share and that of the other Korean shareholders in KPCC. As a consequence, Hanyang became a wholly Korean company in ownership as in personnel. The progression, which began 14 years earlier as a transfer of technology, expanded to become one of total costs and benefits. The Korean body economic now possesses entirely the techniques it adopted and absorbed.

NOTES

1. The summary of Arthur D. Little's report is reprinted, in English, in the *10-year history of petrochemical industry in Korea, 1967-1976*, Seoul: Korea Petrochemical Industry Association, 1977, pp. 249-86. The rest of the text of this volume is in Korean.

2. The investment in Hanyang was approximately $41,000,000 (ibid., Table 2.1, p. 65), and provided approximately 500 jobs, representing a capital to labour ratio of about $80,000 per man. This ratio is similar to that encountered in petrochemicals in developed countries, and in one underdeveloped country, Columbia (D. Morawitz, 'Output composition, technology, and employment: petrochemicals in Columbia', in D. Morawitz et al., *Studies of inappropriate technologies for development*, Cambridge: Harvard University Center for International Affairs, 1974).

3. *10-year history of petrochemical industry in Korea*, Table 1.16, p. 48.

4. ICI, BASF, du Pont, SNPA, ATO Chemie, SNAM, UCC, Dow, Dart, ND, Distillers, Gulf, SIR; ibid. Table 3.4, p. 105. There were also 13 alternatives for high density polyethylene.

5. Goodrich, SD, Monsanto, Stauffer, PPG, Dow; ibid., Table 3.4, p. 106.

6. In the case of Hanyang, 70 per cent of the total investment was raised by international borrowings from the British merchant banking firm Kleinwort Benson and the American Citibank and Bank of America.

5

Case Study: Synthetic Fibres

INTRODUCTION

Lying immediately downstream of the petrochemical industry are several light industries which convert bulk petrochemicals into intermediate or even final products. One such industry converts plastics and resins into fibres, which then compete with natural fibres in all their uses. Two of the most important synthetic fibres are nylon and polyester, with whose conversion this chapter is concerned. The objective is to explore the adoption, absorption and diffusion of imported technology in nylon and polyester production and to reveal the sources of technical change. As in the preceding chapter, so in this chapter one company's experience will be analysed: this section provides a brief history of that company. Subsequent sections will cover the technology of nylon manufacture and its adoption and absorption by the company, followed by the technology of polyester manufacture and its adoption and absorption. The company's recent developments in synthetic fibres will then be described, and the diffusion of the technology into the rest of the Korean economy and abroad will be plotted. The final section will summarise what we have learned, adding observations from other companies in the industry.

The company whose experience will be reported is the Kolon Company Limited, a private company with fairly widely distributed shareholdings. Kolon has its main office in Seoul and its two synthetic fibre plants approximately 250 kilometres to the south-east, in the industrial cities of Taegu and Kumi. Overall the company currently employs about 5,000 persons and secures revenues of US $300 million per year.

Kolon was chosen from among the three nylon- and eight polyester-producing firms for four chief reasons: first, Kolon has the longest history of production of nylon and polyster filament in Korea. Secondly, because of its longevity and its keeping up with technological advance, the types of facilities that it has adopted are quite diverse. One engineer in the plant described the variety of Kolon's nylon facilities as 'a museum of nylon production engineering'. The co-existence of old and new types of equipment testifies to the introduction of imported technology. Thirdly, the company has a long history of technological and financial contacts with two foreign suppliers of synthetic fibre technology, Chemtex of the United States and Toray of Japan. Transactions with these foreign companies at the various stages of Kolon's history are particularly interesting, since these two foreign countries have played the most important roles in providing technology and finance for the development of the Korean economy. Lastly, the authors have been acquainted with the plant personnel of Kolon for several years and are on close terms with them.

It was in Japan that the founder of Kolon began his business, through the agency of the Sam Kyung Company. In 1953 Sam Kyung (Japan) began to import stretched nylon filament yarns into Korea, and a year later the Korea Sam Kyung Company was established as its local representative. In 1956 the local company conceived of stretching nylon filament yarns itself and in 1957 the Korea Nylon Company (abbreviated as Kolon) was founded, to manufacture yarns from stretched nylon, and to finish and distribute nylon textiles. In 1958, the nylon-stretching plant was built; it had 55 Italian twisters (each with 200 spindles), winders, ply twisters, hank winders and steam setters. There were 200 employees initially, including 120 women. Production was 440 Kg/day, mainly for the company's own use.

In 1960, Kolon expanded its nylon-stretching capacity, adding two 'Primatex' machines with 480 spindles each. With 'Primatex' machines, the production line was shortened and the quality of the products improved. Production of stretched nylon yarns was 411 Kg/day in the first section (Italian twisters) and 423 Kg/day in the second (Primatex). There were 110 operating personnel in the first section and 40 in the second. The raw nylon yarns for stretching were imported from Toray (Japan) and Chemstrand & du Pont (USA).

As it was expanding its nylon-stretching capacity, Kolon decided to integrate backwards into the production of nylon filament yarns. It made contact with Chemtex, which possessed the technology and which was willing to enter into a joint venture, on the typical terms of sharing equally in the equity. Chemtex sent engineers to Kolon's plant during 1959 and 1960, and participated in the raising of $3.2 millions, chiefly in the United States, for the construction of a 'Nylon 6' filament yarn plant of 2.5 metric tons per day capacity. Two spinning machines (each with 112 spindles) were incorporated. It was estimated then that there would be a saving of about $2.5 millions per year in foreign exchange through the substitution of domestic for imported nylon filament. Construction began in 1960 and was completed in 1963.

Production commenced in early 1963; up to September the total time spent by Chemtex's engineers in design, construction and production of the nylon filament plant was 850 man-days. The Korean workforce, including technicians, at that time was about 200. From the beginning the plant's operation was troublesome, the main difficulties arising from lack of experience of Kolon's technicians, a mistake in Chemtex's design, and failures on the part of the engineers assigned by Chemtex. To overcome these shortcomings, Kolon decided, in September 1983, to purchase technical advice from Toray (Japan). Also from September 1969 Kolon began to concentrate on the production of nylon yarn, letting other medium and small

Table 5.1: Total capacity, output, revenues, costs and profits Kolon Inc., 1974-84

Year	Capacity (metric tons per day)		Production (metric tons per day)		Financial data (billions of current prices)		
	Nylon	Polyester	Nylon	Polyester	Total revenues	Total manufacturing costs	Gross profit
1974	n.a.	87	42.6	36.5	n.a.	n.a.	n.a.
1975	n.a.	87	n.a.	n.a.	42.8	36.6	6.2
1976	n.a.	87	n.a.	n.a.	52.1	42.2	9.9
1977	n.a.	87	75.1	67.5	64.8	51.5	13.3
1978	n.a.	87	n.a.	n.a.	88.0	68.5	19.5
1979	n.a.	162	n.a.	n.a.	104.6	81.7	22.9
1980	n.a.	n.a.	99.0	93.1	150.5	126.9	23.6
1981	n.a.	n.a.	n.a.	n.a.	188.4	159.3	30.2
1982	n.a.	n.a.	99.8	125.7	184.5	156.3	27.8
1983	n.a.	n.a.	n.a.	n.a.	202.0	169.0	32.9
1984	83.1	215	107.5	160.7	258.1	208.1	50.1

companies stretch nylon yarns. In 1964 Kolon stopped stretching nylon yarns altogether.

In 1964, total Korean nylon yarn production increased to 3.8 tons/day, but this amount was estimated as less than one-third of total national demand. Therefore, Kolon applied to the American Agency for International Development (AID) for a loan of $580,000 to increase its capacity by 7.5 tons/day. In April 1967, the company began to expand the plant; in May 1968, the expansion was completed and production capacity reached 10 tons/day. In October 1968 a second expansion, financed by a loan of $3,420,000 from the EXIM Bank of the USA, was initiated, adding 5 tons/day more capacity. In 1970, a further expansion of 2.5 tons/day was carried out, bringing total capacity to 17.5 tons/day. Sales reached 1,904 million won (US $6 million) in that year, and the firm employed 1,014 persons.

In 1968, the construction of a nylon fish-net plant of 7.5 tons/day capacity was commenced. The first polyester plant came on stream in 1971. In June 1973 a nylon tyre cord plant of 5.4 tons/day started production with the loan of $4,040,000 from Chemtex. Subsequent expansions are indicated in Table 5.1.

NYLON TECHNOLOGY

The production of nylon fibres requires three operations in series: polymerisation, spinning and drawing or stretching. The raw material is caprolactam of 99.5 per cent purity (see Chapter 4, where caprolactam manufacture is referred to). The caprolactam is melted in a heated vessel, into which catalysts, diluting agents and light stabilising materials are fed in proper proportions. The melted solution is then transferred to the continuous polymeriser and is converted into polymer pellets of 0.110" dia × 0.120" long. The pellets are washed, dried and conveyed to the spinning section. In the spinning operation the polymerised caprolactam, now called nylon, is remelted and converted into fibre. A special finish oil is applied and the undrawn, intermediate yarn is wound on bobbins. The bobbins are weighted, conditioned, creeled and conveyed to the drawing machines or draw twisters, where the third process is carried out. After the yarn is drawn, it is inspected and tested, then packaged and conveyed to the warehouse. The sequence of processes is shown in Figure 5.1.

Figure 5.1: Nylon filament manufacturing operations (as of the 1960s)

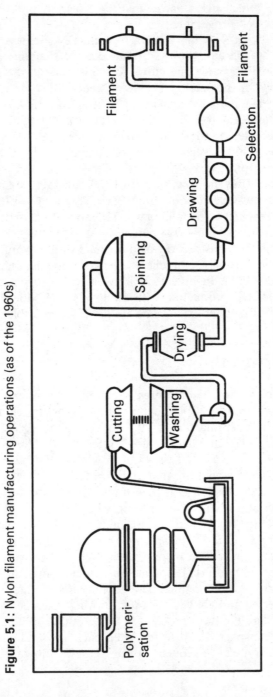

Source: A. Alexander, *Man-made fiber processing* (Noyes Development Corp), 1966.

The three operations of the first plant at Taegu will now be described in more detail. Caprolactam is melted and then fed batchwise to a mixer; the catalyst and a chain terminator are added. The monomer is then filtered and fed to a hold tank. From the hold tank, the mixture is extracted to a mixing system and a delustrant added. The mixture continues through an autoclave where the caprolactam is polymerised under pressure. The reaction in the autoclave consists of initiation, propagation and termination. Initiation is the hydrolysis of E-caprolactam, yielding E-aminocaproic acid, which is then polymerised. In propagation, the polymerisation continues until the molecules are of sufficient length. The polymer is then pelletised and washed to remove low molecular components. Next, the pellets are dried in a vacuum drier, and stored or conveyed to the spinning area. In the spinning of the nylon filament various techniques are available. Originally, prior to 1968, Kolon used the conventional grid type spinning (see Figure 5.2), but subsequently extruder spinning (Figure 5.3) of filament yarns supplanted it. Extrusion is more controllable and also more sensitive to automatic handling than the melt grid type. Moreover, extrusion may be readily adapted for spinning other high polymers, such as polyesters and polypropylene, with only a few minor changes in screws, pumps and spare parts. The molten polymer in the extruder is metred through pumps to spinnerets and is spun straight into atmosphere; the spinning speed is usually over 1,000 metres/min. The polymer freezes at once in cold air and the fibres which result from the freezing are passed round two rollers; the first applies water and a wetting agent and the second an oil-water emulsion, which conditions the yarn. Drawing is carried out on a machine which essentially consists of two rollers, one running faster than the other. The yarn is wrapped round each of these rollers a sufficient number of times and is stretched by a ratio equal to the ratio of the roller speeds.

Subsequent developments at the plant at Taegu consisted of extensions of Kolon's nylon product line. The first extension, begun in 1969, involved the production of yarn for fishing nets. This new product required yarn of higher tenacity, obtained by subjecting the polymer to heat. Three steps are required: pre-polymerisation, in which E-caprolactam is polymerised at 250-280°C for one to two hours; continuous poly-merisation, in which the residence time is about eight hours

119

Figure 5.2: Melt grid-type spinning of nylon filament and polyester filament

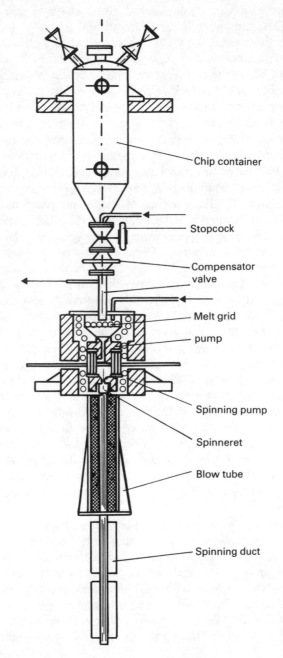

and conversion of the polymer almost complete; and finish polymerisation, in which the polymer is stabilised at a temperature of 265°C for six hours. All three steps are carried out in a single vessel, with baffles between the sections.

The second extension of the company's nylon product line was to tyre cord. In 1973, three years after fishing-net yarn was produced, the first nylon tyre cords were manufactured, at an average rate of 5.4 tons per day. The production process involved a three-step polymerisation similar to that for fish-net yarn, followed by drying, spinning, cable-twisting, weaving, dipping, drying in two temperature zones, winding and a final dipping.

One year before the first new products were added at the Taegu plant, Kolon completed construction of a second factory at Gumi. Nylon chips and yarn were the first products to be manufactured, the former utilising the same production scheme as at Taegu, but with three times the capacity on the single production line. Nylon yarn could also be produced on this line, but in a continuous rather than a discontinuous manner. At Taegu, the yarn was spun from chips, being re-melted before being extruded through the spinneret (see Figure 5.2); at Gumi, the fluid nylon from the reactor was fed directly into the extruder, eliminating the drying and re-melting stages (see Figure 5.3). The continuous process had three advantages over the discontinuous: first, reduced labour, capital and energy costs from the elimination of the drying and re-melting stages; second, reduced storage space for chips; and third, a 5 per cent increase in output, via the elimination of waste in the cutting of chips.

THE ABSORPTION OF NYLON TECHNOLOGY

The process of absorption of nylon technology can be observed at Kolon moving from almost complete dependence on foreign assistance at the beginning to independence at the end. The process began in 1960, after Kolon had decided to integrate backwards into nylon polymerisation and had raised the capital needed to build the first production line. The first action undertaken was to hire five Korean engineers, whose task it was to learn as much as possible about polymerisation from personal contacts and from the literature. These engineers formed a small

121

Figure 5.3: Extruder-type spinning of nylon filament

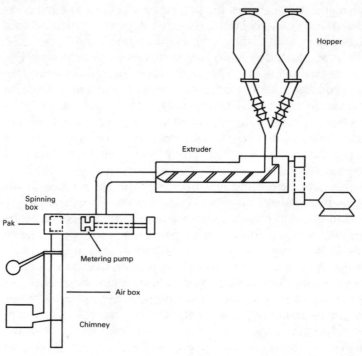

research and development section; simultaneously the company began to hire additional graduate engineers and clerical staff in order to prepare for the design and construction of the Taegu plant. When interviewed subsequently, one of these original engineers recalled that the entire group had been very enthusiastic, keen to acquire all the information they could that was pertinent to the manufacturing techniques.

Once it became known abroad that Kolon was determined to polymerise nylon, several foreign process design and production companies approached them, offering their services. Because it already had drawn upon the Japanese textile firm Toyo Rayon (Toray) for assistance in nylon-spinning, and because Toray had itself begun, seven years earlier in 1953, to polymerise nylon, Kolon selected Toray for technical assistance in the construction, operation and maintenance of the first polymerisation line. For assistance in the process design, in the procurement of finance and equipment, and in its installation, Kolon chose the American firm Chemtex, which had earlier carried out the same functions for Toray.

122

The planning of the polymerisation production line was initiated in 1962, and its design, by Chemtex's engineers, conducted immediately. Construction began in early 1963; the first foreign engineer — a mechanical engineer employed by Chemtex — arrived at the end of March. By the end of July, construction was completed, and on 8 August the opening ceremony was held.

The division of labour among the different nationalities — Korean, Japanese and American — employed in the design, start-up and operation of the first production line was approximately 20, 13 and five respectively. The bulk of the Korean engineers was hired during the design stage and remained in employment during the subsequent stages; six Japanese engineers and one American were assigned for the construction stage, and a different collection of seven Japanese and four American engineers for the start-up and for continuing operation. All the Japanese engineers were employees of Toray, all the Americans of Chemtex. Of the foreigners assigned to construction, two were electrical engineers and six mechanical; of the foreigners assigned to the start-up and operation, three worked on polymerisation, three on spinning and drawing, two on analysis and testing, and the remaining two had general, supervisory duties. In the first column of Table 5.2 the relative contributions of Korean and foreign engineers in the absorption of the initial nylon polymerisation technology is summarised.

By the end of 1963 most of the foreign engineers had been replaced by Koreans. One or two senior engineers from Toray remained, as well as one engineer from Chemtex, with the status of director on the Kolon board, who worked as assistant to the plant manager. In the case of Toray's engineers, one stayed at the head office and up to nine at the plant during the period 1963-78. The average period of stay was about two years. Their backgrounds were as follows: four were university graduates and five were two-year technical college graduates. The engineers from Toray had accumulated much experience, mostly longer than 15 years. Two were treated as directors and seven as department chiefs. Their costs were paid by the Kolon company. By 1979, foreign participation had been reduced to one Toray engineer, positioned at the Gumi plant in polyester production and visiting the Taegu plant twice a week (Wednesday and Saturday). By 1985, all foreigners had departed.

123

Table 5.2: Participation of Korean engineers and managers in the absorption of nylon and polyester technology

Stages in process in absorption	Nylon polymerisation (per cent Korean)				Polyester polymerisation (per cent Korean)		
	Production line 1 Taegu, 1963 2.5 t/d[a] %	Production lines 1,2 Gumi, 1969,70 30 t/d[b] %	Production line 5 Taegu, 1973 5.4 t/d[c] %	Production line 3 Gumi, 1985 30 t/d[d] %	Production line Gumi, 1971 17 t/d[a] %	Production line 2 Gumi, 1975 70 t/d[a] %	Production lines 3,4 Gumi, 1979 75 t/d each[a,b,e] %
Basic design	0 (2)	50 (4)	50	100	0	100	33 (3)
Detailed design	0 (5)	67 (8)	67	100	0	100	50 (6)
Construction	43 (12)	75 (12)	75	100	67	100	50 (14)
Start-up	58 (26)	83 (18)	83	100	81 (26)	100	54 (13)
Operation	58 (26)	83 (18)	83	100	81 (26)	100 (9)	70 (10)
Improvements	88 (17)	88 (17)	88	100	75 (12)	100 (9)	100 (7)

The numbers in brackets are the total number of participants, Korean and foreign.
[a] discontinuous processes for the production of filament.
[b] continuous process for the production of filament.
[c] discontinuous process, with extruder, for the production of tyre cord.
[d] continuous process for the production of film.
[e] operating one production line at a rate of 30 tons per day.

By 1979 Toray's engineers were not staying on at Kolon in order to introduce new technology. According to our findings, the reasons for their stay were otherwise: first of all, since the plant and its auxiliary buildings was completely open to them, they could gather first-hand information on production, inventories and all the other managerial affairs of the plant. With this knowledge they could advise their own firm (Toray) as to what kind of know-how should or should not be offered to Kolon and when. Secondly, since Kolon shared its technology with Chemtex, Toray could watch out for technical changes that stemmed from advances in the USA. Thirdly, the engineers acted as a conduit for the dissemination of up-to-date information generated by Toray in Japan. The Japanese engineers had established friendships with Kolon personnel, so Kolon was able to get substantial technological assistance through personal contact. For example, suppose that Kolon tried to examine a new method which Toray had already developed and adopted. Even after trial and error, Kolon's team might have been faced by unknown factors; in such an event it would have been very hard for Toray's engineers not to have given a hint as to the cause. When we started interviewing the senior plant engineers of Kolon, their responses to the question of whether the stay of Toray engineers helped them or not were inclined towards the negative. However, when allowance was made for the vague but sometimes useful hints they got from the Japanese engineers, they rephrased their responses more positively.

During the interviews we were also told a story which suggests again the multi-purpose aspect of the stay of Toray personnel at Kolon's plants. In 1972-3, during their construction of a nylon plant for a firm in Indonesia, Toray was found to have adopted several methods which Kolon developed by itself, improving the performance of the extruder which Kolon introduced in 1968. Using a different manufacturing process, Toray had not conceived of the improvements before. So in this case Toray's engineers channelled know-how back to their employer.

An alternative to the employment of foreign engineers in Korean plants is the sending of Korean engineers overseas, to acquire knowledge of the imported technology. Besides the on-the-spot technical training they received from foreign engineers at the time of plant construction start-up and early operation, many of Kolon's young engineers were assigned to the Japanese plant of Toray. During the period October 1965-June 1978

30 engineers participated: their average period of training abroad was 22.1 days. In Japan they had the opportunity to learn the plant lay-out, operating system and management procedures as well as specific technical information. Table 5.3 summarises the overseas assignments. Toray did not open its plant to these trainees without reservation, but it is believed that the fact that Kolon and Toray were involved in a joint venture raised the level of technological disclosure. In turn, such overseas training seems to have contributed to the absorption process of imported technology.

Upon their return to Kolon from training overseas the Korean engineers are assigned or reassigned to one of three

Table 5.3: Overseas training of Kolon's Korean engineers, 1965-78

Month and year	Persons	Contents of training	Period (days)	Japanese firm
Oct. 1965	1	Plant inspection	22	Toray
Apr. 1967	1	Plant inspection	17	Toray
Oct. 1967	2	General production	30	Toray
Oct. 1967	2	Test and analysis	30	Toray
Jan. 1969	2	Technology of the spinning process	30	Toray
Nov. 1969	2	Technology related to oiling the filament	27	Matsumoto Oil & Fat, and Toray
Aug. 1970	1	Maintenance techniques and their management	10	Toray
Aug. 1970	1	Polymerisation and water disposal	10	Toray
Aug. 1970	2	Technology of the spinning process	10	Toray
Dec. 1970	1	Technology of the yarn-winding process	10	Toray
Dec. 1970	4	General production	21	Toray
Feb. 1973	3	General production	42	Toray
Oct. 1975	2	Technology of the draw winder	15	Toray
Jun. 1975	3	Maintenance system and polymerisation process	21	Toray
Jul. 1977	1	Technology of the spinning process	12	Toray
Oct. 1977	1	Techniques of product analysis	11	Toray
Jan. 1978	1	'PSY' technique	13	Matsumoto Oil & Fat

Source: Kolon Inc., for the Taegu plant.

groups. The first group is composed of highly experienced personnel working at the head office of the firm, the second of technicians and engineers undertaking research and development at the Technical Research Institute of the company, and the third of personnel working in the production and maintenance departments of the plants.

There are about 30 college graduate engineers in total working in the first group at the Bureau of Technology of the company's head office, including one standing director in charge of technology, one bureau manager and six section chiefs. Most of them have more than ten years' experience on the job. They are responsible for all important matters related to technology, including the areas of planning, implementation, maintenance, service, research and development and patents and licensing. The manpower in the second group consists of about 30 college graduates and about 40 technical high school graduates. The Kolon Technical Research Institute was established in 1975, and a new independent building with modern testing equipment was constructed in 1977 in the Gumi plant site: its major job is research and development for both nylon and polyester products. The researchers at the Institute have also accumulated considerable experience on the development of new products and on technical servicing of customers. The motives for establishing the Technical Research Institute were twofold; to consolidate the increasing amount of technical work which Kolon was carrying out as technology increased in sophistication, and to exploit economies of scale in production. The increased scale of production of both nylon and polyester fibres provided the incentive.

The third group of engineers at Kolon are those employed at the manufacturing plants. The plants are the places where on-the-job training is provided, and where the technology so far accumulated is executed. The numbers of technical workers at the Taegu plant in 1979, by grade and department, are listed in Table 5.4: most of those of the third class are graduates of engineering colleges and enter Kolon at this level; the remainder, 20 to 30 per cent, of the third class, are technical high school graduates promoted from the fourth class. Third class engineers usually assist the section chiefs in routine line activities of planning, ordering and supervising; they also are responsible for the staff activities of trouble-shooting, development of new products, process improvement and the evaluation of new

Table 5.4: Number of workers at the Taegu plant by skill level (as of June 1978)

	Dep't of general affairs[a]	Production	Maintenance	Total (percentage of the total)	
Director	1			1	(0.1)
1st class (manager)	2	1	1	4	(0.5)
2nd class (section chief)	7	4	3	14	(1.6)
3rd class (chief engineer)	14	14	9	37	(4.2)
4th class (group leader)	19	18	19	56	(6.4)
5th class (Male)	67	240	147	454	(52.1)
5th class (Female	27	268	10	305	(35.0)
Total	137	545	189	871	(100.0)

[a]Individuals belonging to the sections of Safety Control and Reserve Army Administration, four and six persons respectively, are included in the Department of General Affairs.
Source: Kolon Inc., for the Taegu plant.

equipment and facilities. Third-class engineers promoted from the fourth class usually work as supervisors on the spot. Fourth-class technicians work as group leaders or shift leaders in charge of personnel management and direct supervision of operators. Their average length of experience is about ten years. The third-class chief engineers and the fourth-class technicians constitute the main technical force of the plant.

Under fourth-class technicians are fifth-class operators. In the case of male workers, less than half are middle school (junior high school) graduates, more than half are high school graduates. Those fifth-class operators working in the maintenance department are required to be technical high school graduates. The rest of the male fifth-class operators work in the polymerisation and spinning sections. In the case of females in the fifth class, about 20 to 30 per cent are high school graduates; they work at inspection and packing.

When a new worker is hired, he usually undergoes two months' general training and six months' probationary training on the job. In the case of female workers they are given two months' general training and three months' on-the-job training,

Table 5.5: Number of workers in the production and maintenance departments by education and experience (as of June 1978)

Educational level	Work experience				Total number
	Less than 3 years	3 to less than 5 years	5 to less than 10 years	More than 10 years	
College or university	10	3	4	3	20
Technical senior high school	35	16	27	9	87
Junior high school (Male)	59	114	132	32	337
Junior high school (Female)	220	34	24	—	278
Total	324	167	187	44	722

Source: Kolon Inc., for the Taegu plant.

before being assigned to a department. Initial wages are 80 per cent of those for regular workers up to three months, and 90 per cent up to four to six months.

The number of workers by education and experience in the production and maintenance departments is shown in Table 5.5 and the training they received within the plant is summarised in Table 5.6. The total number of man-hours of technical training over the four years 1974-7 was an impressive 88,872; averaged over the total employment of the plant (722 persons) it amounted to 32.5 hours per employee each year.

THE ABSORPTION OF POLYESTER TECHNOLOGY

The production of polyester resin and fibre at Kolon has followed the same pattern as did that of nylon, involving the design, construction and operation of three production lines of ever-increasing scale and technical sophistication. In outline, the technology of polyester fibre production is identical to that of nylon, with an initial stage of polymerisation followed, either immediately or after chipping and drying, by spinning, drawing

Table 5.6: Technical training for Kolon's employees with the Taegu plant, 1974-7

Year	Number of persons attending	Contents of Training	Length of programme (per person)
1974	300	Production and maintenance	30 times (60 hrs)
1975	30	Engineering technology	64 hrs
1975	31	Inflammable synthetic fibre (seminar)	8 hrs
1975	8	Anti-static nylon (production)	24 hrs
1975	300	Production and maintenance	60 hrs
1976	25	Drawing technique	56 hrs
1976	32	EDPS	24 hrs
1976	4	Heat management	150 days
1976	300	Production and maintenance	30 times (60 hrs)
1977	48	Mechanical engineering drawing	128 hrs
1977	300	Production and maintenance	30 times (60 hrs)

Source: Kolon Inc., for the Taegu plant.

and winding. The first two polyester lines were designed with discontinuous processing; the third with both discontinuous (50 per cent by volume) and continuous (the other 50 per cent) processing. The dates of completion of the three lines were 1971, 1975 and 1979 respectively and the original design capacities 17, 70 and 75 metric tons per day. The first line has been expanded over the years so that in mid-1985 it was capable of producing 70 tons per day; the third line has not yet been utilised to its full extent, but is expected to be expanded to 150 tons per day in the next few years, as soon as extra demand for the product materialises.

The ability of Kolon's employees to utilise the technology of polyester polymerisation and spinning has also followed the same pattern as that of nylon. Once again, many foreign suppliers of the technology approached Kolon when it became known that Kolon intended to build and operate a plant. Once again, for the first production line, Kolon chose the American firm Chemtex for the provision of process design and finance and the Japanese firm Toray for assistance in construction and operation. Once again, the basic design of the process was carried out entirely by Chemtex and the construction by a single contractor under Chemtex's supervision. The procurement and installation of equipment were the responsibility of the contractor, who released the production line to Kolon only when it was complete, under the so-called 'turn-key' contract. Finally, once again, Toray's engineers performed the chief tasks during the start-up and ensuing operation.

Whereas Kolon's engineers and managers were mainly observers during the design and construction stages of the first polyester production line, by the time the second line was conceived, four years later, they had amassed sufficient knowledge and experience to carry out both of these functions unaided. The polymerisation and spinning processes incorporated in the second line were identical to those in the first; the only advance was an increase in scale from 17 to 70 metric tons per day. There were not too many difficulties in scaling up, for equipment of the appropriate size had already been produced for Western European and American chemical firms, and the discontinuous scheme of production (with the break, for chipping and drying, between polymerisation and spinning) meant that synchronisation of the two main processing steps was not necessary.

131

In the final two production lines, whose design and construction were undertaken together, Kolon had to seek foreign assistance once more. The reason was not that capacity increased still further, as both the third and fourth production lines were of approximately the same size — 75 tons per day versus 70 for the second production line. The reasons were twofold: first, a newer polymerisation process was to be incorporated; and secondly, one of the production lines was to be continuous, with the molten polymer from the reactors passing directly to the spinnerets, and then to the drawers and winders. To synchronise the processes required much more careful control, which in turn required much more instrumentation. Instrumentation was provided by two American firms, Honeywell and Brown, and the reactor design by the Japanese firm Hitachi. Construction of two of the five reactors was assigned to the Korean firm Dae Woo (see Chapter 6), but the manufacture of complex, delicate instruments could (and can) only be achieved abroad. Likewise, the spinnerets and drawing equipment still had to be imported from abroad, from Britain in Kolon's case.

The participation of Korean and foreign engineers in the design, construction and operation of the polyester production lines is summarised in Table 5.1. As in the case of nylon polymerisation, so in polyester there has been a steady progress towards independence, until there is a substantial advance in technique, at which point Kolon had to revert to a dependence on foreign suppliers: the shift from discontinuous to continuous processing marked the reversion in both cases.

IMPROVEMENTS

Technically trained employees of a company determined to improve its performance can generate improvements that reduce the costs of producing current output and that enable new products and capacity to be added to future output. It is the function of the company's administration to mobilise the technical and managerial skills of its employees so as to achieve beneficial change. In this section we will ask what methods Kolon's administration has utilised and what results it has obtained.

We will start with methods directed chiefly at improving existing equipment. One formal method is the organisation of

workers into quality control centres or circles. Every production, engineering, maintenance and research worker is assigned
to a circle which comprises his immediate colleagues, the
numbers in a circle varying from five to 20 (see Table 5.7,
a typical sample of the accomplishments of Taegu's circles in
the second half of 1970, when there were three nylon production lines in operation). Almost all the circles are represented in
Table 5.7, implying that improvements in activities were nearly
universal. As capacity is expanded and new employees hired,
new circles are formed and their objectives and accomplishments celebrated.

An informal method is the suggestion system, operating in all
departments. The procedure is as follows: as technicians work
in a plant, they often think of ways of simplifying their jobs.
They write them down and hand the proposals to the plant
manager. The manager collects them over a period, for example
one month, and discusses with department heads and section
chiefs whether or not the proposals are desirable. Such a suggestion system was adopted in 1969, and has secured the participation, mainly of fourth-class technicians. Since 1969, many
suggestions have been adopted leading to speedier production,
fewer defects, less waste and increases in quality. A sample
taken in 1975 revealed one suggestion adopted was increasing
the size of bobbins. (The normal size was 1 Kg/bobbin, but
adopting the proposal, package size increased to 1.2, 1.3, 1.8
and finally a 2.0 Kg/bobbin, with a resulting increase in
production rate.) Another example was the change to pinless
drawing from pin-drawing, which makes the yarn more nearly
uniform. Take-up speed also increased to 1,500 m/min from
1,200 m/min without a reduction in quality. Additional
improvements obtained through the operation of the suggestion
system in 1975 were the development of a two-cap take-up
device; a shortened polymerisation time; and better solvent
recovery.

It is difficult to evaluate the effects of direct technical change
on production costs, but an attempt can be made for one
isolated year, 1975 (see Table 5.8).

The outcome of such devices as the quality control circles
and the suggestion system is lower costs of production. We were
not able to measure the benefits received from specific improvements in Kolon's production of nylon and polyester, but we
were able to obtain accounting data which permitted compari-

Table 5.7: Activities of quality control circles, July-December 1970

Department	Section	Subject	Name of circle	Leader	No. of members	Control items	Improvement (%)	Month
Production	Polymerisation	Caprolactam loss decrease	Bull	K.W. Lee	10	Reducing the Caprolactam loss	90-40	July, 1970
		Polymer waste decrease	Noodle	H.M. Bae	7	Spaghetti	50-15	July
Production	Spinning Drawing (1)	Waste decrease	n.a.	J.O. Kim	9	Waste	7.600-3.600 (Kg)	September
		Reduce filament decrease	n.a.	Y.H. Son	8	Pin oil, cut filament	100-30	September
		Stain decrease	Lily	J.H. Park	7	Stain (%)	35-15	September
		Draw waste decrease	n.a.	S.K. Choi	14	Waste yarn	3.000-2.000 (Kg)	September
		Initial cut filament decrease	n.a.	T.K. Oh	16	Initial cut filament	10.3-5.0	August
		Poor transfer tail decrease	T.Q.	S.J. Cho	12	Transfer oil	2.0-	July
		Draw guide control	K.S.	W.S. Kim	13			November
Production	Spinning Drawing (2)	Stain decrease		Y.J. Lee	18	Grade 'A' percentage	7500. 0.62-0.4 500. 0.86-0.4	July
		Weight control	Elephant	E.T. Kim	10	Weight	53-20	August
		Initial cut filament decrease	Morning star	C.O. Lim	17	Initial cut filament	28-14	September
		Stain decrease	P.S. 77	J.I. Han	9	Stain (%)	25-15	September
		Full drum ratio and take-up guide damage decrease	Bear	W.B. Lee	6	Drum ratio, take-up guide damage	85-50	July

Division	Section	Project theme	Circle	Leader	Members	Control item	Effect	Month
Production	Inspection	Bad yarn winding	Hibiscus	S.B. Sock	14			September
		Relative viscosity decrease	Analyst B	B.O. Chio	7			
	Machine	Ether recovery increase	Analyst A	Y.K. Kim	6	Ether recovery	40-80	September
		PD4 limit in waste pump grand	Steam engine	N.S. Moon	7	PD_4 limit	10-20 (p.p.m)	October
		Backing-life increase	Maintenance	J.R. Kim	7	Packing change period	10-60 (days)	June
Engineering		Removal of impurity in compressed air	Industrial water	S.H. Chon	7	Moisture in compressed air	20-10	July
		Water quality uniformity and cost down	n.a.	N.S. Moon	7	Water treatment cost	$48-45_3$ (Won/m^3)	October
		Decrease of change in colour of chip	n.a.	H.T. Kim	6			
		Bad bobbin	Rainbow	T.K. Yu	10	Winding from grade	A. 26-66 / B. 40-20 / C. 34-14	October / October
Engineering	Engineering	Pipe leak decrease	Camel	K.Y. Lee	11			July
		Decrease of bad filter screen gasket	Lion	S.B. Kim	9	Bad chip	50-20	October
		Decrease of fluorescent lamp	Thunder	J.T. Kim	8	Waste number	400-200	December
R&D	Development	Work level raise of warp piecing	Development group	E.K. Ahn	11	Warp piecing		December

Source: *20-year history of Kolon*, p. 221.

Table 5.8: Productivity of labour and energy, and costs of production 1974-84: nylon filament at Kolon's Taegu plant (per metric ton of product)

| Year | Productivity of labour | | Productivity of energy[a] | | Costs of production | | | | | | |
| | | | | | Average variable cost | | Average fixed cost | | Average total cost | | |
	Man-hours per ton	Index: 1980=100	000kCal per ton	Index: 1980=100	Won, current prices	Index at constant prices, 1980=100	Won, current prices	Index at constant prices, 1980=100	Won, current prices	Won, constant prices	Index at constant prices, 1980=100
1974[b]	24.5	166	15,565	140	551	131	295	186	846	2,410	146
1977	19.3	131	12,144	109	622	96	311	125	933	1,720	104
1980	14.7	100	11,109	100	1,195	100	459	100	1,654	1,654	100
1982	14.3	97	9,590	86	1,243	82.5	608	105	1,851	1,470	89
1984	11.5	79	8,989	81	1,258	82.5	636	109	1,894	1,488	90
Average annual rate of reduction	7.7%		5.7%		4.6%		5.3%		5.0%		

[a]Includes tyre cord.
[b]Excludes production line 6, which did not come on stream until 1975.
Current prices were converted to constant prices by means of the wholesale price index: 1974 = 35.1; 1977 = 54.3; 1982 = 126.0;1984 = 127.2.

sons of the productivity of certain inputs, and the costs of certain outputs, at different points in time. Having analysed the data, we present summaries of the results in Tables 5.8 through 5.10, the first two tables referring to the production of nylon and the third to the production of polyester. Each table differs only in the product concerned: the measures provided — of the productivity of labour and energy, and of average-variable, average-fixed and average-total costs — are identical.

Discussing the tables in numerical order, the first, Table 5.8, measures improvements in the production of nylon filament at Taegu, the plant where it was introduced. The years covered are 1974, 1977, 1980, 1982 and 1984; during the period, production rose from approximately 15 metric tons per day to 50, 20 tons of which increase was contributed by the sixth production line coming into operation in 1975 and 15 tons of which was through the expansion of the first three production lines. (Production lines four and five were devoted to the manufacture of fish-net and tyre cord, respectively, whose output is not reported separately in Kolon's statistics.) The data in Table 5.8 for 1974 thus relate to the first three production lines, while the data for subsequent years relate to the first three plus the sixth, in what appeared to be approximately equal volume.

Looking at changes in the productivity of two main inputs, labour and energy, we find a reduction in the former of a little over half during the ten years 1974-84, and in the latter of a little less than half. Expressed in terms of average annual rates of reduction, the figure for labour is 7.7 per cent, and for energy 5.7 per cent. Turning to reductions in costs, Table 5.8 reveals that these can be broken down into reductions in average-variable cost, average-fixed cost and average-total cost. Over the ten years these annual reductions were 4.6 per cent, 5.3 per cent and 5.0 per cent respectively, impressive accomplishments considering that the production lines were being operated at or beyond their design capacities for almost the entire period.

One other set of data is available measuring labour productivity on a different, and unfortunately incomparable basis, namely persons employed per metric ton of nylon filament produced. At the Taegu plant in 1970, when only the first three production lines were in operation, 20 persons were employed in nylon filament manufacture for each ton made; in 1978 this number had fallen to eleven. At the same later date, in one plant of Toray in Japan, only eight persons were

Table 5.9: Productivity of labour and energy, and costs of production, 1974-84: nylon filament at Kolon's Gumi plant (per metric ton of product)

Year	Productivity of labour		Productivity of energy		Costs of production						
					Average variable cost		Average fixed cost		Average total cost		
	Man-hours per ton	Index: 1980=100	000kCal per ton	Index: 1980=100	Won, current prices	Index at constant prices, 1980=100	Won, current prices	Index at constant prices, 1980=100	Won, current prices	Won, constant prices	Index at constant prices, 1980=100
1974	26.7	247	22,737	196	661	154	449	257	1,110	3,160	184
1977	15.5	142	14,124	122	598	91	317	117	915	1,680	98
1980	10.9	100	11,595	100	1,220	100	498	100	1,718	1,718	100
1982	9.7	89	10,062	87	1,216	79	624	99	1,840	1,460	85
1984	9.3	85	9,898	85	n.a.	n.a.	n.a.	n.a.	1,842	1,448	84
Average annual rate of reduction		11.3%		8.7%		8.7%		12.6%			8.3%

Note: Current prices were converted to constant prices by means of the wholesale price index: 1974 = 35.1; 1977 = 54.3; 1982 = 126.0; 1984 = 127.2.

Table 5.10: Productivity of labour and energy, and costs of production, 1974-84: polyester filament at Kolon's Gumi plant (per metric ton of product)

Year	Productivity of labour		Productivity of energy[a]		Costs of production						
					Average variable cost[b]		Average fixed cost[b]		Average total cost[b]		
	Man-hours per ton	Index: 1980=100	000kCal per ton	Index: 1980=100	Won, current prices	Index at constant prices, 1980=100	Won, current prices	Index at constant prices, 1980=100	Won, current prices	Won, constant prices	Index at constant prices, 1980=100
1974[a]	22.4	207	20,710	193	529	227	260	130	789	2,240	184
1977	15.7	143	13,577	126	426	118	366	120	792	1,460	119
1980	11.0	100	10,714	100	644	100	562	100	1,226	1,226	100
1982	9.9	90	9,903	92	721	86	670	94.5	1,390	1,102	89.5
1984	7.8	71.5	8,831	82	n.a.	n.a.	n.a.	n.a.	n.a.	n.a.	n.a.
Average annual rate of reduction		11.2%		8.9%		12.9%		4.1%			7.5%

[a] line 1 only; thereafter both lines 1 and 2.
[b] Ditto, with equal weights to the two lines.
Current prices were converted to constant prices by means of the wholesale price index: 1974 = 35.1; 1977 = 54.3; 1982 = 126.0;1984 = 127.2.

employed per ton of output. The explanations given by Kolon's engineers for Toray's higher labour efficiency were longer experience in fibre manufacture and an all-male labour force, rather than one like Kolon's which is about 40 per cent female.

In 1978, when the productivity of labour at Kolon's Taegu plant was eleven employees per metric ton of filament, the productivity at Kolon's Gumi plant was nine to ten employees per ton, some 10 to 20 per cent higher. The reasons were partly product heterogeneity at Taegu, and partly assorted equipment of smaller scale. At Taegu, a variety of nylon filaments was produced, at Gumi only filament of 70 denier; at Taegu there were, in 1978, four production lines ranging in age from three to 15 years, at Gumi just two parallel lines, of the same design and capacity installed nine years previously.

The production of nylon filament at Kolon's newer plant at Gumi is not seen to be more efficient overall than that at the older plant at Taegu when the data in Table 5.9 are compared with those in the previous table. To be sure, labour productivity remains higher at Gumi, but energy productivity is lower, and average costs of production — variable, fixed and total — display no general tendency. Average total costs were lower at Gumi in three years (1977, 1982 and 1984) of the five in the sample, but higher in the other two.

The next table, 5.10, summarises the results of improvements in the production of polyester at Gumi. For the first year in the compilation, 1974, the first production line was on stream; for the remaining years, both the first and the second. Since the two production lines are almost identical in design and have been almost identical in output, the whole period 1974-84 can be considered as a single entity. In almost all dimensions — labour and energy productivities and average total cost — the rates of improvement in polyester production at Gumi are close to those in nylon production at the same plant. The only difference is in the proportions of the overall reduction in costs attributable to fixed and variable cost items; in nylon the larger savings occurred in fixed-cost items, in polyester in variable-cost items. The engineers at Kolon did not attach any significance to these differences, and our research did not isolate the contributing factors.

Considering all three sets of data together, we find a considerable similarity in the pattern of improvements across products, plants and time. Generally, the rate of improvement, measured either in physical or in cost terms, was more rapid in the first years of operation of new facilities, tapering off in later years. Improvements did not cease, according to our figures, at the Gumi plant, nor did they at the Taegu plant when allowance is made for the production of finer denier filament and of such special yarns as anti-static, electro-conductive, computer ribbon, sewing thread, dope-dyed, pre-shrinkage and soft-touch, all of which yield higher unit values when sold. Operating profits, therefore, when also measured per metric ton of output, would reveal a more nearly constant rate of increase throughout the entire period.

This proliferation of products has been the result of advances both within Kolon and without. Up until roughly 1978 the Korean textile manufacturing industry — the users of Kolon's artificial fibres — was not sufficiently skilled to be able to utilise the finest denier filaments and the specialised fibres; improvements in the industry's finishing technology, such as in weaving, knitting, dyeing and sewing, were necessary before Kolon's new products could be assimilated. Kolon's production therefore was concentrated on the standard forms of nylon yarns and tyre cord, and Kolon's improvements were derived from better production and quality control.

Since 1978, Kolon's efforts have been directed more towards the adoption of advanced products developed by textile firms abroad. In April 1978, when the R & D centre being was established, there was a staff of 57 employees and an expenditure, relative to total sales, of 0.65 per cent to be expended on product development. Since then, expenditures have risen year by year, to 1.2 per cent of total sales in 1982 and 2.6 per cent in 1985. Employment in the Centre has risen too, to 109 persons in 1982 and 153 in 1985. Of the staff in 1985, six have PhDs (all were hired with MScs, and were then seconded to the Korean Advanced Institute of Science and Technology for their doctoral training), 33 have MScs, 37 BScs and the remainder technical training at secondary school.

Indicative of Kolon's improvements have been the patents applied for. Through 1978, Kolon had eleven patents registered in the Korean patent office, almost all representing process or product improvements. After 1978, the balance of patent applications shifted towards products new to Korea; this shift was celebrated in 1985 when Kolon received its first patent in the United States of America, on the characteristics of an improved version of aramid pulp, an aromatic polyamide invented by du Pont.

THE DIFFUSION OF THE TECHNOLOGY

As the first producer in Korea of nylon and polyester fibres, the Kolon company has been the source of some of the technological advances in the artificial fibre industry. Examples of techniques that have diffused from Kolon have been the molten caprolactam system, which dispenses with the step of melting chips of resin, and the three-step polymerisation-depolymerisation system, which has even been exported to Thailand (in 1979).

Doped yarn, which was dyed before spinning, and ballow fibre technology were introduced first by Kolon and have diffused to the Jeil synthetic fibre company and others. Silk-like fibre was also made first by Kolon and has been diffused throughout the synthetic fibre companies in Korea. The direct 'spin-draw' system and POY-DTX (pre-oriented yarn draw texturing) were used first by Kolon 1975 and have now been adopted by Tong Yang, Sunkyong and others in Korea.

Top-level engineers at the Kolon plant, in interviews, seemed quite confident that they could provide full-scale engineering and know-how to foreign as well as domestic buyers. Moreover, they emphasised that they had already participated in the start-up of the plant Chemtex built for the Hantex nylon company in Thailand. Similar joint ventures have been undertaken in countries such as India and Taiwan (see Table 5.11). In the domestic market, Kolon's technicians supervised a project to build a dryer facility at Koryo Synthetic Fibre Co., which spins nylon yarns.

In the course of diffusion, several problems arose for Kolon. One set affected exports of technology, when its subsidiary the Kolon Engineering Co. (KEC), attempted to provide nylon filament plants, chiefly to African countries. The buyers, without exception, demanded loans, as had the Koreans a decade or more earlier. Kolon does not have the capital to extend loans.

Second, problems arise in attempting to sell know-how to domestic firms. Since the domestic nylon yarn market is divided

Table 5.11: Kolon's technological exports to foreign countries

Month and year	Company name and country	Technical assistance
Nov. 1972	Shree Synthetics Ltd, India	Start-up operation of nylon plant
Jan. 1975	Ta Shung Chemical Fiber, Taiwan	Start-up operation of nylon plant
Nov. 1975	Hantex, Thailand	Start-up operation of nylon plant
April 1979	Hantex, Thailand	Nylon plant improvement programme

Source: Kolon Co.

among three strong firms, competing with each other, the opportunity to sell know-how is limited. It is further restricted when we consider secrecy, as an example will reveal. The example involves the production, in Korea, of spinnerets. Spinnerets are necessary in production, and every firm demands quite a large number. Thus far, nylon yarn-producing firms have ordered them from Japanese factories; if a Korean firm attempts to establish a plant for spinneret production, it must compete with the Japanese. In ordering spinnerets, the ordering company must disclose the size (denier) and number of spinnerets needed. The spinneret-producing firm would thereby get confidential information on the produce mix and output rates of the ordering firms. The Korean nylon producers would not risk releasing this information and so would continue to buy from abroad. Of course the problem would be reduced if spinnerets were produced by many local firms, but this possibility is not feasible, simply because there would not be enough demand to support more than one producer.

Secrecy prohibits diffusion. It was revealed by the case study that Kolon has been paying increasingly more attention to the security of its know-how, as the level of its accumulated technology has risen. As was mentioned earlier, the case of Toray's sale of Kolon's know-how to an Indonesian firm is thought to justify attention to such matters. As the state of technology rises in the future, diffusion may be even further hindered.

Among the three nylon yarn-producing companies there is in existence an anti-pirating clause in order to prevent the leakage of confidential 'know-how'. By a clause in his contract an engineer who is employed by company A cannot move directly to other nylon-producing companies B or C within three years, unless he moves to another non-nylon company first. It is said that this clause is observed by the three companies. The clause seems to have two conflicting effects on the development and diffusion of technology. On the one hand, if secrecy reduces the leakage of 'know-how', it will tend to provide a greater incentive for research and development. On the other hand, secrecy reduces diffusion. There appears to be no way to evaluate the net effect of the anti-pirating clause, although we judge that the first factor is the most significant and that the anti-pirating clause contributes to the general absorption of technology in the nylon industry.

CONCLUSION

The Korean First Five-year Economic Development Plan, which began in 1962, included a project for nylon filament production. The government facilitated the completion of the project by helping to mobilise both foreign and domestic capital. A high and rapidly expanding demand for nylon textile products was also present. Kolon, the firm we studied, led the industry during the 1950s and the 1960s. Their management skill and general knowledge of the technology brought success to the company.

In entering into nylon polymerisation Kolon drew upon the engineering designs of Chemtex of the United States and the know-how of Toray of Japan. Of these two partners the engineers at Kolon believed and the researchers agreed that the 'know-how' provided by Toray played a more important role. Chemtex and Toray contribute to Kolon's management, capital and knowledge through the contracts involving technical co-operation and investment. Chemtex entered into technical co-operation with Kolon in 1961 and was permitted by the Korean government to invest in a joint venture on the basis of 50:50 ownership. Chemtex supplied seven directors out of 14 on the board and the sole auditor. Chemtex also participated in the design and construction stages for the nylon and polyester facilities in the Gumi plant of Kolon.

Toray (then Toyo Rayon) was awarded a contract involving technical co-operation after the completion of Kolon's first support plant and was also allowed to participate in the investment. The first Kolon-Toray meeting on technology was held at Taegu plant in May 1969; meetings were repeated almost every year, alternating between Korea and Japan, and had by 1979 totalled eight in number.

The present outstanding shares of stock of the Kolon Company held by Chemtex and Toray amount to 23.3 per cent of the total in nylon and 28.8 per cent in polyester. Kolon currently maintains its technical relationship with Chemtex on an *ad hoc* basis, engaging in project-by-project contracts. Under this arrangement, Chemtex joins Kolon in nylon or polyester expansion projects. In return, Chemtex has provided several opportunities for Kolon to sell Kolon's know-how to foreign firms, in Thailand, India and Taiwan. This is a very similar situation to that in 1963 when Chemtex engineering and Toray know-how were combined at the time of the first of Kolon's plant construction projects.

As for Toray, the direct investment by Toray seems to have made many things possible. One result is the appointment of one standing director and one common director on Kolon's board. Another is the Kolon-Toray technology meetings. Overseas training and visits from Toray's engineers to the Kolon plant also seem to have been of benefit. Thirdly, although Toray never disclosed top-class 'know-how', which could accelerate competition between Kolon and Toray in overseas markets, they nevertheless made accessible a substantial amount of lower-level know-how. Finally, Toray participated in Kolon's profits. For these reasons, we conclude that direct investment by co-operating foreign firms is mutually beneficial and promotes the absorption and diffusion of imported technology. The hypothesis of a positive correlation between direct investment and technological co-operation seems to be borne out in this case study of Kolon.

The absorption and adaptation process of nylon technology at Kolon seems to have been successful. The company absorbed the knowledge relating to start-up, operation and maintenance. Nevertheless the company has still relied on Chemtex engineering for design and construction. Much of the success stems from Kolon's technical training schemes — on-the-job training for the newly hired, overseas training, etc. Also significant have been the improvement proposal system, quality control activities, intermittent drive for cost reduction, the establishment of a patent section and of a research and development department.

It would be safe to say that Kolon did not follow any unusual policy in absorbing the foreign technology. Nevertheless, we might possibly draw some policy implications about technology absorption from Kolon's experience. First, especially at the early stage of technology absorption, it may be better for the importing firm to maintain as intimate a relationship as possible with co-operating firms. Secondly, although it may not always be the case, joint ventures can help smooth the transfer of foreign technology. Thirdly, we have seen that the accumulation of minor technological changes and of plant expansion at Kolon contributed very much to increases in productivity. Finally, as the general level of accumulated technology of a firm increases to an internationally acceptable one, the firm may consider establishing a subsidiary engineering firm, since an engineering firm backed by a large-scale, technically advanced mother company can diffuse technology abroad. Assistance from government, in the form of loans or guarantees, may, however, be necessary for the export to take place.

6

Case Study: Machinery

INTRODUCTION

A case study on the adoption, absorption and diffusion of imported technology in the machinery sector is presented in this chapter. Machinery was chosen because of its important role in enhancing industrial independence through increased domestic production of capital goods. Although the machinery sector in the Republic of Korea exhibited a fairly rapid rate of absorption of its first set of foreign techniques, it has not been able to keep up with subsequent developments from abroad. The industry has achieved only a modest rate of diffusion of its specialised knowledge. These main findings, and others less controversial, will follow.

The approach in this case study has been to study one company in depth and as many others superficially as time and resources permitted. The first part of this chapter will deal briefly with the sources of information. After this, there will be a short section on the history of the company chosen. This same company will provide the data for the next three sections describing the technology that was imported, its absorption and the improvements that were subsequently made upon it. Following these lengthy sections will be a shorter one describing the diffusion of imported technology, and then another shorter one focusing on the degree of sophistication of a technology and its effect upon the absorption and diffusion. This section will involve a comparison between the sophisticated technology analysed in the previous sections and a simpler imported technology, introduced concurrently.

Finally, there will be a conclusion in which the accomplishments of the industry are summarised and their implications for public policy noted.

The firm chosen for detailed study was Daewoo Heavy Industries Ltd, a privately-owned company in which 37 per cent of the shares are owned by the holding company, Daewoo Corporation, 7 per cent by Korean commercial banks and the remaining 57 per cent by a body of Korean citizens. Daewoo Heavy Industries Ltd (DHI) produces a wide range of vehicles — diesel engines, railway wagons, fork-lift trucks, excavators — and a large variety of industrial machinery such as machine tools.

The information from DHI was supplemented by data gathered from other firms, both Korean and international, and from the general knowledge of the authors. The source of most of the information on DHI was the company's employees and their documents; whenever other sources were drawn upon they will be cited. The source of information on the other companies will also be cited where it seems necessary.

HISTORY OF DAEWOO HEAVY INDUSTRIES LTD

The firm concerned in this study was founded in 1937, while Korea was under Japanese occupation, as the Chosun Machine Works. During that era, it produced industrial machines, mining equipment and, occasionally, weapons such as artillery and small-sized submarines. After Japan's retreat in 1945, the firm was nationalised by the government and, as a government workshop, resumed production of industrial machines. In 1963, following the commencement of the nation's economic development plans, the government re-established the company as a corporation, under the name of the Hankook Machine Industrial Co. Ltd. In 1968 its shares and management were transferred to private hands.

Since then, the company has gradually extended its business areas and diversified its main products. In 1973 the company merged with the Bugok Rolling Stocks plant and added railroad cars and coaches to its products. In 1975, the company established the diesel engine plant and began to produce MAN engines, in technical collaboration with the Maschinenfabrik Augsburg-Nüernberg Aktiengesselschaft and with financial assistance from the German government. In 1976, Hankook merged with the Daewoo Machinery Company. Through these successive mergers, the company has grown to the extent that it operates four major plants: the industrial machine plant, the diesel engine plant, the rolling stocks plant and the precision machine plant.

So far as management was concerned, the year 1975 marked the end of an epoch for the company. Despite its leading role in Korean industry, the company had been in chronic deficit in prior years, mainly due to a lack of domestic demand and to unstable direction. However, in 1976, the holding company Daewoo Industrial Company Ltd, together with its affiliates, took over 44.8 per cent of the total shares of the company and began participating in management. Daewoo Industrial Company, the parent, is one of the largest trading companies in the orient, with annual international sales over US$1 billion currently, and is rated highly for its excellent managerial ability.

IMPORT OF DIESEL ENGINE TECHNOLOGY

The story of diesel engines in Korea begins seven years earlier, in 1969. With government encouragement, as described in Chapter 3, Hankook began an investigation into the German diesel engine manufacturing industry, with the aim of manufacturing, under licence, water-cooled diesel engines in the power range from 50 to 200 HP. The investigation continued until July 1970 and showed that engine types produced by MAN and Daimler Benz AG coincided most nearly with those conceived of by Hankook.

On 31 August 1970, as the result of speedier negotiations and more favourable financial conditions offered by the former of the two potential foreign suppliers, a licence agreement was concluded between Maschinenfabrik Augsburg-Nüernberg AG (MAN), Augsburg, Federal Republic of Germany, as the licensor, and Hankook Machine Industrial Co. Ltd, Inchon, Korea, as the licensee. The subject matter of the agreement concerned the following diesel engines built by MAN: type D 0844 M, power 50 to 90 HP (DIN), and type D 0845 HM, power 130 to 160 HP (DIN), plus all modifications and improvements to the engines effected by MAN during the period covered by the agreement. The licence authorised Hankook to manufacture the said engines, to draw relevant engine parts from third parties, to market the engines throughout Asia, with the exception of India and Turkey, and to manufacture and market single parts as spares for the said engines.

The licensor was required to provide accurate information and documents covering the objects of the agreement. The licensor also assured the licensee that the latter could use his patents and declared his willingness to make available foreign rights used by himself to the licensee under the most favourable conditions which could be obtained. In addition, a skeleton agreement was drawn up relating to the residence of specialists employed by the licensee in the country of the licensor and vice versa.

The duration of the licence agreement was five years from the date production began but could be renewed. For the first five years royalties were to be subdivided into a single basic fee of DM 500,000 and a piece rate which declined with increasing production. The basic fee of DM 500,000 was to be payed in three instalments: the first instalment (DM 200,000) within two months of authorisation by the Korean government and at the latest three months after the granting of a credit by the Kreditanstalt für Wiederaufbau, Frankfurt/Main, for the acquisition of equipment to manufacture the objects of the agreement; the second instalment (DM 200,000) within two years of signing the licence agreement; and the third instalment (DM 100,000) within three years of signing the licence agreement.

The royalty rates on current output were as follows: for the first 15,000 litres of cylinder capacity, in one year of contract, DM 22.50 per litre; for the next 15,000 litres of cylinder capacity, in the same year of contract, DM 18.75 per litre; for the third 15,000 litres of cylinder capacity, in the same year of contract, DM 15.00 per litre; for the fourth 15,000 litres of cylinder capacity, in the same year of contract, DM. 11.25 per litre; and for all further engines in the same year of contract, DM 7.50 per litre. After the initial period of five years, royalty rates could be renegotiated; after ten, discontinued.

For spare parts, a licence fee of 5 per cent of the respective MAN list price was agreed upon. In the event that MAN supplied Hankook with more than 50 per cent (in terms of value) of the parts for the engines to be manufactured under licence and providing that at least 1,500 pieces were supplied per annum, Hankook was required to pay only 50 per cent of the minimum royalties. In the event that Hankook exported engines to Asian countries, the royalties were increased.

The skeleton contract concluded between Hankook and MAN on 28 October 1970 provided for the employment of 500 Korean skilled workers by MAN at its engine and truck manufacturing plant in Germany. According to the terms of this contract, the first Koreans, 20 in all, commenced work at MAN on 1 January 1971; the number was to increase by approximately 70 men later in the year. Further increases in the number of Korean workers were to depend upon the success of the initial experiment.

PRODUCTION PROCESS FOR DIESEL ENGINES

The flow diagram of Figure 6.1 shows in schematic form the ideal production cycle, assuming proper co-ordination of pre-production, production and storage, plus the associated subsidiary functions. This technologically conditioned material flow was worked out during the first planning section, and, on the occasion of the talks in Inchon in 1970, accepted by the company.

A rough division of the main production stages is shown along the top edge of Figure 6.1, these being receiving, storage, preliminary operations, intermediate storage, machine production, assembly lines, finishing shop and completed products. The material flow is indicated by arrows. The stages through which materials pass are named in sequence from left to right. From the store for purchased and produced parts the material travels directly to the corresponding preliminary or final assembly point. The raw materials required for casting are taken from the raw materials store to the foundry, via the foundry cleaning room. Completed castings are then placed in intermediate storage. At this point the material flow for casting diverges, according to the component. Subsequently, the cast material flows to preliminary and then final assembly.

Starting at the sheet steel, strip material and rod material store, those materials which must be forged pass through the forge and hardening shop, are primed and finished up in the forged parts store. Initially, the foraged components were purchased from MAN: it was not until the second expansion stage (1976) that the forge was built. The most important forged parts of a water-cooled diesel engine are the crank shaft, counter weights, rocker gear, rocker gear bracket, gears, gear

Figure 6.1: Production flow sheet for diesel engines

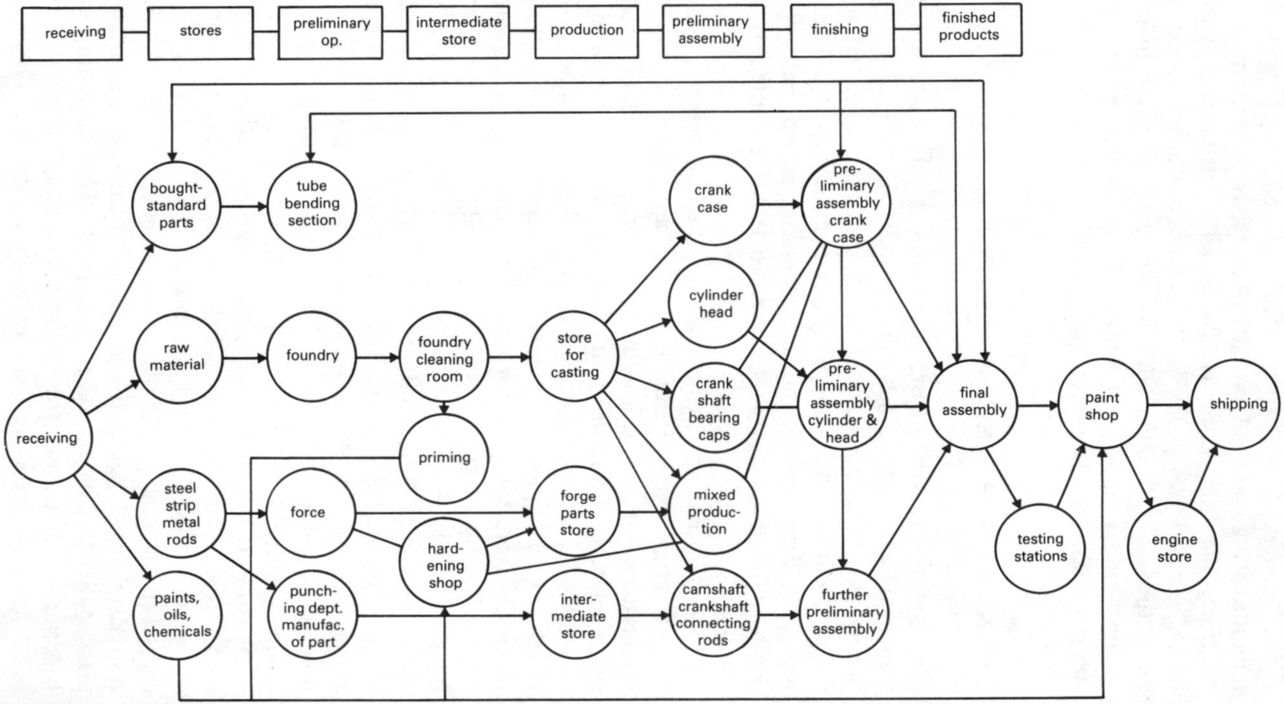

Table 6.1: Forging operations in the diesel engine plant

Processing shop	Operations	Machinery
Hammer mill	Cutting, hand forging Pressing, upsetting	Cold circular saw High-speed swaging hammers Upsetting machines
Drop forge	Initial heating Initial upsetting Drop forging	Pre-heating (gas or induction heated) Friction screw presses Die-stamping presses
Straightening	Upsetting Pressing Calibrating Grinding and polishing Surface treatment Aligning	Friction screw presses Eccentric presses Sizing presses Grinding and polishing machines Cleaning drums Sand-blasting equipment Aligning machines or benches
Re-annealing	Re-annealing Treatment of surfaces	Iso-thermal annealing equipment Blasting equipment Bonding equipment

rings, connecting rods, camshaft and values. Some idea of the complexity of manufacture can be gained from Table 6.1, which lists the various forging operations and the machinery used in carrying them out, and from Table 6.2, which lists the subsequent machining operations.

SCALE AND RATES OF OUTPUT

At the outset of the project a feasibility study was commissioned by Hankook and carried out by the German consulting firm Aktiengesellschaft für Entwicklungsplanung, of Essen. In the course of predicting the profitability of the proposed plant in Korea, the consultant projected sales figures for the firm's diesel engines, recorded in the first three columns of Table 6.3. Actual production and sales figures are shown in the final two columns of the table.

Against the production and sales figures must be set the capacity of the plant, 24,000 diesel engines per year with one shift per day, or 72,000 per year with three shifts. Capacity was calculated by the German engineers who designed the plant, based upon assumptions that production would occur at the pace maintained in German facilities, with raw materials and

Table 6.2: Machining operations in the diesel engine plant

Processing line	Operations
Crankshaft	Cutting to length
	Centring
	Turning
	Circular threading
	Drilling
	Induction hardening
	Balancing
	Washing
Camshaft	Centring and aligning
	Turning
	Drilling
	Shaping
	Induction hardening and unstressing
	Grinding with circular and cam grinding machines
	Checking, testing and washing
Counter weights for crankshafts	Milling
	Drilling
	Trimming
	Weighing
Connecting rods	Milling
	Grinding
Flywheel and gear ring	Turning
	Tracer turning
	Drilling
	Milling and shaping of gear ring teeth

components up to the standard of those supplied to MAN in Germany. Comparison of production and sales figures, on the one hand, and capacity on the others, reveals that the diesel engine plant has failed to achieve its potential. Build-up of production was gradual over the first four years of operation, by which time the plant was operating at 63 per cent of capacity, and a peak of 68 per cent was obtained in the following year (1979); but since then it has showed a decline. Such disparities demand an explanation.

The simplest explanation for the failure of Daewoo to exploit the potential of their diesel engine plant is that there has been insufficient demand for the products. In 1975 there were two manufacturers of commercial vehicles in Korea: Shinjin, which then used Toyota/Hino engines in their chasses, and Hyundai, which used Ford. Both were reluctant to substitute Korean for foreign engines, for technical and economic reasons. Initially, the technical problem encountered in trying to sell to local

Table 6.3: Prospective and actual rates of output and sales of MAN diesel engines, 1970-84

Year	Prospective sales figures for medium-sized diesel engines in Korea			Actual figures for MAN diesel engines, all applications	
	For trucks	For buses	Total	Production	Sales
1970	9,000	3,000	12,000	—	—
1971	10,000	3,600	13,600	—	—
1972	10,000	3,400	14,300	—	—
1973	11,000	3,700	14,700	—	—
1974	11,500	4,300	15,800	—	—
1975	13,000	4,900	17,900	1,120[a]	285
1976	15,500	5,650	21,150	2,578	3,119
1977	18,500	6,375	24,875	9,385	9,313
1978	21,000	7,300	28,300	15,206	15,041
1979	22,500	8,300	30,800	16,281	16,963
1980	24,000	9,100	33,100	13,665	13,650
1981	25,000	10,250	35,250	13,100	13,101
1982	37,000	21,000	58,000	13,876	14,020
1983	53,000	26,000	79,000	15,925[b]	14,642[b]
1984	59,000	26,000	85,000	15,085[b]	14,518[b]

[a] Production began in May 1975, in the horsepower range 100-281 HP.
[b] Includes, as well, large-sized diesel engines (from 310 to 675 HP).

Source: Daewoo.

manufacturers was that the engines could not be mounted on their vehicles. Engines are not final products by themselves: an engine is a sub-system of a bigger system. Hence, there always exists a certain degree of inter-relationship between the sub-system and its total system. In mounting an engine on a vehicle it is necessary to integrate the two into a functioning system, unless the two were designed initially as an integrated system. However, since Korean vehicle manufacturers were already producing trucks and buses with imported engines by 1975, it was technically not immediately possible for Daewoo's engines to be mounted on the vehicles which were then being produced. The licensing agreement did not contain any clause addressed to, or mention anything about, this adaptation problem, an unfortunate omission.

When Daewoo bought the controlling part of Hankook's equity, it immediately launched a project to eliminate the mounting problem. First, Daewoo's project team worked in close contact with KIST (Korean Institute of Science and Technology), a research institute established by the Korean government to help business firms and industries solve technical problems. Furthermore, Daewoo asked MAN for specific technical assistance. In the beginning, MAN was reluctant to give extra assistance not included in the original licensing agreement. However, after Daewoo's repeated requests and after having learned about the serious market barrier due to this mounting problem, MAN began to help Daewoo by giving technical information thereon. After a year's hard work, Daewoo resolved most of the problems, so that vehicle manufacturers were able to mount their engines on buses, trucks and other heavy-duty vehicles being manufactured in Korea.

The specific technical problem of mounting having been eliminated, the company still faced the general technical problem of low quality and the economic problem of high price. The prices of local diesel engines were initially set to recover costs, which were high chiefly because of the small scale of operation. Overheads — e.g. interest payments on the foreign loans undertaken to purchase machinery — were spread over few engines, and imported raw materials and components were purchased in such small lots that quantity discounts could not be negotiated. In addition, the inexperience of management and the poor quality of the product raised the average costs of those engines that could be sold.

It was the problem of high costs, and consequently prices, that had led to the takeover of Hankook Machine Industrial Co. by the Korean Development Bank, its main creditor, and to its subsequent assignment to Daewoo. It was Daewoo's reputation for skilful management and technical competence that led to its being selected by the Korean government, in the expectation that Daewoo would be able to curb costs.

Upon acquisition in 1976, Daewoo asked the government to impose a ban against the import of competing foreign diesel engines. The government acquiesced to this request, in exchange for the right to control the price of diesel engines to local vehicle manufacturers. The price was set at approximately the price of imported diesel engines and imports ceased, so that by 1978 the domestic market for medium-sized engines was being supplied entirely by Daewoo.

Displacing foreign diesel engines, Daewoo's production and sales of MAN diesels rose rapidly in 1977 and 1978, although not sufficiently to utilise all the plant capacity. By then, the demand forecasts (of Table 6.3) for medium-sized engines were seen to have been overly optimistic, chiefly because it was proving possible to substitute engines of lower horse-power in less powerful trucks. Some of these smaller-sized engines were even being produced by Daewoo, who, before absorbing Hankook, had independently entered into a licence agreement with the Japanese firm Isuzu to produce Isuzu diesel engines in the horsepower range 85-145. Given the overlap in power ratings of the MAN and Isuzu engines, Daewoo decided to concentrate on producing MAN diesels in the medium-range 100-281 HP; in the years 1976-9 the ratio of production of medium (MAN) to small-sized (Isuzu) engines was approximately 1.0 to 1.5, and the ratio of the revenues from their sales was approximately 2.0 to 1.0.

Daewoo might have continued to produce and sell medium- and small-sized engines in these ratios had not the government, in an effort to rationalise engine production, decreed in 1979 that Daewoo should not have access to the new market created by the growing production of small automobiles in Korea. This exclusion, combined with the recession of 1980-2, produced a collapse in the demand for Daewoo's Isuzu engines; from a peak output of approximately 26,000 engines in 1979, production had fallen to 1,500 in 1982, from which figure it has not recovered. One price that Daewoo paid for its monopoly in the market for medium-size diesel engines was the loss of an oligopolistic position, shared with other Korean manufacturers, in the market for small-size engines.

ABSORPTION OF THE TECHNOLOGY

In order to accelerate the absorption of diesel engine manufacturing technology, Hankook had arranged for the training of engineers and skilled workers in Germany. The original contract with MAN, concluded in 1970, provided for a limited exchange of personnel, in the case of Koreans not to exceed six months for any one person nor a total of five persons in MAN's engineering offices or factories at any one time. The majority of Koreans sent to Germany under this provision were engineers; the total over the first five years of the agreement was 30 (see the top row of Table 6.4).

There was nothing extraordinary in MAN's training Korean engineers, but there was something extraordinary in MAN's bringing over Korean skilled workers. In a separate contract, also concluded in 1970, MAN undertook to provide employment for up to 500 skilled workers in its engine and truck manufacturing plant. The third through the sixth rows of Table 6.4 summarise the experience; it can be seen that the number of Koreans involved were far larger than is usual for a training programme and their stay in Germany was much longer than is

Table 6.4: Number of Koreans receiving training and employment in MAN's diesel engine plant in Germany

Status of Koreans	Numbers departed	Numbers returned	Date of departure	Date of return
Engineers	30	30	1970-5	
"	32	32	1976-85	
Skilled workers	20	16	Jan. 1971	Jan. 1973
" "	70	51	July 1971	July 1973
" "	100	73	Feb. 1972	Feb. 1975 to 1975
" "	160	108	July 1972	July 1974
" "	11	11	1976-85	
Total skilled workers	361	259		
Per cent returned		72%		

Source: Daewoo.

customary. Moreover, while they were working for MAN, the Korean workers were treated as its employees.

Remembering that in the early 1970s there was a shortage of skilled workers in Germany, the advantage to MAN of being able to draw at will upon a pool of industrious and technically educated workers was substantial. To Hankook, the advantage would also have been substantial, provided that the Koreans acquired the skills they would need to utilise when they returned. To the individual Koreans who remained through marriage to native Germans, or who emigrated to other industrialised countries like the United States, the advantage was presumably the higher income that could be earned. Since nearly 31 per cent of the Korean workers sent to Germany failed to return to Korea to apply the skills they had acquired, the brain drain was fairly high.

Nevertheless, in spite of the loss of trained workers, the Korean firm felt that the employment programme was worthwhile. At the end of the first year of operation of the newly erected plant in Inchon, by which time only one expatriate engineer remained, it felt that the Korean engineers and skilled workers had absorbed those portions of the imported technology relating to the start-up, operation and maintenance of the diesel engine manufacturing processes, and to have made some small progress in absorbing the knowledge required for the prior stages of equipment design and procurement and plant construction. Basic process design had not been encountered; nor, deliberately, had research and development. Some of the Korean engineers sent to Germany for training had requested assignment to MAN's R & D department, where they might learn about the design of new engines, but this was denied.

There is some additional evidence to support the firm's claim for a rapid absorption of the imported technology governing the production stage, stemming from an ever-decreasing rate of defective items. In the year 1975, when production began, the defective rate was 30.8 per cent; this fell to 27.2 per cent in 1976, 20.5 per cent in 1977, 15.4 per cent in 1978, 14.5 per cent in 1979, 13.6 per cent in 1980 and 12.5 per cent in 1981. In what Daewoo believes to be a better indication of performance, their 'Engine Quality Index', calculated first in 1981, and equal to $[1 - (\text{Number Defective} + \text{Number Downgraded})/290] \times 100$, the value rose from 92.4 per cent in 1981 to 96.8 per cent in 1982 and 98.6 per cent in 1983. By assuming that the two different values for 1981 are equivalent, we can link the two indexes, deriving values of the percentage defective for 1982 and 1983 of 5.3 per cent and 2.3 per cent respectively. The contrast between the last percentage and that for the initial year of production, 30.8 per cent, is striking. (The means by which some of the improvements in product quality were obtained are described in the next section.)

There are two other indicators of the degree to which Daewoo has absorbed the technology of diesel engine manufacture, both referring to later years of production. The first is the fraction of engines sold on which the purchaser subsequently makes claims for repairs or renewal: that has fallen from 0.53 per cent in 1980 to 0.50 per cent in 1981, 0.46 per cent in 1982 and 0.29 per cent in 1983. The other, more comprehensive indicator is the index of direct labour productivity, measured as the number of acceptable engines produced per man-hour worked. Based upon 1978 = 100, the index advanced to 125 in 1979, 139 in 1980, 156 in 1981 and 175 in 1982.

These are all the quantitative measures available to us to judge the extent to which Daewoo has absorbed the technology underlying the design of MAN's diesel engines and the design, construction and operation of the facilities in which they are produced. They do not provide much indication, though, on the extent to which Daewoo's designers and engineers could substitute for foreigners in performing the various activities, being related as they are entirely to continuing production. What we would like to have are data on the design and operation of subsequent diesel engine plants, such as we have on subsequent plants in the petrochemical, artificial fibre and iron and steel industries, but no subsequent diesel engine plant has been, or is scheduled to be, built. The chief reason is the lack of demand, even after ten years, for the products of the first diesel engine plant built by Daewoo. This failure of demand to materialise seems to have had an influence upon the rate of absorption of the technology.

To the authors, it is significant that the improvements which have been secured were initiated during the years 1976-9, when the output of diesel engines was growing rapidly. In the first few years of operation there appears to be a close association between quality and quantity of production. When production moves in response to demand, and demand is growing, skilled personnel can be continuously employed in the same activity, accumulating and applying experience. The application of experience in a systematic way leads, among other things, to increases in the rate of output which the facilities can produce. If the market is expanding, this additional output can be profitably sold. In mechanical industries, in the absence of growing demand at levels sufficient to operate the facilities fully, skilled personnel originally trained to operate the facilities cannot all be continuously employed. They may be transferred to other projects and their specific skills lost. Such a situation arose after the first years of the diesel engine plant when Daewoo, in an attempt to control costs, had to transfer some of those Koreans trained in MAN's German plant to other assignments.

Our conclusion with regard to the relative success of the absorption of the imported technology of diesel engines must therefore be qualified. On the one hand, most of those to whom the authors spoke in the course of gathering their information agreed that manufacturing know-how had steadily accumulated once Daewoo had taken over, to an extent sufficient to enable the Koreans to dispense with all but one of the expatriate engineers. On the other hand, the failure to operate the facilities at full capacity and to produce at design cost suggests that the technology involved in operation has not been wholly absorbed. There remains a dependency on some components which must still be imported from abroad (carburettors are one example) and on foreign firms which must be enlisted for alterations in engine design (to achieve a reduction in weight or an increase in power, for example). In sum, it can probably be said that Daewoo's engineers have absorbed those portions of the imported technology relating to the start-up, operation and maintenance of the diesel engine manufacturing process; and, at the same time, have made some progress in absorbing the knowledge required for equipment selection, lay-out and plant construction. The basic design of engines and of the facilities within which they can be produced has yet to be mastered.

IMPROVEMENTS IN DESIGN AND PRODUCTION

Another way in which the relative success of absorbing technology can be assessed is by observing then importing firm's improvements in design and operation. The ability to carry out improvements requires a prior knowledge of the techniques

161

being currently applied, the pieces of equipment that constitute them and the mode of operation. It also requires a fundamental knowledge of the principles of mechanical engineering and physics, and a willingness to change.

Six early but typical improvements will be described, the first involving the local production of a raw material, the second the re-working of a formerly rejected component, the third the renewal of a worn tool, the fourth the redesigning of a component, the fifth the alteration of a machining operation, and the sixth the removing of a bottleneck in the production flow. The motivation in each of these cases was to reduce production costs, through either savings in materials or reduction in defects: where the data are available, the specific reductions in costs will be reported.

The first improvement was made in 1976, when three engineers working in Daewoo's foundry were assigned the task of producing ductile cast iron, then imported from Japan. At the end of 1977, after nearly two years of study and experimentation, they succeeded in producing three different sorts of iron, each suitable for one set of specifications. To take an example, one of the engine components made from cast iron is an end plate, each one of which, in 1977, cost 7,300 won when imported. The alternative cost at Daewoo, calculated at a unit cost of 321 won per kilogram of iron and a unit weight of twelve kilograms, was 3,852 won, a reduction in cost of nearly 50 per cent, and a consequent elimination of foreign exchange.

The second improvement was made shortly afterwards, when it was discovered, after some experiments, that some rejected cylinder heads could be reworked. A cylinder head contains valve seats, head bolt holes and a cold water jacket. After machining, the cylinder head is subjected to a pressure test, to ensure that there is no leakage of cooling water onto the valve seats or into the bolt holes. At the time of the study, about 20 out of each 1,000 cylinder heads failed to pass the hydraulic test, leaking water into the bolt holes, and were cast aside as scrap iron.

The improvement consisted of reaming out the bolt hole and inserting a seamless pipe, proof against oxygenation of water. The pipe was then fixed to the bolt hole with a metal adhesive. After this treatment, on the average, 18 of the 20 cylinder heads that had previously failed were acceptable. The cost saving attributable to the reworking of the cylinder heads can be estimated by subtracting from the average production cost of a failed item (19,600 won for material and 14,000 for labour, or 33,600 each) the additional cost of the repair (90 won for seamless pipe, 425 won for adhesive, and 200 won for labour, or 715 won each), the difference (33,600 — 715, or 32,885 won) being the saving obtained by recovering an otherwise worthless cylinder head. On the basis of an annual production of 24,000 cylinder heads, and a reduction in rejects of 1.8 per cent (18/20 × 2%), the total yearly saving was 14,200,000 won or, at the US dollar exchange rate then ruling, $31,100. This saving represented approximately 0.002 per cent of the annual revenues from Daewoo's sale of MAN diesels.

The third improvement involved the reusing of worn tools which would otherwise have been discarded. Most machine tools, particularly boring tips and turning bites, are imported from Germany. By investigating the machining processes and re-programming the uses of tools at their different stages, it was found possible to reuse, in rough machining processes, tools too worn to be of further use in fine processes. Cost reduction was minimal, but foreign exchange up to a few million won per year was saved.

The fourth improvement involved the redesign of the fly-wheel housing to eliminate the use of cores in their casting. The cost saving, through a reduction in production time of 48 minutes per piece and in material of 889 won per piece amounted to 49 million won per year, or US$ 49,000, equivalent to 0.003 per cent of total value of sales of diesel engines.

The fifth improvement came about through the analysis, in 1977, of the causes of defects in the machining of the cylinder blocks mentioned before. Of 48 defects encountered between 1 May and 10 June, 36, or three-quarters, were traced to faulty alignment of tappet holes, which channel the tappets between push rod and cam. (No more than two defects out of the 48 were traced to any other single factor.)

The remedy consisted of subsituting a different type of drilling process (an end mill) for the existing one (a conventional vertical drill); the savings, through a reduction of 2.5 per cent in defective cylinder blocks, were 157,050 won per piece in material, 51,600 won per piece in labour, and 18,960 won per piece in other costs, totalling 227,610 won per piece, or, annually, 68 million won (US$ 31,600). Of equal magnitude to the savings from the second improvement, this amounted to 0.002 per cent of total sales.

The sixth and final improvement removed a bottleneck in the crank-shaft machining process. At one of the work stations in the crank-shaft line, the oil pump driving gear shaft, pilot bearing hole and flange slot were formed. This station became a bottleneck in the machine shop since the operation required a more frequent change of tools than at any other station. An investigation into the differences between Korean vehicles and those of Western countries revealed that transmission centre shafts are shorter in Korean vehicles than in Western ones. This finding suggested that there was no need for machining the pilot bearing hole at the rear of the crank shaft. (According to the original MAN design, there was machining on this hole.) So the engineers redesigned the machining process and changed the shape of bites to be utilised in the station. With this change in the process, machining time was reduced from 32 minutes to 19 minutes per piece.

Improvements such as the six described above do not come about by accident but by the deliberate actions of skilled individuals. Through time, the skills of Daewoo's diesel engine production and engineering workers have increased both through experience and through formal education. Experience is codified in output statistics (see Table 6.1); education in the scholastic attainments of Daewoo's employees are summarised in Table 6.5. Most noticeable is the reduction, over the five years 1978-83, in that portion of all employees with minimal attainments, by approximately one-third.

AUGMENTATION OF THE PRODUCT LINE

The final illustration of the absorption of diesel engine technology within Daewoo is offered by the extensions of the product line. These extensions were twofold, the first historically, into new uses for the existing engines, and the second into new engine sizes. The motive behind the first extension was to increase sales of engines, so as more fully to utilise plant capacity; the motive behind the second extension was to meet the demand for more powerful prime movers.

The extensions into new product lines began in earnest when Daewoo Heavy Industries took over management of the diesel engine plant. Two new product lines — marine engines and stationary engines for compressors and electric generators —

Table 6.5: Educational attainments of all engineers and skilled workers in Daewoo's diesel engine plant, 1978 and 1983

Status	Primary school	Middle school	High school	Junior college	Four-year college	Graduate school	Total
1978							
Engineers	—	—	93	16	162	3	274
Skilled workers	70	264	563	10	—	—	907
Total	70	264	656	26	162	3	1,181
Per cent	28.3		55.5	2.2	14.0		100.0
1983							
Per cent	19.0		60.0	4.0	16.0		100.0

Source: Daewoo.

required relatively little alteration of the engines and addition of components; but two more — excavators and forklift trucks — required major programmes. For the design and production of large-size excavators (with a lifting capacity exceeding 0.2 cubic metres) Daewoo sought a licence from Hitachi and, in 1983, of small-sized excavators from Kubota. Since production commenced, Daewoo's excavators and forklift trucks have taken over the Korean domestic market. Some excavators have also been exported, although they are at a disadvantage with respect to Japanese machines, which incorporate diesel engines of a more advanced design. The advantages of the more advanced diesel engines are lighter weight per horsepower delivered, with consequently greater fuel economy and lower emission of pollutants.

THE DIFFUSION OF THE IMPORTED TECHNOLOGY

Having described the absorption of the diesel engine technology within Daewoo Heavy Industries Ltd, it remains to describe its diffusion outside the importing form. This means describing first diffusion of the technology to firms competing with Daewoo, second to other firms which supply inputs to Daewoo, and third to the rest of the Korean economy.

Diffusion of the first sort — to other competing firms — has taken place through the movement of engineers tempted by the prospect of promotion and higher salaries in other firms. Since Daewoo built the first diesel engine plant in Korea, there was to begin with no immediate competitor. However, Hyundai Motor Company, under licence from Perkins in the USA, prepared to enter the field only a year after Daewoo started its operation. Engineers are vulnerable to inducements from competing firms when they have accumulated about three years' service; by then they are eager for advancement, and by then they have acquired enough know-how to make them valuable acquisitions. When they move from one company to another, they usually do so not individually but as a group — the group in which they worked together as a team in the previous company. This kind of manpower movement, which was prevalent during the boom years of 1975 through 1978, may well have been detrimental to the accumulation of technological capabilities within the departing firm. During the period there were even incidents or

Table 6.6: Loss of technically-trained employees from Daewoo heavy industries, 1976-84

Year	Skilled workers	Junior engineers	Senior engineers	Total number employed	Turnover rate (per cent)
	Number turned over				
1976	399	34	2	1,205	36
1977	430	38	4	1,385	34
1978	425	23	4	1,290	35
1979	552	93	n.a.	n.a.	n.a.
1980	349	94	n.a.	725[a]	61[a]
1981	318	92	n.a.	595[a]	69[a]
1982	299	91	n.a.	533[a]	73[a]
1983	263	78	n.a.	471[a]	71[a]
1984	259	72	n.a.	n.a.	n.a.

[a] Employment at Daewoo Heavy Industries' Inchon plant only; these figures exclude employment at Daewoo's home office in Seoul.

Source: Daewoo.

disputes between the firms involved over what was called 'technical manpower robbery', sometimes accompanied by burglary of blueprints. Daewoo Heavy Industries Ltd suffered such a loss of technically trained employees, as Table 6.6 shows.

Diffusion of the second sort — to or from firms supplying machinery, parts or components to Daewoo — has taken place slowly. This kind of diffusion might be described as 'quasi-forced diffusion', deriving from the nature of machine manufacturing. To discuss diffusion of this sort, one should start by looking into the nature of machine manufacturing. A machine is an assemblage of a large number of parts or components functioning together systematically to perform a specified job. A sewing machine, for example, comprises from 200 to 500 parts, according to its sophistication. As far as machine manufacturing is concerned, it is neither technically nor economically feasible to manufacture all the needed parts within the firm which produces the machine. In other words, the number of parts needed for a machine is in general too great for one firm to produce all of them, regardless of the size of the firm. So, even in industrially advanced countries like Japan, Western Germany, etc., the functioning of the machine industry is based on co-ordination and co-operation among multitudes of firms, the large firms being served by small ones producing components. For example, as of 1971, in Japan 66.1 per cent of the total 166,127 machine shops were small-sized firms with employees of less than nine. In West Germany, the corresponding percentage was 44.5 for the same year.

In a machine, components or parts function together systematically to perform a specified job. Hence, the quality level of a machine depends on that of each functioning part. Sometimes the quality level of the machine as a whole is determined by the part with the lowest quality level. In these circumstances, the economics of specialisation comes into play; that is, smaller machine shops specialise in parts production and supply the parts to their contractors on a long-term basis, while large firms like Daewoo specialise in major assembly works, research, development and design.

Daewoo, fortunately, recognised the need for this coordination and co-operation among machine manufacturing firms. In 1975, the company, in line with government directives, established a programme for the localisation of materials, equipment and parts. This programme has achieved some success, in localising the supply of a few materials and a large number of parts. These accomplishments, which were made possible by assisting smaller firms with technical know-how and financial support, have made significant contributions in reducing costs and saving foreign currency. A list compiled for the year 1978 displayed the following items whose manufacture had been undertaken domestically through technical assistance provided by Daewoo: connecting rod material, push rods, tappets, cylinder head bolts, gaskets (except head gaskets), water pumps and rocker arms assemblies (all completed); oil pumps (a sample produced); and oil coolers (project for localisation initiated). The overall result of the attempt to localise production of items supplied to Daewoo is known for this year, 1978, when the purchased value of domestic capital equipment used in producing diesel engines was US$ 6.4 million, and when the cost of components, parts and materials used in the assembly of the diesel engines was US$22.5 million, the latter representing 27 per cent of the total cost of purchases, domestic and foreign.

In that year the company was working under a government guideline that domestically produced components, parts and materials should be 50 per cent of the total, the percentage having been established at 30 per cent in 1976, and having risen

Table 6.7: Localisation of components and parts for three types of diesel engine, 1975-84

Localisation (purchases from domestic suppliers, as a per cent of total value of purchased components and parts)

Year	Engine number and application		
	D 0846 M used in trucks, buses, generator sets, portable air compressors, stationary engines and ships	D 2156 AM, same as D 0846 M	D 2156 MT, turbocharged engine used in trucks only
	%	%	%
1975	40	37	38
1976	43	46	45
1977	50	49	48
1978	59	55	49
1979	66	63	53
1980	73	69	58
1981	77	74	61
1982	78	75	63
1983	89	75	64
1984	90	86	76

Source: Daewoo.

to 40 per cent in 1977. Although the outcome came short of the guideline in these early years of production, localisation in subsequent years for the main types of diesel engines shown in Table 6.7 has advanced steadily, reaching an approximate average of 85 per cent in 1984. Components still supplied from abroad today are fuel vaporisation and control instruments such as carburettors and turbochargers.

A COMPARATIVE CASE: TISSUE PAPER MANUFACTURE

Our preceding diesel engine manufacturing case was one which involved a sophisticated technology. Another case with rather simpler technology is reported here for the sake of comparison. This second case study was done at the Yuhan-Kimberly Co. Ltd (302-75 Dongbu-Ichon-Dong Yongsan-Ku, Seoul), a cosmetic and sanitary tissue manufacturing form, in technical collaboration with the Kimberly-Clark Corporation of the USA.

169

Since 1968 the Kimberly-Clark Corporation of the United States of America had been searching for investment opportunities in Korea. From the US embassy in Seoul, Kimberly-Clark learned that the Yuhan Corporation was known as a pharmaceutical company of high repute for their skill in public relations and for their efficient marketing channels.

At that time Yuhan was considering the production of sanitary (feminine) napkins. As negotiations between the two parties proceeded, Yuhan learned that they would have to import large volumes of what is called 'warding', the semi-finished absorbent tissue material which is used in sanitary pads. Eventually, Yuhan concluded that it would be more profitable to set up warding production facilities in Korea, while Kimberly-Clark maintained that the market size was too small in Korea to justify capital expenditure in a warding production plant.

While negotiations proceeded, Kimberly-Clark's team began to learn about 'the Korean style of getting things done' — for example, they noticed that most of the bodies of street buses on Seoul were built by many small diverse companies with low capital and ill-equipped facilities, using unorthodox manufacturing processes. They learned that the ingenuity, sincerity and diligence of Korean people could somehow get things done which to the eyes of Western people might appear impossible. This growing confidence in the Korean 'people' led Kimberly-Clark's team to understand Yuhan's assertion and finally they agreed to establish a joint-venture company (Kimberly-Clark 60 per cent, Yuhan 40 per cent) in a warding manufacturing plant, for which Kimberly-Clark would supply the needed technical know-how.

By early 1970, the status of tissue-manufacturing in Korea was still at a primitive stage. Bathroom tissue rolls were produced using machinery designed and manufactured in Korea based on traditional methods. Yuhan managed to hire several engineers who were able to design and construct the old-style equipment. These engineers were sent to Kimberly-Clark in the USA on a mission to learn the 'modern' technology for cosmetic tissue manufacture. They made tours to several paper mills and collected information about the design, construction and assembly of tissue-manufacturing machinery. Above all, they learned that, as far as paper-tissue manufacturing is concerned, the basic principles of 'modern' techniques were not too far from those of traditional ones.

After returning home, they started to construct the machinery to produce absorbent paper tissue on the basis of the blueprints, information and other technical assistance supplied by Kimberly-Clark. They tried to design the simplest possible system. Some parts were produced in their own machine shop, while many others were made through sub-contracts with local machine shops. Some very critical parts were sent to the USA for tests. Those parts whose manufacture was beyond the capability of domestic producers were imported.

In December 1970, the machinery was set up and operation started. The system was much simpler than those in advanced countries; production speed was slower than with the 'advanced' machines. However, the quality of the product was about the same. Considering the small capital expenditure involved in constructing the machinery, the result came as a surprise to Kimberly-Clark.

Yuhan-Kimberly's next project was to set up felt-producing machinery. Most felt product had been imported from abroad. Kimberly-Clark agreed to supply the needed technical assistance, including drawings, blueprints and information about parts and assembly of the system. Given the Korean engineers' experience, gained during the first mission, the felt-producing machinery system was set up without much difficulty in February 1972.

With the fast-growing national income and rising standard of living in Korea in the late 1960s and early 1970s, the demand for cosmetic tissues, sanitary feminine pads and felt products was growing at about 50 to 60 per cent annually. To keep up with market growth, Yuhan-Kimberly decided to expand their production facilities. A threefold expansion project was approved by the government in January 1972 and the project was completed by July 1974. The company's growth is shown below:

	1971	1974	1977	1978
Exports ($1,000)	235	650	2,300	1,700
Assets (million won)	397	1,880	3,196	5,753
Employees	206	417	430	536

The year 1975 was a turning point: Kimberly-Clark Co., which now had complete confidence in Yuhan-Kimberly's machine manufacturing capability, decided to use Yuhan-Kimberly as the source of supply for its paper-making machinery. Yuhan-Kimberly's capability in design, its manual skill in machining, its willingness to learn, and above all its cheap labour costs were the major factors which led them to this decision.

The first development took the form of machinery parts export to Iran in 1975. In the same year, Korean engineers and operators of tissue manufacturing machinery were sent to Iran under a technical assistance programme. In 1976 Yuhan-Kimberly exported machines for cosmetic tissue and felt manufacturing, plus some major parts, to the Philippines and Thailand. In 1977, Yuhan-Kimberly exported a whole manufacturing plant to Columbia and sent five engineers for its operation. Recently, Yuhan-Kimberly has functioned as a development laboratory for Kimberly-Clark, and has advanced to a higher stage of technology in the paper industry.

SUMMARY AND CONCLUSIONS

In the previous section, a rather brief sketch was given of the history of Yuhan-Kimberly as a paper machinery manufacturer. Let us now compare the two cases — Yuhan-Kimberly and Daewoo — and draw some conclusions.

Very often when one thinks of machine technology, one thinks only of Western, large-scale, centralised, capital- and energy-intensive technology. However, it is only possible for such a technology to exist in a society where a host of specialised conditions are satisfied. Indeed, it is often argued that Western technology is inappropriate to underdeveloped countries and that Western aid should not concentrate on helping underdeveloped countries acquire the kind of technology that developed countries rely upon. The following reasons are used to support this claim: (1) Western technology is capital intensive; (2) Western technology depends on a supply of highly-skilled labour of all kinds, from skilled manual workers to managers, which cannot be provided by most underdeveloped countries. For this reason, imported plant is either run inefficiently or else its running depends upon a team of foreign experts; and (3) Western technology is extremely expensive and its import by an underdeveloped country means a significant drain on its foreign reserves.

Interestingly, executives and top managers of Daewoo Heavy Industries are in agreement that Daewoo's diesel engine technology deserved all the criticisms above. As for the first point, capital intensivity, Daewoo would like to resolve the problem by running the plant on a three-shift basis instead of one-shift; and would do so, given sufficient demand. But the demand is deficient.

As for the second point, Western technology's high demand for skilled labour, this problem has afflicted the company since the initial operation of the plant. Concerning the third point, there is no question about the validity of the argument on foreign currency drainage. The initial contract specified payment of DM 500,000, plus royalties, to MAN, and the loan for imported machinery amounted annually to an approximately equal sum, as interest and repayment of principal.

Thus, our case analysis on diesel engine technology has confirmed the validity of argument concerning the hazards of selecting highly advanced Western technologies on the machine industries in underdeveloped countries. However, as we saw in the Yuhan-Kimberly case, with a less advanced or less sophisticated technology, fewer problems arose. What the comparison between the complicated diesel engine technology and the rather simple tissue-manufacturing one suggests is that when a developing nation wishes to accelerate learning, absorption and diffusion of imported technologies, she might be advised to start with the simpler ones. Needless to say, simpler technologies can be absorbed more easily than sophisticated ones, since the principles exploited by the former are in general more elementary than the latter. When they are easier to learn, they can be quickly indigenised, duplicated and further adapted to local conditions. This reasoning was verified by the Yuhan-Kimberly experiment. Executives and top managers of the Yuhan-Kimberly Corporation emphasised that their phenomenal success in machine manufacturing was primarily attributed to the fact that they adhered to a simpler technology in the beginning.

A qualification must be made when high product quality is vital. For products like engines, precision, standardisation and consistency in manufacturing processes are primary determinants for the final quality of the products. Without these characteristics, manufacturing processes will yield products of low quality, which cannot be sold abroad. The capital-poor developing country which aspires to compete in international markets for the sale of sophisticated goods is thus in a dilemma: importing advanced technologies consumes very scarce resources in large amounts and even then the technologies may not be successfully absorbed, whereas importing less advanced technologies may not enable the manufacture of internationally acceptable products.

In the course of the case study of diesel engines, the conclusion was drawn that the absorption of imported technology is highly dependent upon continuity of demand for the products of the technology. During the earliest stage of diesel engine production, there was not enough demand for the engines to support production at more than a small fraction of capacity. Hence, personnel who were employed in the diesel engine project were transferred to other projects; the company could not afford to keep personnel in a project where they were losing money. The continuity of men engaged in the technical activities was broken and the accumulation of technical knowledge hampered.

Since the technology involved in the production of diesel engines is very sophisticated, it is not to be expected that Korean engineers could accomplish major technical changes in a short period of time. However, with reasonably intensive operation of the plant, there can be technological improvement; the study identified six such improvements motivated by attempts to save raw materials and prevent defects. These and subsequent attempts have been integrated into the Saemaeul Movement, a government-sponsored, nation-wide activity encouraging greater productivity and inspiring new attitudes and spirits.

Diffusion of the imported technology to other competing firms has taken place primarily through the movement of engineers attracted by competing firms with the prospect of promotions and higher salaries. Furthermore, when they moved from one company to another, they moved together with others who had formed a team in the previous company. This kind of manpower movement, which was prevalent especially during the boom years of 1975 through 1978, was sometimes detrimental to the accumulation of technological capabilities within the losing firm.

Diffusion of the technology to input suppliers has taken place slowly. This diffusion came from a need which is intrinsic to the machinery sector. Since a machine is an assemblage of a large number of parts or components functioning together systematically to perform a specified task, the quality level of a machine is likely to be determined by that of the parts with the lowest quality level. A machine manufacturer should, therefore, recognise the need for co-operation and co-ordination among all firms engaged in machinery manufacturing. Daewoo, fortunately, was aware of this need and established, in line with government directives, a programme for the localisation of materials, equipment and parts by assisting smaller parts manufacturers with technical know-how and, sometimes, financial support. The successful accomplishment of the programme has made significant contributions to costs and savings in foreign currency.

As for the sophistication of the technology, it can be said that engineers at Daewoo have absorbed those portions of the imported technology relating to the start-up, operation and maintenance of the diesel engine manufacturing processes. However, basic design and R and D areas are still far from having been absorbed or diffused.

Another case in an industry with much simpler technology was also studied in order to see the impact of the degree of sophistication of technology on its absorption and diffusion. What the comparison between the complicated technology and a rather simpler one suggests is that simpler technologies can be absorbed and understood with much greater ease than sophisticated ones. However, when developing countries hope their machinery products to be competitive in international markets, the requirements of quality may call for the import of foreign techniques which are unusally sophisticated. Thus, in the machinery industry, a developing country appears to face a choice between simple technologies, easily absorbed and cheaply exploited, on the one hand, and complex technologies, absorbed only with difficulty but yielding internationally competitive machinery products, on the other.

7

Case Study: Iron and Steel

INTRODUCTION

The Pohang Iron and Steel Company Ltd (POSCO), selected for a detailed case study, is the nation's first integrated iron and steel mill, with a modern, large-scale, continuous production system of iron- and steel-making and rolling.

Prior to the analysis of the absorption and diffusion of the imported technology, we will deal with the establishment and expansion of POSCO. Following the section on absorption, the effects of technological improvements will be analysed and an explanation of the diffusion of the technology will be presented.

General information on the iron and steel industry in Korea has been drawn upon, as have POSCO's internal documents. There were three sets of interviews with POSCO's engineers, from which a considerable amount of experimental knowledge was acquired. The source of information derived from these interviews will be cited where necessary. There are some comparisons between POSCO and other steel mills.

ESTABLISHMENT AND EXPANSION OF POSCO

POSCO was incorporated in 1968 and has undergone three subsequent stages of expansion. The initial paid-in share capital was US$5,861,000 and the initial number of employees 101. Construction of the plant began in April 1970, with a capacity of 1,030 thousand metric tons per year of crude steel. In the first expansion of capacity, completed in May 1976, steel capacity was increased to 2,600 thousand tons; in the second,

176

completed in December 1978, to 5,500 thousand tons; and in the third, completed in February 1981, to 8,500 thousand tons, POSCO is today the eleventh largest steel company in the entire world, operating 80 individual plants and incorporating machinery supplied from Japan, Austria, West Germany, France and Belgium. Its total assets, in 1981, were 1,892 billion won, of which US$1,957 million were in foreign countries and 881 billion won were in Korea.

POSCO's history can be divided into four periods according to the establishment and expansion of facilities: such a division will be adopted in the following analysis, since the import of technology in POSCO is closely related to the expansions. In the next section, we will describe the expansions, noticing each import of technology and its characteristics. First to be referred to will be the terms and conditions of the import of the technology at the initial stage.

CONDITIONS GOVERNING THE INITIAL IMPORT OF TECHNOLOGY

In Korea experience with integrated steel-making was non-existent prior to the incorporation of POSCO. Capital, particularly in the amount necessary to finance an integrated steel plant, was very scarce. The Korean government consequently felt wholly dependent on foreign sources of capital and technology.

Before the construction of POSCO, the Korean government had tried several times to create an integrated steel mill, only to fail to secure the required capital through foreign loans. Two early plans involved establishing steel mills with annual production capacities of 300,000 and 600,000 tons of crude steel respectively. The failure of the latter plan to materialise is instructive; it involved the consortium Korea International Steel Associates (KISA), consisting of seven members from four countries: Koppers, Blaw Knox and Westinghouse Electric International from the USA; DEMAG and Siemens from West Germany; Societa Italiana Impianti from Italy; and Wellman Steel Works Engineering from England. Initially, Japan was also to participate but instead, France joined later. According to the contract agreed between KISA and the Korean government in October 1967, KISA was to have raised an international loan by 1969, and dedicated the integrated mill by 1972. The expected capital requirements for the equipment and facilities was estimated to be about US$100 million. However, the consortium was dissolved in 1969 because Koppers, the leading consulting firm, could not raise the required investment capital, and because KISA, because of its complicated composition, could not make prompt decisions.

After this and other failures in securing funds, the Korean government shifted to the raising of a foreign loan for construction. Successful negotiations were undertaken with Japan; agreement to support the project was made at the annual conference of Korean and Japanese ministers on August 1969, and detailed inter-government negotiations were conducted during the rest of the year. According to the contract signed, Japan would provide loans to Korea, totalling US$123 million as well as all the major technology and facilities. The breakdown of the foreign loans supplied to POSCO at each stage are shown in Table 7.1.

Since there was no knowledge of the technology of steel-making on a large scale it all had to be imported into Korea. Contracts with foreign suppliers had to be arranged at each stage. To illustrate the extent of the knowledge that had to be acquired we summarise below the contents of the contract agreed between POSCO and the 'Japan Group' in 1970,

Table 7.1: Sources of foreign loans for POSCO, 1969-85 (in thousand US dollars)

	Initial stage	2nd stage	3rd stage	4th stage
Japan	122,507	152,164	398,710	
EX-IM Bank	52,498	35,177	—	
Economic Co-operation Fund	46,428	41,521	—	
Commercial loan	23,581	75,466	398,710	
USA	—	61,659	—	
Syndicated loan	—	21,429	—	
Citicorp	—	13,410	—	
EX-IM Bank	—	13.410	—	
Private export finance	—	13,410	—	
Others	24,345	127,431	367,590	
Total	146,852	341,254	766,300	670,000

Source: POSCO, July 1985.

covering the technology underlying the initial construction. The Japan Group consisted of Nippon Kohan (NKK) and Nippon Steel Corp (NSC), two Japanese steel-producers with large-scale, modern plants on the seaboard.

The contract specified the following:

(1) Planning and consulting project

a. Preparation of the time schedule from construction to operation.

b. Supervision of plant construction and plant lay-out, and preparation of main flow charts and skeleton diagrams.

c. Specification of the construction work and estimation of the required amount of construction work and main raw materials during each construction period.

d. Planning of operation, production scale by month, and consumption and inventories of main raw materials.

e. Inspection and technical evaluation of financial management plan, and project and expansion plan suggested by POSCO.

(2) Purchasing and construction contract project

a. Recommendation of proper contract units in ordering of equipment and facilities.

b. Preparation of the purchase specification of equipment.

c. Explanation of the specifications to suppliers and technical inspection of bids submitted by the suppliers.

d. Inspection and evaluation of progress of plant construction by domestic construction firms.

e. Training of engineers and specialists for the construction of the integrated steel mill.

(3) Assistance and guide to the purchase of equipment, its installation and the related civil engineering and construction.

(4) Planning and execution of the construction and overall constructional management system.

(5) On-site assistance for start-up and operation.

The amount of technical assistance provided by foreign suppliers has shrunk in subsequent stages. In the third stage, for example, POSCO depended solely on the Japan Group for the master engineering plan. Other authors have calculated the progressive reduction in expenditure on foreign project engineering, on the basis of each ton of additional capacity installed. Initially, it was US$6.13; for the first expansion (labelled second stage in Table 7.1) it was $3.81; for the second $2.42; and for the third, $0.13 (Westphal, Kim, Lin-Su and Dahlman, 1984). All told, for the initial steel mill and its three expansions, 20 contracts for the provision of technology were signed, and royalties of US$21 million paid.

The initial project of POSCO comprised an integrated steel-making system equipped with a blast furnace and Linz-Donawitz converters (see Meyer and Herregat, 1974 and Ray, 1984). The blast furnace had an inner volume of $1,660m^3$ and an initial production capacity of 949,000 tons, while two LD converters had a steel production capacity of 1,032,000 tons. In addition, there was a foundry pig iron furnace with an inner volume of $330m^3$ and a production capacity of 150,000 tons. A blooming and slabbing mill, billet mill, plate mill and hot rolling mill were also included.

In the first stage of expansion in 1974, completed in 1976, POSCO added another furnace and LD converter, increasing capacities by 1,416,000 tons and 1,568,000 tons respectively. The new technology of continuous casting, producing slab and bloom directly from the molten steel, was also introduced. Production capacity of slab and bloom, by continuous casting, was established at 400,000 tons and 300,000 tons respectively. The hot strip rolling mill was expanded, and a cold rolling mill was newly set up with a production capacity of 485,000 tons. In general the first expansion project duplicated the initial plant. (Figure 7.1 and Table 7.2 depict POSCO's plant at this stage.)

The next expansion project was started two years later in 1976 and completed at the end of 1978. Technological change took place with the expansion in product capacity: while the first two blast furnaces had an inner volume of $1,660m^3$ and $2,254m^3$ respectively, the third furnace had an inner volume of $3,795m^3$, and a capacity of 2,752,000 tons, exceeding the combined capacity of the two earlier furnaces. In addition, LD converters were added, rolling facilities were greatly expanded and the capacity of bloom and slab billet and plate were increased by 2,200,000 tons 524,000 tons and 1,176,000 tons respectively. A wire rod mill with an annual production capacity

Figure 7.1: Flow diagram of POSCO's plant upon completion of the first expansion of capacity, 1976

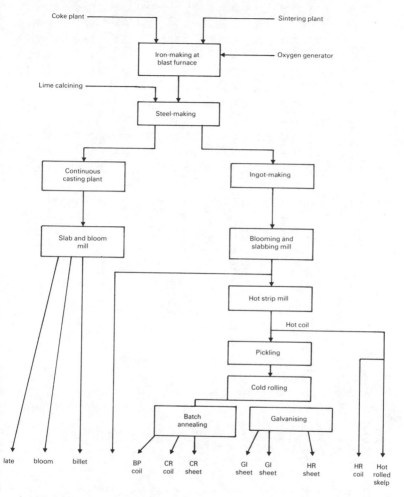

of 446,000 tons was also established.

The third expansion, the last of the four stages of construction at Pohang, was begun in 1979, almost immediately after the third stage was finished. In scale, the iron- and steel-making equipment was exactly equal to that of the third stage.

The major products of POSCO at its initial stage were hot rolled steel such as the KSD 3501, HRSI, KSD 3503 and SB 41, etc., used for general structural purposes. Greater emphasis

181

Table 7.2: Design capacity and output of POSCO, 1972-84

Facility	Capacity (in thousand ton/year)	Output												
		72	73	74	75	76	77	78	79	80	81	82	83	84
1st furnace	1,095		456	988	982	1,073	926	912	825	1,044	1,020	1,033	1,052	1,063
2nd furnace	1,697					735	1,330	1,486	1,499	1,464	1,431	1,427	1,268	1,822
3rd furnace	2,920							94	2,544	2,860	2,903	2,886	2,607	2,781
4th furnace	2,920										2,367	2,902	2,902	2,902
Pig iron plant	200			36	213	203	170	197	209	215	214	195	196	195
1st steel making plant	2,300		449	1,153	1,234	2,037	2,412	2,720	2,367	2,401	2,229	2,165	1,837	2,220
2nd steel making plant	6,800							87	2,912	3,502	5,976	6,616	6,601	6,975
1st continuous casting plant	1,029					266	601	758	959	987	927	928	806	951
2nd continuous casting plant	3,544										1,862	2,525	2,898	3,536
1st blooming and slabbing mill	1,524		383	1,018	1,101	1,553	1,593	1,753	1,825	1,761	1,684	1,587	1,301	1,398
2nd blooming and slabbing mill	3,086							19	1,955	2,532	3,119	3,309	2,931	2,809
Billet mill	845		38	115	134	130	218	144	540	700	732	751	737	800
1st wire rod mill	446								134	376	458	481	483	488
2nd wire rod mill	350													5
1st hot strip rolling mill	1,707	15	418	661	733	1,232	1,619	1,861	1,881	1,694	1,490	1,610	1,581	1,717
2nd hot strip rolling mill	3,268									441	2,981	3,311	3,379	3,429
1st plate mill	336	33	157	280	284	340	386	299	385	365	359	372	373	385
2nd plate mill	1,243								897	929	1,065	1,107	1,076	1,162
Cold rolling mill	686						164	423	453	413	507	606	646	705
Silicon steel mill	80								1	20	37	34	59	70

Source: POSCO.

was placed on the production of even-quality, plain carbon steels, than on the development of new products. High-tensile strength steel of 50Kg/mm^2 was developed in 1975, providing a basis for the first expansion of output in the following year. In the expanded facilities, low sulphur clean steel was used as the basic material, and, through the introduction of equipment for bottom pouring and desulphurising, boiler and pressure vessels could be produced. Subsequently, POSCO engineers succeeded in learning the technology of making high carbon steel, producing high tension steel of 55Kg/mm^2 and 0.3 per cent C class medium carbon steel. In 1977, cold rolling coils and sheet, and galvanised coils and sheet were added to the product lines, as well as low sulphur clean sheet and steel plate, both used for high-pressure gas vessels. In 1978 POSCO acquired the technology for producing low alloy, high tension steel of 60Kg/mm^2. Along with the accumulation of iron- and steel-making techniques, the number of new products was gradually increased, totalling 131 by the end of 1977, 300 by the end of 1981, and by 364 the end of 1984.

THE ABSORPTION OF IMPORTED TECHNOLOGY

At its initial stage, the most important tasks for POSCO were seen to be the prompt construction of the mills and the normal operation of facilities. At an early stage, POSCO had sent its engineers to Japan for field training, where they participated actively in the construction and operation of local mills with their Japanese counterparts. As a result, experience in the techniques used in operation and production management was gained.

In operating the first blast furnace, the 'normal' rate of output was achieved in 107 days after the burning-in. Table 7.3 shows the monthly production record from the point of burning-in to the time of achievement of the design rate (2,600 tons per day). In view of their own experience in Japan the Japan Group had originally expected that it would take at least twelve months to achieve 'normal' operation, yet POSCO achieved 'normal' operation within four months.

It is possible to compare POSCO's achievements in the first year of operating its first blast furnace with that of five Japanese steel firms. Figure 7.2 plots the tapping ratios attained through-

Table 7.3: Production records for the initial blast furnace after burning-in (June-November 1973)

	June 1973	July	Aug.	Sep.	Oct.	Nov.
Amount tapped (tons per day)	1,142	1,742	2,216	2,409	2,557	2,620
Tapping ratio (tons per day per cubic metre of inner volume)	0.67	1.05	1.33	1.45	1.54	1.58

Note: The blast furnace was designed in 1973 with a tapping ratio of 1.52; in 1979, after re-lining, the tapping ratio was increased to 1.67.

Figure 7.2: Operating plans and production record for POSCO's first blast furnace, with comparative data for Japanese companies

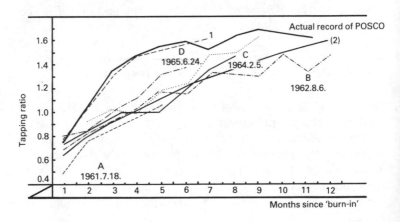

Note: 1 refers to POSCO's operation plan; 2 refers to plan suggested by Japan Group; A, B, C, D, E, refer to the experience of Japanese companies. Tapping ratio was designed to be 1.52; yielding a design output of 2,500 metric tons from the blast furnace's inner volume of 1,660 cu. metres.

out the year, revealing that with one exception (Japanese firm D, for slightly more than one month) POSCO surpassed all the others' results.

The ability to bring new blast furnaces quickly on tap and to their design capacity has also been displayed by POSCO for the three subsequent furnaces. The second blast furnace was brought to its original design capacity (1,416,000 tons per year) within 80 days, and the third and fourth within even shorter intervals (70 and 29 days respectively). The achievement was particularly impressive in the case of the third blast furnace, whose scale was double that of the second. In part the speedy working-in of the third blast furnace was due to the large number of foreign engineers on site at the time of the start-up (to be described later), but in part it was due to the know-how accumulated by the Korean engineers from the first two projects.

The speed with which the steel-making facilities — the Linz-Donawitz converters — had been brought into operation is equally impressive, as the figures in Table 7.3 show. However, because they involve both chemical and mechanical processing, steel-working facilities have taken longer to bring to full-capacity operation. The figures in Table 7.2 show that the typical interval between initial operation and the attainment of 'normal' production rates is two to three years, or 700 to 1,000 days. POSCO's experience in exploiting the potential of iron- and steel-making plants is similar to that of the petrochemical firm in Chapter 4 and the artificial fibre firm in Chapter 5; the common element is that all are employing chemical processes: POSCO's experience in exploiting the potential of steel-working plants is similar to that of the machinery firm in Chapter 6; the common element is that both are employing mechanical processes.

If POSCO can be said to have been successful in bringing its plant to, and maintaining it at, its full potential, it can also be said to have been successful in carrying out the construction of the plant. In our previous cases, the difficulties inherent in construction were less than those in operation, chiefly because of the relatively small size of the individual pieces of equipment: at a guess, all of the equipment comprising the first artificial fibre plant would fit within a single blast furnace, and all that comprising the first polyethylene and diesel engine plants within two blast furnaces. Yet the blast furnaces are only the first massive pieces of equipment in the iron- and steel-making and -working facilities, as Figure 7.1 indicates. Capital costs, too, provide an indication of the differences in size and complexity of construction; the total capital cost of the petrochemical plant of the Hanyang Company, described in Chapter 4, was US$41 million; the cost of the foreign component of capital for the initial stage of POSCO's plant was over three times as much (see Table 7.1), and the total capital cost, foreign plus domestic, approximately seven times.

Great expenditures on huge pieces of equipment, if not carried out skilfully and rapidly, can saddle a firm with excessive costs from its initial date of operation. Taking US$500 million as the capital cost of a million ton per year iron and steel plant (see Hogan (1985); POSCO's plant cost less, as we shall see when we discuss Table 7.5), an extra year spent on construction would add somewhere in the value of US$10 million to US$20 million to capital cost, US$1 to US$2 to each ton of steel produced. Avoiding such a penalty is a considerable incentive to speedy completion of construction projects.

Even though they had no previous experience with iron and steel mill erection, POSCO's personnel with the first plant firmly established a tradition of early project completion (see Table 7.4). The construction volume of the initial stage project, 1,030,000 tons per year, was relatively small; it took 38 months, 29 months were required for the third stage, of more than double the volume, and 24 for the fourth. The early completion of the fourth stage saved an estimated 55 billion won.

But in constructing such a facility as an integrated steel works, a high-risk project for any developing country, POSCO has encountered many twists and turns right from the planning stage. For the initial mill, no fewer than four separate construction plans were devised. The construction of the first-stage facilities was a succession of challenges and trials. Especially noteworthy was the two-month-long emergency works, necessary to make up for a delay in the laying of concrete at the site of a hot strip rolling mill. Round-the-clock work exemplified the determination and stamina of POSCO's workers. After No.1 Blast Furnace was ignited in a ceremony on 8 June 1979, POSCO officials and employees wondered whether molten iron would really pour out of the furnace: when bright golden molten pig iron rushed out, the construction workers burst into shouts of rejoicing. It was a memorable occasion.

During the period of the second expansion, which was completed five months ahead of schedule, work continued throughout the night. Workers even skipped Chusok holiday leave. In order to prevent a possible decline in the quality of work due to the transfer of many skilled workers to middle eastern oil-producing countries, even operating staff were mobilised as special supervisors.

Table 7.4: Construction time for steel mills of several nations

	POSCO				Italy (Taronto)	France (FOS)	India (Bokaro)	Brazil (Usiminas)
	1st stage	2nd stage	3rd stage	4th stage				
Capacity (in thousand metric tons per year)	1,030	1,570	2,920	2,920	2,600	3,500	1,700	1,400
Construction period (months)	38 (4/1/70-6/8/73)	30 (12/1/73-5/31/76)	29 (8/2/76-12/8/78)	24 (2/1/79-2/18/81)	49	50	100	74
Early completion (months in advance of scheduled date)	1	1	5	10	—	—	—	—

Source: POSCO.

187

In the third expansion, a technical inspection system was introduced for major areas of work so as to ensure that the quality of work was adequate. When the countdown began on 1 November 1980, situation rooms were set up at various construction sites to ensure speedy progress. As a result of this and other provisions the expansion was completed ten months ahead of the originally planned date.

Not surprisingly, construction costs in Korea have been lower than elsewhere. Table 7.5 provides a comparison with costs in developed countries (columns 3-5) and developing countries (column 6). Most of the difference between Korea, on the one hand, and Japan, the USA and the EEC, on the other, is probably the result of Korea's much lower labour costs; most of the difference between Korea and other developing countries is probably the result of Korea's skill and propensity for hard work.

Retreating to earlier steps in the process of incorporating a technology — namely to process design, equipment design and procurement and construction planning — we find that the contribution of Korean engineers and managers has been less prominent. The third step has not been identified separately in previous chapters because construction of petrochemical, artificial fibre and diesel engine plants involves chiefly the installation of equipment built elsewhere, but the construction of iron- and steel-making plant involves much building of equipment on-site. As a consequence, greater attention was given to planning construction at POSCO.

The replacement of Korean for foreign engineers in the planning of construction has been gradual, as Table 7.6 shows. The most difficult task, that of formulating the general engineering plan, was only assumed by POSCO's staff at the

Table 7.5: International comparison of construction costs (current US dollars per metric ton of steel capacity)

Stage	POSCO	Japan	USA	EEC	Developing countries
1st	287	450	550	500	550
2nd	352	550	800	600	550-800
3rd	469	588	820	728	600-850
4th	460				

Source: POSCO special report, 1981.

Table 7.6: Contributions of foreign and Korean engineers in construction planning

Activity	1st stage (1970)	2nd stage (1974)	3rd stage (1976)	4th stage (1979)
General engineering plan	0	0	0	X
Material balance and specification of facilities	0	0	X	X
Inspection of specifications	S	S	X	X
Inspection of drawings	0	0	X	X

Key: 0 : foreign engineers only; S : mixture of foreign and Korean engineers; X : Korean engineers only.

time of the fourth stage, which we recall was a duplicate of the third stage so far as the longest piece of equipment built on-site, the blast furnace, was concerned.

The reduced contribution of foreign engineers from stage to stage can also be judged by the falling level of royalties paid to the Japan Group, the prime contractor throughout.

From US$6.2 million for the construction and operating technology of the first stage, POSCO's royalty payments decreased to US$5.8 million for the second stage, to US$4.8 million for the much-applauded third stage and to nothing for the fourth.

Royalty payments remain only for those foreign firms which provide process and equipment design. These first and second steps in the process of incorporating the technology are, even after four stages, still undertaken entirely by foreign suppliers. This continued dependence upon foreign suppliers for process and equipment design of iron- and steel-making plant is deliberate; the reasons are the infrequency of construction of new plants — only four in Korea in ten years — the high degree of competition among foreign design firms anxious to secure contracts to supply plant, and the greater returns to the allocation of the limited supply of Korean engineers to exploit to the full the potential of plant already installed. The absence of Koreans in the design steps of incorporating iron- and steel-making technology is explained, in part at least, by their presence in adequate numbers in the steps of equipment start-up, operation and improvement.

189

IMPROVEMENTS IN TECHNOLOGY

In this section, we shall describe some of the improvements in productivity that have been obtained at POSCO. In the years of successful operation of the iron and steel mills there have been various cases of technological improvements. We have chosen six representative examples of improvements carried out by the Korean engineers engaged directly in production. Where possible, we will measure the changes in productivity, focusing on consumption of raw materials, product quality and production costs.

(Case 1) Local construction by the gas cutting group in the hot rolling mill

The group made gas cutting beds using their own scrap from slab (see Figures 7.3 and 7.4). In outline, the development of local manufacture was as follows:

(a) Motives:
    a. Saving on the high cost of imported gas cutting beds.
    b. Combatting lowering of quality and the rejected product of slab, due to the occurrence of flaws on the cutting surface and off-perpendicularity in the cutting point.
(b) Functions of the gas cutting group:
    a. Cutting of slab thicker than 20m/m.
    b. Cutting of scrap.
    c. Measurement of dimensions of product.
    d. Management of usage of oxygen and LP gas.
(c) Analysis of cause of poor quality:
    The group found out that the inferior quality was attributable to the inexperience of its operators and to the bad state of the cutting bed. The reasons for the latter were:
    a. Wearing and superannuation of bed mounting due to the continuous use since the installation of the equipment in 1972, thus causing inaccurate horizontal angle and bed perpendicularity on the cutting surface.
    b. As the horizontal angle of the bed was not uniform (variations of over ± 5m/m), the torch of the gas cutter was not in perfect alignment with the surface of the slab and the torch was damaged.

Figure 7.3: Set-up of gas cutting beds

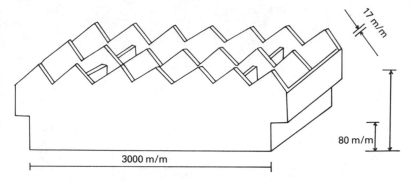

17 m/m

80 m/m

3000 m/m

c. As a mounting of the bed was worn by about 70m/m, the working condition was unstable, with lowered cutting speed.

(d) Establishment of counter plan:

a. The bed should be replaced.

b. Name tag of the cutter should be attached after cutting, to urge a sense of responsibility.

c. As the cost of the bed was too high and the delivery too late, beds would be made with scrap.

d. It was calculated that a total of 400 hours would be required to make 60 sets of bed. Members of the group should be utilised in the manufacture of beds when they were otherwise free.

(e) Detailed procedure of manufacture:

a. Steel plates of thickness ranging from 160m/m to 19m/m were collected and moved to the cutting yard.

b. Mountings of bed were prepared by cutting the steel plate according to a standard model made by the most skilled technician. Short plates were welded together to get a bed 3,000m/m long.

c. Since steel plates were twisted by the heat of welding, supporting plates were attached.

(f) Effects:

The manufacturing and replacement of 60 sets of beds by the group members themselves saved annually 3,457,000 won over the cost of beds purchased abroad or US$7,143. Also, the improvement in bed design reduced wearing rate of the beds, increased efficiency of working, increased the quality of cutting and reduced the rupture rate of torches.

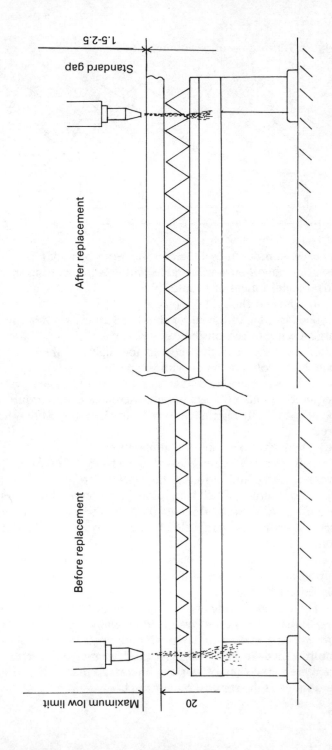

Figure 7.4: Shapes of cuttings before and after replacement

192

Case 2. Operating improvements by the calcination group in the steel-making plant

Long charging-time consumed large amounts of electricity, and caused wear on the conveyor, so the objective of the group was to cut down shaft kiln charging time from 9 min/charge to 5 min/charge. In outline the improvements were:

(a) Functions of the calcination group:
    a. Charging limestone to the shaft kiln.
    b. Crushing limestone to the proper size.
    c. Operating the oil pressure pump of the gas compressor, the blower and the dust collector.
(b) Analysis of causes:
The group analysed the reason of the prolonged charging time. The reasons were:
    a. Un-uniform size of limestone.
    b. Overweight charge in hopper.
    c. A fixed feeder volume (regardless of the size of the lumps of limestone).
(c) Appropriate measures adopted:
    a. Controlling the feeder volume according to the size of the lumps of limestone. (When the size of the lumps of limestone were very small, feeder volume should be increased.)
    b. Attaching to the charging belt an 'introducing plate' to deflect the limestone falling from the hopper, as is shown in Figure 7.5.
(d) Effects:
These measures made it possible to reduce the average charging time to 5 minutes, and to prevent defacement of the charge belt.

Case 3. Technical management accomplished in the third blast furnace

Technically, the third blast furnace is different from the first and second blast furnaces mainly in pressurised operation and a high tapping ratio. As the capacity of the third blast furnace is much larger than the first and second ones, the amount of charge through the top of the furnace at any one time is large. The stacking of coke and ore inside the blast furnace is also different

Figure 7.5: Drawing of deflecting plate on the limestone feed belt

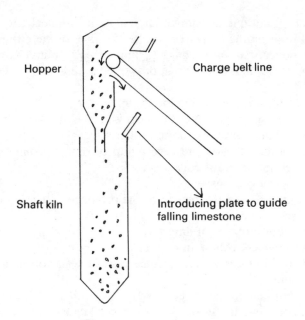

Hopper

Charge belt line

Shaft kiln

Introducing plate to guide
falling limestone

from that inside the previous two blast furnaces, in that wedge formation (depicted in Figure 7.6) is at a steeper angle. To reduce the steepness of angle of stacking, movable armour was attached to the top wall of the blast furnace. As the name indicates, movable armour can be shifted so that the area between the inner wall of blast furnace and the triangular wedge is controlled. The charge is delivered in such a way that coke is stacked in the middle part of the blast furnace to reduce the contact of coke with the refractory liner, since contact of the coke with the refractory wall can induce corrosion of the wall. As the coke is gathered in the middle part of the blast furnace, the temperature around the refractory wall is relatively low and the ore is not molten. The pile-up of the solid ore along the wall puts pressure to the tuyere inlet (made of copper tube) prolonged towards the centre of the blast furnace.

There is a possibility that the outer part of the tuyere might be twisted and tilted upward due to the high pressure of the solid ore. In anticipation of this, a supporting rim was attached to the lower part of the outside tuyere. Without this supporting rim,

194

Figure 7.6: Illustration of stacking angle and tuyere inlet in the third blast furnace

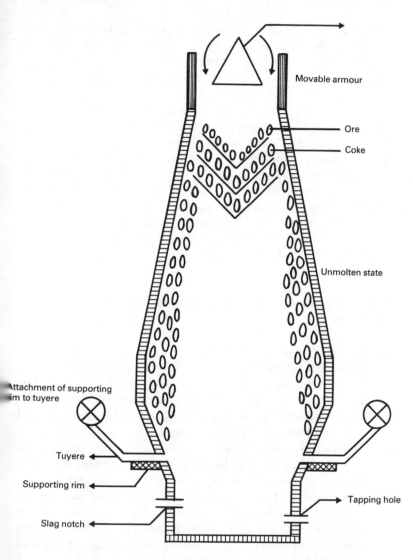

molten steel might have overflown through the tuyere. Figure 7.6 shows the supporting rim at the outside tuyere and the stacking manner of coke and charge. This component was not originally included in the foreign supplier's design, through ignorance of the need for it.

Case 4. Removing the scrap chute in the shear cutter at the slabbing mill

In the process of shear cutting, scrap tended to become stuck at a side trimmer. To free the scrap required heating it by means of a torch, held by hand; while the heating took place, the rolling operations had to be halted. The top drawing in Figure 7.7 shows the location of the fault.

It was believed that separating the original chute cover into two parts would leave a space between them through which the operators could observe the flow of scrap with the naked eye. Furthermore, any entanglement of scrap might be freed without removing the covers and halting operations. To achieve this separation, two covers of a size 25m/m by 200m/m by 300m/m were fabricated and installed, as shown in the bottom half of Figure 7.7. The alteration in the design of the scrap chute was successful, enabling output of rolled steel to be raised by approximately 1,400 tons per year.

Case 5. Installation of skew volume for tail-out in the cold rolling mill

(a) Original status and problem:
    When tailing-out, the end of a strip of steel can fold up, due to its free movement after passing the fore stand. The operator of the back stand is not able to observe the fold-up. If folded up, the tail part of the coil cannot be cold rolled, for it would damage the roller.

(b) Resolution of the problem:
    One skew volume is attached to each stand. The skew volume controls the rolling road on the work side and the drive side of the rolling stand. Another skew volume was attached to each stand, as shown in Figure 7.8, so that the operator of the fore stand could observe the tail part and thus control the rolling road of the next rolling stand. The appended skew volume is engaged when tailing-out.

(c) Effects:
    (i)   Since the operator of the fore stand could now control the rolling road and observe the situation of the tail part of the coil, the tail part could be completely rolled and 30 seconds operating time saved per coil.

196

Figure 7.7: Original and remodelled scrap chute covers

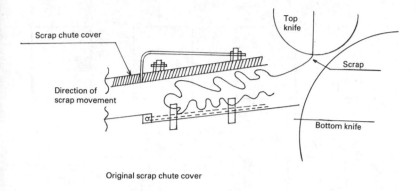

Original scrap chute cover

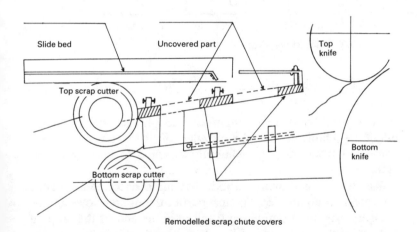

Remodelled scrap chute covers

(ii)   As all the coil could be rolled, about 825 tons of strip per month were saved.

Case 6. Remodelling the mud gun nozzle

Problems arose in both the fore furnace to the blast furnace and the foundry pig-iron furnace during the plugging of the tapping holes with mud guns. Occasionally, in the second and third blast furnaces which operate at higher pressures than the first, the mud failed completely to plug the hole, releasing an ejection of

197

Figure 7.8: Original and redesigned skew volumes

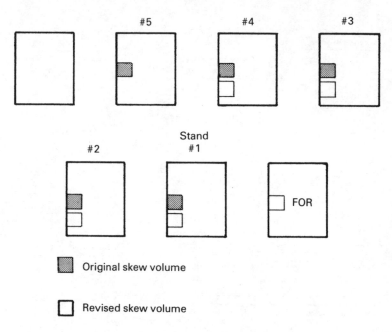

Original skew volume

Revised skew volume

molten iron. The Korean engineers thought that the problems might be eliminated if the nozzles of the mud guns were converted from being permanently attached to being replaceable.

The nozzles and their method of attachment to the mud guns are shown in Figure 7.9. The top part of the figure shows an oil-pressure-type mud gun being fitted over the end of the tapping hole, with the last drops of the flow of molten iron escaping at top and bottom. Before the improvements, with repeated pressing against the tapping hole, the bottom end of the nozzle eroded and a tight seal was impossible to obtain. Without a tight seal, the plugging of the tapping hole was incomplete.

The remoulding of the nozzle involved thickening the walls from 30m/m to 45m/m, attaching a replaceable tip, and reducing the clearance between nozzle and tip to less than 0.03m/m. In addition, operating procedures were re-written to respond better to emergencies: if the tip of the nozzle melted, the molten tip was to be knocked off with a handhammer and exchanged for a new one. The new tip was to be attached tightly. If the fore end of the nozzle melted the tip was first to be exchanged and

Figure 7.9: Original and remodelled mud nozzle tips

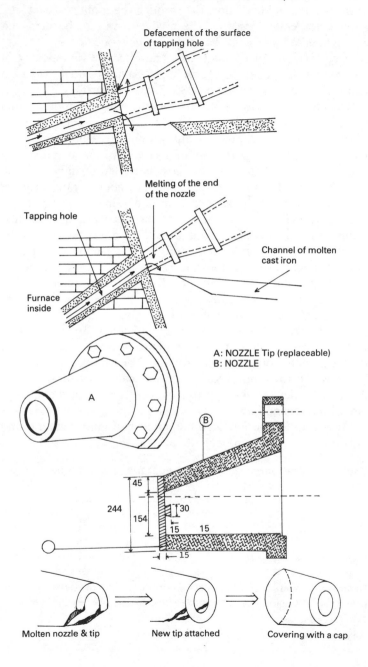

Defacement of the surface
of tapping hole

Melting of the end
of the nozzle

Tapping hole

Furnace
inside

Channel of molten
cast iron

A: NOZZLE Tip (replaceable)
B: NOZZLE

A

B

45
244
154
30
15   15
15

Molten nozzle & tip   New tip attached   Covering with a cap

199

then the fore end of the nozzle covered with a cap and bolted, so that mud would not flow out through the molten vacant site. After emergency measures, the mud gun was to be detached and the melted nozzle exchanged for a new one.

A comparison of events before and after the remodelling of the nozzle is given in Table 7.7. Savings attributable to remodelling corresponded to US$77,000 per year.

The above six cases of improvement in equipment design and operating procedures came about under two schemes called 'zero defect' and 'improvement proposal', which enlist the voluntary efforts of personnel in production, maintenance and management. These schemes have been led mainly by field engineers and technicians, and therefore concentrate on practical problems. Their achievements are remarkable: in 1977, under the zero defect scheme, 564 cases were investigated, resulting in savings of US$754,000 at the then exchange rate. Through the improvement proposal system, substantial improvements were made in 37 cases; savings amounted to US$2,994,000. According to Table 7.8 the major effects of 'zero defect' activities were to reduce costs and to improve efficiency and quality, while those of the improvement proposal system were to improve efficiency and to reduce waste. As part of those two programmes, POSCO introduced a reward system for excellent proposals, providing an attractive incentive for the employees. Such systematic back-ups for zero defect activities are thought to have contributed to the absorption of the technology.

Over a longer period both the number of improvements and

Table 7.7: Comparison of accidents at the tapping hole before and after remodelling

Item	Before remodelling	After remodelling
Blast off, due to failure of plugging	2 times	—
Pressure loss, due to failure of plugging	11 times	1 time
Flowing out of mud	26 times/month	9 times/month
Defacement of tapping hole	28 times/month	10 times/month
Exchange of nozzle	6 times	—
Welding of nozzle	15 times/month	—

Table 7.8: Nature of improvements gained through the 'zero defect' and 'improvement proposal' schemes for the year 1977

Scheme	Cost reduction	Efficiency improvement	Prevention of obstacles	Stable maintenance	Quality improvement	Reduction in waste	Total
'Zero rated'							
Number of proposals registered	300	258	127	83	86	72	967
Number of projects accomplished	159	142	65	50	37	32	565
Amount saved, estimated (in US$)	402,000	116,000	18,000	17,000	126,000	17,000	754,000
'Improvement proposal'							
Number of proposals registered	9	25	2	1	1	5	43
Number of projects accomplished	7	21	2	1	1	5	56
Amount saved, estimated (in US$)	100,000	2,162,000	90,000	—	—	598,000	2,949,000
Total savings (in US$)	502,000	2,278,000	108,000	17,000	126,000	615,000	3,703,000

Source: POSCO.

their contribution to reduced costs can be seen to have fluctuated year by year. Table 7.9 summarises the data; 1977, the year covered in detail in Table 7.8, can be seen to be fairly typical of the interval from 1974 through 1981. In 1980, midway between the completion of the third and fourth stages of POSCO's plant and coincidental with the recession that struck all of Korea's heavy industry, the number of improvements undertaken increased dramatically. This increase was followed two years later by an equally dramatic increase in the savings effected. It appears that programmes for improvements require several years to get fully underway, and that a sharp down-turn in overall economic activity can provide a powerful stimulus to their attainment.

The above improvements in operation led to reductions in costs which were primarily those of fixed cost elements; there have also been improvements leading to reductions in the elements that vary with output. Table 7.10 reports the data for new material and energy consumption, per unit of output of the product (intermediate or final) identified in the first column. So far as raw material input is concerned, there were no appreciable unit savings in three of the operations — those producing hot rolled sheets, plate and billets. The raw material savings in the other three operations — those producing pig iron, wire rods and cold rolled sheets — were of the annual order of 1 per cent, 2 per cent and 2.5 per cent respectively.

Energy savings were substantial in the production of plates, billets and wire rods; and, after the first year of operation, of hot rolled sheets. In the production of cold rolled sheets there appears to have been some substitution of one form of energy, fuel, for another, electricity.

The data in Tables 7.9 and 7.10 are interesting in themselves but unrelated to the total cost of operations. To gain a better impression of the overall significance of improvements we must turn to POSCO's cost records, summarised in Table 7.11. The data begin in 1973, the initial year of production, and end in 1983, at the time of our enquiry the last year for which there were complete results. The first conclusion to be drawn concerns the relative importance of the improvements emerging from the zero defect and improvement proposal schemes, aggregated in Table 7.9. Taking 1983, the next to last year, we see that improvements resulted in an estimated saving of 18 billion won, out of total manufacturing costs of 1,263 billion, or

Table 7.9: Number of proposals for improvements arising within POSCO's plant, and savings therefrom, 1974-84

Year	Number of proposals		Distribution of proposals by objective (per cent)									Savings (million won)	
	Registered	Carried out	Cost reduction	Quality increase	Efficiency increase	Equipment operation	New techniques	Labour saving	Energy saving	Environment and safety	Others	Current prices	Constant 1980 prices
1974	28	28	25	11	11	22	—	3	—	6	—	121	350
1975	24	24	13	17	17	46	—	—	—	8	—	180	410
1976	34	34	9	12	24	32	—	9	—	12	3	587	1,180
1977	41	41	24	7	44	7	—	5	—	7	5	238	440
1978	41	41	29	22	24	2	—	—	—	5	17	331	550
1979	87	87	14	6	21	41	—	14	—	3	1	686	950
1980	745	745	19	3	18	23	—	22	1	11	2	229	230
1981	1,085	1,085	13	7	17	36	2	14	2	7	1	1,158	960
1982	2,056	2,056	16	8	22	30	—	13	1	10	—	12,838	10,200
1983	8,756	8,251	8	4	17	45	1	12	—	13	1	18,276	14,560
1984	12,635	12,355	19	4	14	34	—	12	—	14	3	18,590	14,600
Total, 1974-84	25,534	25,017	15	4	16	37	1	12	—	13	2	53,234	44,430

Source: POSCO. Current prices were deflated by the wholesale price index.

Table 7.10: Changes in raw material and energy consumption, 1974-84

Manufactured product	Raw material	Unit	74	75	76	77	78	79	80	81	82	83	84
Pig iron	Sintered ore	Ore/ton of iron	1.27	1.32	1.31	1.34	1.32	1.35	1.36	1.33	1.33	1.31	1.28
	Indian iron ore	Ore/ton of iron	0.43	0.38	0.37	0.34	0.36	0.36	0.33	0.35	0.33	0.34	0.32
Hot rolled	Slab	Slab/hour	1.04	1.08	1.05	1.05	1.05	1.06	1.06	1.05	1.05	1.05	1.04
	Electricity	kwh/ton of iron						98.8	166.3	125.7	121.4	120.7	117.5
	Fuel	10^3 kcal/ton						400.8	521.5	445.9	413.8	413.1	406
Plate	Slab	Slab/plate	1.16	1.17	1.16	1.15	1.16	1.15	1.15	1.15	1.13	1.13	1.14
	Electricity	kwh/ton of plate						73.6	76.2	75.3	72.2	76.7	72.3
	Fuel	10^3 kcal/ton of plate						442.2	398.7	399	391	396.7	375.8
Billet	Bloom	Bloom/billet	1.03	1.02	1.03	1.03	1.04	1.04	1.03	1.03	1.03	1.03	1.03
	Electricity	kwh/ton of billet						44.9	41.0	41.7	42.8	45.7	45.0
	Fuel	10^3 kcal/ton of billet						443.6	372	307.3	284.4	284.4	296.5
Wire rod	Billet	Billet/wire						1.15	1.08	1.03	1.02	1.02	1.02
	Electricity	kwh/ton of wire						190.8	136.0	125.7	122.4	127.5	123.9
	Fuel	10^3 kcal/ton of wire						454.8	363	317.3	318.8	313.4	307.8
Cold rolled	Slab	Hours/ton of CR				1.30	1.12	1.09	1.08	1.11	1.10	1.10	1.08
	Electricity	kwh/ton of CR						139.5	144.6	135.6	128.1	130.0	110.1
	Fuel	10^3 kcal/ton of CR						29	28.5	39.5	35.5	43	38

Source: POSCO.

1.5 per cent. Taking 1974, the estimated savings were 0.2 per cent; and taking the intermediate year 1979, just before the great expansion of the schemes, 0.2 per cent again.

The second conclusion concerns the overall reductions in manufacturing costs, not only those arising out of improvements in operations in raw materials and energy consumption, but also out of the expansion of capacity. To estimate the overall reductions we will need to correct the cost data in column four of Table 7.11 for increases in the price level and in the volume of output. This is done in column five, using the wholesale price index in column three. The total manufacturing costs of column five are converted to average cost per metric ton of steel in the final column. Taking a weighted average of the 1973 and 1974 costs (equal to 190,500 won per ton) as representative of the first year of full production, and 1983 as the last, the average annual rate of cost reduction over the nine-year interval is 5.1 per cent compounded or 6.6 per cent in simple terms.

Year-by-year comparisons of costs are not generally revealing, because of the inflation that occurred during the decade 1973-4 and 1984 and the consequent difficulty of converting rapidly rising to constant prices with any price index. There does appear to be one discontinuity in the average cost data,

Table 7.11: Total and average manufacturing costs of POSCO, 1974-83

Year	Steel production (million metric tons)	Wholesale price index (1980 = 100)	Total manufacturing costs (billions of won)		Average cost of manufacture (thousand won of 1980 per metric ton)
			Current prices	Constant 1980 prices	
1973	0.449	24.7	32.6	132	295
1974	1.157	35.1	60.7	173	150
1975	1.234	44.4	86.7	196	159
1976	2.037	49.8	133.3	268	132
1977	2.412	54.3	193.9	357	148
1978	2.807	60.6	277.2	457	163
1979	5.278	72.0	417.6	580	110
1980	5.903	100	619.4	619	105
1981	8.185	120.4	1,059.7	879	107
1982	8.781	126.0	1,269.4	1,009	115
1983	8.438	126.3	1,263.5	1,001	119
1984	9.195	127.2	n.a.	n.a.	n.a.

Source: POSCO.

however, between 1978 and 1979; this must be associated with the bringing on tap, in December 1978, of the third and much larger blast furnace and its associated converter and processing equipment.

In order to make allowance for the substantial increase in scale, and, presumably, the economies that the much larger sized blast furnaces, converters and other pieces of equipment brought, we will need to utilise the method devised in Chapter 2. The appropriate equation is (8), with the division between the first and second terms in the sequence conveniently occurring at the end of December 1978, when the third blast furnace, the second steel-making plant, and the second slabbing and blooming mill had all just been brought on stream. Given our data in Table 7.11, the end of the interval (t in equation 8) is 1983; the date and design capacity of the first step are 1973-4 and 2,800,000 metric tons respectively (t_1 and q_1); the date and design capacity of the second step are 1979 and 5,600,000 metric tons respectively (t_2 and q_2); and the total costs of operating the first step equipment in 1973-4 and in 1979 ($C_1(t_1)$ and $C_1(t_2)$) are 535 billion won (adding total costs for 1973 (132 billion won) and 1974 (173 billion won)), then multiplying the sum by the design capacity of the first step (2,800,000 metric tons) and dividing by the total output achieved in 1973 and 1974 (0.449 and 1.157 million metric tons respectively) and 457 billion won respectively.

At this point in the analysis we are faced with two alternatives: we can estimate either the cost reduction attributable to scale economies (the β_1 of equation 8), or we can estimate the scale parameter delta (δ in the equation 8); but not both. Since our main purpose is to subtract from the overall rate of reduction of manufacturing cost, per metric ton of steel (already estimated at 5.2 per cent per year) that portion attributable to the exploitation of scale economies in successively larger-sized equipment, in order to derive the residual, attributable to all improvements, we will choose the first alternative. Hence we will need to draw on measures of delta independent of our own study.

It is not easy to find estimates of the scale parameter for manufacturing costs. Estimates for delta for construction costs are readily available from information published in trade journals, but those for operating costs are held confidential by the firms that incur them. The estimates that are in our possession suggest values for delta in the range 0.8 to 0.9 (Yotopoulos and Nugent, 1976, Table 9.1, pp. 152, 153); we shall insert both extremes into equation (8), obtaining thereby a high (0.7 per cent) and a low (0.3 per cent) estimate of β_1; and by subtraction, a low and a high estimate of the residual ($\beta - \beta_1$). These, which we ascribe to all the efforts within POSCO to improve operating performance, amount as a simple rate to 5.9 and 6.3 per cent annually. Compounded, the rates are 4.4 and 4.8 per cent per year.

We will leave an evaluation of the rates of cost reduction through improvements to our concluding Chapter 9; but we might draw one conclusion here, namely that the building of larger-scale plants and their operation at, or above, design capacity does contribute to lowering average costs of production, but so also do improvements in current operation. In industries like iron and steel, whose plants are gigantic to begin with, new and still larger plants are going to be constructed only occasionally, whereas improvements in operation can be sought at every instant. Steady pressure to achieve improvements is required for success, as well as dramatic moves to expand capacity.

THE DEVELOPMENT OF NEW PRODUCTS AND PROCESSES

Up until this point we have been considering chiefly new processes, and their absorption into POSCO: it is now time to focus on new products produced by POSCO. During the first two stages, up till the end of 1978, POSCO concentrated on the production of ordinary iron and steel, in relatively simple shapes. It was only into the design of the third stage that POSCO introduced the production of special steels. Two points are worth remarking in relation to the development of special steels: first, the slow development of special steels can be attributed to the fact that the technology POSCO had absorbed did not reach the level of those products and that the demand for special steels had been relatively small. The demand for special steels recorded only 29,000 tons in 1976, and increased to 70,000 tons in 1977, but even then represented only 3.7 per cent of the total steel production. The demands for special steels, however, were expected to increase sharply with the rapid development of defence industries and of exports.

Second, the development of special steels could only be achieved through the introduction of foreign know-how; POSCO has not concentrated on the development of the technology itself. Table 7.12 gives some idea of the extent of the knowledge that had to be imported.

Although POSCO was content to go abroad for the technology needed to produce special steels, it was determined to create internally an ability generally to develop new products and to improve upon the design of existing processes. Simultaneously, therefore, it established a research laboratory, consolidating in one centre developmental work that had previously been done throughout the firm, and increasing substantially the resources devoted to it. An analysis of tasks completed by the R and D centre in 1984 revealed twelve themes within the category of new techniques and products

Table 7.12: Import of 'know-how' for the development of special steels

Contract	Specification	Contents
Technical co-operation agreement between POSCO & Japan Group	SMA 41A	Techniques for the addition of alloying elements
	50A	Techniques to improve recovery of alloying elements
		Techniques to produce clean steels and to improve weldability
	SB 46M	Techniques to produce clean steels and to improve weldability
	AP 15LX	Heat treatment technique
	−X60	Baushinger effect
	AP 15LX	Techniques for controlled rolling
	−X65	Heat treatment techniques
Know-how agreement	SPCEN	Techniques to improve formability
		Heat treatment techniques
Agreement for making of hi-carbon steel	SWRH 82 SWRS 92	Low-P, high-C steel production techniques
	SWRCH 52	Cooling techniques for high-C steel
	SWRY 11	Wire drawing techniques for high-C steels

Note: Special steels are defined as: plain carbon steel whose tensile strength exceeds $50\,Kg/mm^2$; steels which need alloying elements other than the five most common; steels whose carbon content exceeds 0.5 per cent; steels which need heat treatment; steels for rigid forming, like deep drawing; and non-ageing steels, etc.

(improvement in the solidification structures of continuously-casted products by means of an electromagnetic stirrer, desulphurisation and dephosphorisation of hot metal by means of a CaO flux, development of carbon steel wire rods for automatic welding by a controlling cooling process, and development of line pipe steel for transporting sour gas); 39 themes within the category of quality improvement (including the reduction of silicon content in molten iron, the development of a coating solution for non-oriented silicon steel, the determination of the effect of pre-annealing conditions upon the formability of galvanised sheet, and the establishment of quality control procedures in the making of milling powder and continuous casting); 14 themes within the category of process improvements (including the determination of optimum reheating time in the furnace for steel plate, and the improvement of granulation of sintered feed); three themes within the category of energy-saving (including the use of the continuous annealing production line for the manufacture of high-grade black plate); and 20 themes within a residual category (including the investigation of shell cracks in the blast furnaces, a study of the preferred treatment of coke plant waste water, and a general enquiry into the behaviour of sulphide inclusions in steel). The programme for 1985 was larger still, extending over 203 themes and focusing on steel rolling in addition to the categories of the previous year.

That the programme for 1985 should have exceeded that for 1984 is not surprising, given the close correlation between POSCO's expenditures on research and development, on the one hand, and its current prosperity on the other. Table 7.12 shows that although expenditures on research and development have generally risen in absolute terms throughout the years, they have fluctuated quite widely, in relative terms, along with the firm's profitability. The correlation is closer for pre-tax profits, shown in Table 7.12, than it is for total revenues, total costs or post-tax profits.

THE DIFFUSION OF THE TECHNOLOGY

POSCO has largely depended upon foreign technology. The absorption of technology necessary for the construction of mills and their operations was rapid. The absorption and assimilation of the core technology necessary for process and equipment design has, however, been sluggish. Similarly, it has been construction and operating technology that has successfully been diffused. Diffusion will be considered below in the following two ways — diffusion to other companies and diffusion abroad.

In analysing the diffusion of technology to other steel mills within Korea, we should notice that POSCO is the only integrated steel mill in the country. Diffusion can only be to unintegrated or specialised mills. As there is no anti-pirating clause in the industry, POSCO technicians and engineers can move freely to other companies. As shown in Table 7.13, the departure of POSCO's technicians and engineers, chiefly to other mills, occurred on a fairly large scale during those years for which there are data. Because of the intensive training programmes POSCO introduced in its first years of operation, those who left would have been much more skilled than the employees of the smaller firms they joined. Even though they are not equipped with an integrated steel-making system and so utilise processes somewhat different from those of POSCO, other steel mills have been able to benefit from the knowledge accumulated by the company's former employees.

Some of the persons quitting POSCO have taken employment with capital goods producers, particularly those located on the periphery of POSCO's plant at Pohang. There they have

Table 7.13: Expenditures on research and development, in absolute and relative terms, 1977-84 (billions of current won)

| Year | Expenditures on research and development | | | | | | Profits of of POSCO | Total R & D expenditure ÷ profits (per cent) |
| | Research and development centre | | | | Else-where within POSCO | Total | | |
	Labour costs	Capital cost	Other costs	Total for centre				
1977	0.37	0.17	0.16	0.69	0.44	1.13	15.4	7.3
1978	0.41	0.48	0.04	0.92	0.24	1.16	24.5	4.7
1979	0.45	0.17	0.20	0.82	0.83	1.65	30.8	5.4
1980	0.50	0.25	0.40	1.14	0.14	1.28	12.7	10.0
1981	0.50	0.74	0.26	1.50	1.94	3.44	52.1	6.6
1982	0.97	1.52	0.74	3.23	0.53	3.76	44.1	8.5
1983	1.41	1.32	1.34	4.07	5.71	9.78	77.9	12.5
1984	1.99	1.43	1.54	4.97	n.a.	n.a.	n.a.	n.a.

Source: POSCO.

helped to construct equipment installed in POSCO's plant. With the lack of advanced iron- and steel-fabricating technology in Korea, iron- and steel-making equipment like blast furnaces and LD converters have had to be imported. Domestic industries have been able to supply only unsophisticated equipment: 12.5 per cent of the total equipment by value in the initial stage, 15.5 per cent in the second, 22.6 per cent in the third and 35 per cent in the fourth. As can be seen in Table 7.15, local suppliers have confined themselves to less-important equipment such as cranes, ladles, water pipes, transformers, etc. In the third and fourth stages, however, equipment for water treatment and for dust collection, and the large magnetic crane, were produced by local suppliers. In subsequent construction, a consortium of Korean equipment manufacturers — Hyundai, Daewoo and Samsung — will try to play a greater role.

The heavy dependence on foreign suppliers for sophisticated equipment can be attributed in part to the low level of technology of the domestic machinery industry. The chief argument for the low degree of localisation of equipment can be summarised as follows; because iron- and steel-making facilities are of very large unit capacity, it is expensive to shut them down in emergencies. Emergencies are less likely to occur if the equipment is of high quality. Buyers of equipment, like POSCO, want the highest-quality equipment, which domestic capital goods

Table 7.14: Number of production employees quitting POSCO, 1968-77

Year	Semi-skilled workers	Skilled workers	Persons leaving Technicians	Engineers	Total
1968	1	—	1	4	6
1969	3	—	3	9	15
1970	4	—	2	10	16
1971	12	—	5	12	29
1972	32	—	10	20	62
1973	82	6	47	47	182
1974	169	17	74	41	301
1975	153	20	79	65	317
1976	336	27	121	100	584
1977	361	60	203	156	780

Note: In 1977, POSCO's total employment of both technically and non-technically trained was 22,900 persons.
Source: POSCO.

suppliers cannot provide. Moreover, international purchases are financed by foreign loans at low interest rates, whereas domestic purchases have to be financed domestically at higher interest rates.

The second way in which the iron- and steel-making technology has diffused is abroad from Korea. This reversal of flow, initially from Japan and Austria, and to a lesser extent other developed countries, to Korea, and now from Korea to other developing countries, took approximately ten years. Taiwan, engaged in 1978 in constructing an integrated iron- and steel-making plant of 1.5 million tons annual capacity for the Chinese Steel Corporation, negotiated a contract with POSCO in which the latter was to receive a sum of US$300,000 for training 42 Taiwanese in Korea in plant operation and maintenance and for assisting in the new plant's initial production. The link with Taiwan has been maintained by means of annual conferences on operating techniques. A subsequent export of technology from Korea has taken the form of a production control system, computerised, for the hot rolling section of the integrated Krakatoa steel works in Indonesia. A team of six engineers from POSCO designed the system and assisted at its installation and operation; the contract for providing the technology and the training yielded US$2,476,000 to POSCO.

CONCLUSION

In summarising POSCO's experience we will first compare it with that of steel firms in developed countries and second attempt to explain the company's relative success. The comparisons with firms in developed countries are made in Tables 7.16 and 7.17: the former reveals, in the first column, the substantial rate of growth of POSCO's sales since commencing production; and, in the second column, the continued profitability. Retained profits have permitted most of the domestic portion of investment at Pohang to be financed internally, and will even cover part of the foreign component of the capital cost of the next steel mill being built at Gwanyang on the southern coast of Korea.

Even more revealing is a comparison between the rates of return for POSCO and for the largest Japanese and US firms. Columns three, six and nine of Table 7.16 provide the data for

Table 7.15: Localisation of capital equipment by stage of facilities (in billion won)

	1st stage	2nd stage	3rd stage	4th stage	Total and average
Total expenditure on facilities (A)	752	161.4	446.9	442.0	1,125.5
Amount spent on locally-produced equipment (B)	9.4	25.0	100.8	154.7	289.9
Ratio (B/A)	0.125	0.155	0.226	0.350	0.258
Items produced domestically	Small-scale crane, cast iron products, ladle, low-pressure cable	Water piping, transformer, automatic alarm, elevator, dust collector	Equipment for water treatment, 30 ton magnetic crane, 330 ton large-scale ladle, roller table	Plant transportation facilities, special crane	

the comparison, reported as percentages of profits, after tax, *vis-à-vis* revenues from sales. During the period 1980-4, the American firms were collectively losing money, and in one year, 1983, the Japanese firms were too; POSCO was consistently profitable.

Over the period 1980-4 as a whole, however, POSCO was not appreciably more profitable than the Japanese firms, and this demands an explanation. Turning to the latter table, 7.17, we see that POSCO has maintained higher rates of steel output, relative to capacity, than have all other steel-producing countries. The coverage for Japan and the USA in Table 7.17 is greater than that in the preceding table, extending over the entire industry rather than just the largest firms, but the general result holds: POSCO uses its equipment more intensively than do its rivals in world markets. This may explain POSCO's margin over the steel firms in the USA. Another explanation for POSCO's relative success, at least over the US firms, must be its having modern, large-scale equipment located in a single plant on a coastal site.

Where the Japanese firms are concerned, POSCO has no advantage in location or modernity of equipment, and is at a disadvantage in scale of operations. Four of the five firms in the sample for Japan (in Table 7.16) are larger than POSCO, and

213

Table 7.16: Total revenues and profits of POSCO, 1973-84, and of comparable Japanese and US firms, 1980-4

Year	POSCO (billion current won)			Japanese firms[a] (billion current yen)			USA firms[b] (million current dollars)		
	Revenues	Profits after tax	Profits ÷ revenues %	Revenues	Profits after tax	Profits ÷ revenues %	Revenues	Profits after tax	Profits ÷ revenues %
1973	42	4.6	11.0	n.a.	n.a.	n.a.	n.a.	n.a.	n.a.
1974	104	35.5	34.2	n.a.	n.a.	n.a.	n.a.	n.a.	n.a.
1975	110	9.1	8.3	n.a.	n.a.	n.a.	n.a.	n.a.	n.a.
1976	180	15.3	8.5	n.a.	n.a.	n.a.	n.a.	n.a.	n.a.
1977	253	13.7	5.4	n.a.	n.a.	n.a.	n.a.	n.a.	n.a.
1978	360	21.9	6.1	n.a.	n.a.	n.a.	n.a.	n.a.	n.a.
1979	606	26.2	4.2	n.a.	n.a.	n.a.	n.a.	n.a.	n.a.
1980	959	10.8	1.3	8,187	237.3	2.9	37,205	−1,132	−3.1
1981	1,521	44.3	2.9	8,619	169.1	2.0	43,015	−2,112	−4.9
1982	1,742	15.3	0.9	7,860	120.2	1.5	40,030	−2,912	−7.3
1983	1,751	52.1	3.0	7,435	−24.9	−0.3	37,022	−2,444	−6.6
1984	1,963	60.2	3.1	8,019	115.8	1.4	41,763	−676	−1.6

[a] The Japanese firms are Nippon Steel and Nippon Kokan (the two members of 'Japan Group'), Kawasaki Steel, Sumitomo Metals and Kobe Steel.
[b] The US firms are US Steel, Bethlehem, LTV, Armco, Inland and National Steel.

Source: POSCO.

the fifth, Kobe Steel, is only marginally smaller, with 8,807,000 metric tons annual steel capacity compared to 9,100,000 for POSCO. Moreover, it is also at a disadvantage in that steel prices in Korea, its major market, have been lower than those in Japan, the major market for the Japanese firms, throughout the period 1980-4 by as much as US$50 to $100 per ton.

In the light of these factors it is not surprising that POSCO has been little more profitable, on average, than the Japanese firms. In fact, what surprise there is might arise out of POSCO's equalling the performance of the Japanese firms. Given that Korea had to create a steel industry out of nothing, that the creation involved a very rapid expansion of capacity and output, and that all this took place at a time when the steel industry in the rest of the world was in depression, the accomplishment of Korea is even greater.

To the authors of this study two additional explanations for POSCO's relative success are the low capital cost of its facilities and the steady improvement in their operation. Both these factors are tied in with the adoption and absorption of the technology. Capital costs are lower, the more skilful are the choice of technique and the conduct of negotiations with its foreign supplier, and the more expeditious are the construction of the plant and the installation of the equipment. Operating costs are lower, the more rapidly the technology is absorbed.

Some evidence pointing to Korea's skilful adoption of iron- and steel-making technology has been given in this chapter, and is corroborated by another author (Hogan, 1985, pp. 35, 36). Korea was fortunate indeed that its construction projects were

Table 7.17: International comparison of rates of utilisation of capacity in steel, 1977-84 (annual output of steel, as a percentage of rated capacity)

| Year | 1977 | 1978 | 1979 | 1980 | 1981 | 1982 | 1983 | 1984 |
Country	%	%	%	%	%	%	%	%
Korea (POSCO)	96.1	103.9	100.9	107.3	102.3	103.3	99.7	101.0
Japan	61.1	67.3	71.3	70.2	64.2	63.0	62.2	67.2
USA	78.3	86.8	87.8	72.8	78.3	48.4	56.2	68.9
EEC	62.8	65.8	68.9	63.1	63.2	56.2	57.1	66.5
World (excluding communist countries	74.3	78.0	79.7	70.7	69.1	59.6	61.6	68.3

Source: Korea; POSCO. Other countries; *WSD Strategist*, no. 10, December 1984.

215

initiated in an era when steel-making capacity in the rest of the world was shrinking and the competition among suppliers of technology and capital goods was intense. If there was a drawback to the cheapness of the foreign technology it was that it offered little incentive to the Koreans to learn the arts of process and equipment design.

The evidence, in this chapter, pointing to Korea's proficiency in constructing plant, installing equipment and starting up the facilities, is very strong. The data in Table 7.4 reveal the speed with which POSCO was able to build the facilities, those in Figure 7.2 the speed with which POSCO was able to bring them into production. Both indicated a mastery of construction and operating technology, and both reduced the capital requirements of each successive stage.

A further indication of the Koreans' accomplishment in absorbing iron- and steel-making technology is provided by the improvements carried out subsequent to the initial operation of the facilities. Making allowance for the economies associated with increases in plant scale, the annual rate of reduction in production cost over the period from 1973-4 to 1983, covering almost the entire operating history of POSCO, has been in the order of 4.5 per cent. All of this is attributable to improvements: improvements in operating procedures, in raw material utilisation, in energy consumption and in product quality. To secure improvements in productivity of this magnitude, year after year, on facilities already being operated at full capacity, implies a successful absorption of the technology.

8

The Experience of Japan

To the extent that any country has been the model for Korea in its industrialisation it is Japan. Explanations are easy to find; geographical propinquity; recent experience; familiarity with the language, particularly in its written form; recognition that the Japanese have already adapted Western technology to Eastern social and political mores; and, surely a necessary part of the explanation, Japanese success in their own endeavours. So the experience of Japanese in incorporating foreign technology may be useful in understanding Korea's, and may give some indication of the direction in which Korea will move in the future.

In this chapter we shall enquire into Japan's absorption and diffusion of foreign technology, asking the same sorts of questions that we asked of Korea's: whence did it come and on what conditions? how was it chosen? absorbed? diffused? with what consequences? Our aim is thus no different from our aim in carrying out the four Korean case studies — to learn more about the overall process of incorporating a foreign technology within a developing country.

Our means in this chapter are, however, quite different from those of the previous four. We did not conduct the research that we will be reporting; not only this, but most of the research that we will be reporting was not even conducted with the same primary aim. To record achievements was the objective of most of these carrying out the research in Japan and they were employed in this task not by universities, as were we, but by the organisations which incorporated the foreign technology — government agencies, industry associations and individual firms. Moreover, many of these organisations were the very ones which incorporated the technology, and many of the sponsors were the individuals involved. Under such circumstances, the results of research tend to be congratulatory rather than critical, and to give the impression that the Japanese experience has been universally successful. The achievements of the Koreans will seem to be, in comparison, much less so, yet the Koreans' relatively poorer showing may be no more than the consequence of our having utilised a different set of sources. Indeed, some who have studied Japan's import of foreign technology (e.g. Tipten, 1981) have reservations as to Japan's success. In the specific areas of government policy and implementation, in which we judge the Korean government to have excelled, the Japanese government may not have; yet the material that we will cite will not provide any evidence to this effect. The reader of our Korean case studies will, of course, approach them in a critical vein; one's critical faculties should not rest when approaching this chapter too.

In outline, this chapter on the Japanese experience will follow the order in which the Korean cases were presented; first petrochemicals, then synthetic fibres, followed by machinery and, finally, iron and steel. At the end of the chapter there will be a comparison of Japan's experience with Korea's, in which we will attempt to bring out the similarities and dissimilarities in their environments and in their processes of incorporating foreign technology.

PETROCHEMICALS

The Japanese chemical industry came into being at the end of the nineteenth century as a diversified collection of small firms using very simple processes. Little progress, economic or technological, occurred until the 1930s, when the military government encouraged the construction of relatively large-scale plants producing basic chemicals for munitions. Towards the end of the decade, the government also began to undertake, at its own and in university laboratories, research into the production of synthetic rubber. One of the 'zaibatsus', Mitsui Chemical Company, co-operated, and succeeded in reproducing the Malthole process for the production of butadiene rubber, starting with carbide as the raw material. As sole supplier of synthetic rubber to the Japanese Navy, Mitsui constructed a plant with a capacity of one ton per day and, in spite of shortages of power and raw materials, managed to produce 350 tons during the Second World War (Haruo, 1968).

After the end of the war, the Americans, in occupation, forbade the production of synthetic rubber. Mitsui, along with 18 other firms, decided to transfer engineers released from wartime work to the development of plastics, particularly vinyl chloride monomer (VCM). Its plant, constructed in 1949, had a capacity of approximately 6,000 tons per year; its first competitor, Nippon Zeon, which had entered into a joint venture with Goodrich Chemical of the US in 1950 using the latter's technique, also constructed a plant of 3,000 tons capacity, soon expanded to 6,000 tons. Shortly after, three other chemical firms began to produce VCM; one, like Nippon Zeon, drew upon foreign technology, and two, like Mitsui, developed their own.

Although domestic demand for VCM was growing rapidly, the five Japanese producers had difficulty competing with foreign firms, both in quality and in cost. It was not until they shifted the raw material source from carbide to ethylene, thereby becoming petrochemical producers, that the Japanese firms were internationally competitive. In the course of the shift, Mitsui combined with its subsidiary, Toyo High Pressure Company, to develop an oxychlorination process. A little later, in 1962, another Japanese firm, Kureha Chemical Co. Inc., developed a process, called the Kureha-Chiyoda, for the production of VCM using ethylene dichloride as an intermediary (the same route followed by Hanyang) and constructed a plant of some 75,000 tons per year (Hanyang's capacity was 60,000 tons). High costs led this enterprise to fail.

Mitsui Chemical Co. was also the innovator in Japan of the production of polyethylene. The basis of Mitsui's manufacturing technique was the Ziegler process for polymerisation at low pressure. The process had been observed by Mitsui's President, Ishida Ken, during a visit to Germany in 1954. Hoechst and a few other chemical firms in the developed countries had adopted the process only a few years before; Mitsui was the first in any of the less-developed countries, when, in the following year, it licensed the patents describing the Ziegler process and acquired two volumes of note books on laboratory work directly from Dr Ziegler himself, for US$1,200,000. In the same year Mitsui created a subsidiary firm, Mitsui Petrochemical, and initiated work on a pilot plant designed to produce 12 tons per year of polyethylene. Performing successfully, the pilot plant was expanded tenfold in the course of nine months, reaching a commercial scale.

Simultaneously, Mitsui was developing its own technique, inventing around Ziegler's patents. This technique, involving a new catalyst, was incorporated in a commercial plant of 12,000 tons per year, constructed in 1958, but not brought to full capacity operation immediately because of the poor quality of the polyethylene produced. One year's research, in co-operation with the Honda Technical Research Institute, eliminated the problem, so that output could be raised to 7,200 to 8,400 tons per year at the end of 1960, 9,600 at the end of 1961, and full capacity at the end of 1962. By 1968 Mitsui felt confident enough of its understanding of the process and of the growth of the market for its product to construct a plant of 60,000 tons per year. (Hanyang's polyethylene plant, brought into operation in 1973, had a capacity of 50,000 tons per year.)

Mitsui has not been the only Japanese firm to produce polyethylene. Other producers like Showa Denko, employing Philip's method (invented in 1950), and Hurukawa Denko, adopting Standard Oil Indiana's method (invented in 1956), also entered into production in 1959 and 1960, respectively. They are competing, without the exchange of technological know-how, to meet the domestic and foreign demand for polyethylene.

SYNTHETIC FIBRES

As in the manufacture of petrochemicals, so in the manufacture of the synthetic fibre nylon, the innovating firms in Japan had already accumulated a substantial amount of experience through producing similar products. In the case of nylon, the experience was gained in the production of the first synthetic fibre consumed on a large scale, rayon. Invented in England in 1905, viscose rayon was first produced in Japan in 1909 (Habu, 1958 and 1971). By the 1930s, the Japanese rayon industry was large enough to support a few firms with their own research and development departments and a large government-sponsored synthetic fibre research association.

One of the alert firms was Toyo Rayon, a division of the

Mitsui Industrial Group. From scientists at Tokyo Technical University, Toyo learned that du Pont in the United States was in the process of developing a new synthetic fibre. Some of Toyo's R and D personnel were assigned to the investigation of synthetic fibres, in anticipation of du Pont's success; work increased after du Pont filed its patent application for Nylon 66 in 1938 and after Mitsui's office in New York, operating as Mitsui Bussan Trading Company, secured a sample of the material. The sample was analysed at Toyo Rayon, as well as at no fewer than four Japanese universities — Tokyo Imperial, Kyoto Imperial, Osaka Imperial and Tokyo Technical — and found to be based upon a polyamide. The scientist at Toyo Rayon who had been working on polyamides, Hoshino Kohei, set out to invent around du Pont's patents. In 1940 he came up with a different nylon, Nylon 6, which was given the trade name of 'Amiran' (Toyo Rayon, 1977). Amiran was discovered to have properties which made it suitable for use in ropes and fishing nets. A pilot plant of five kilograms per day was constructed, expanded to one ton per day at the request of the Japanese Navy,

The next development occurred after the end of the Second World War, when the Investigation Commission of the occupying forces judged that Amiran was sufficiently different from Nylon 66 so as not to infringe upon du Pont's patents. But although Toyo Rayon now was immune from litigation, it was not capable of integrating backwards into the production of the intermediates used in nylon manufacture nor forwards into the subsequent processes of spinning, dyeing, knitting, etc. In order to familiarise itself with these activities. Toyo Rayon entered into a contract with du Pont in 1951. For blueprints and know-how Toyo paid a lump sum of US$3,000,000, plus a royalty of 3 per cent of the value of the output. Even then the production of Amiran did not progress smoothly at Toyo, the quality of the product being poor and the costs of manufacture high. These problems were eliminated only after Toyo had sent a mission to the United States and had signed another contract, for the provision of technical service, with du Pont.

With improved techniques and with a new variant of nylon called 'Wooly', developed in Toyo's own laboratories in 1951, Toyo Rayon began to prosper. Capacity was increased from 3 tons per day in 1951, to 11 in 1954, and to 36 in 1956; and Toyo's domestic monopoly in the production of nylon, supported until 1954 by the Japanese government, guaranteed profitability.

When competition in nylon emerged it took the form of entry by another rayon producer, Nippon Rayon, supplied with foreign technology. In 1954 Nippon Rayon negotiated a contract with the Swiss firm of Inventor, in which for a cash payment of US$115,000 and a royalty rate of 2.5 per cent of the value of sales, Nippon Rayon would receive Inventor's technology. The technology included licences to manufacture both the intermediates and nylon itself, process and equipment design, assistance in plant construction and operation, and training both in Switzerland and on the site. Rather than acquire foreign technology partially and piece-meal, as did Toyo Rayon, Nippon Rayon bought it in its entirety and at once.

In 1955 Nippon Rayon's nylon plant was built; in the early 1960s the company felt that it had absorbed the operating technology completely. By then, three more Japanese firms, Kanebo-Teijin, Kureha-Boseki and Asahi-Kasei, had joined the two existing producers, following Nippon Rayon's route of complete reliance upon a foreign technology. By 1964 another Japanese firm had entered the market for nylon, making six in all.

Although it was now sharing the domestic market, and competing in the export market, with five other Japanese firms, Toyo Rayon continued to take advantage of its technological lead. In 1950 its scientists had invented an alternative means of producing caprolactam, the chief intermediary in nylon manufacture. Development proceeded slowly, held up by the practicality of the existing technique for caprolactam manufacture and by the unavailability of the light-generating equipment vital for the new technique. The former deterrent disappeared when foreign firms also supplanted the existing technique for caprolactam manufacture with cheaper alternatives, and the latter when Toyo Rayon, in collaboration with Toshiba, developed mercury light sources, in the range of 40-60 kw, which were effective and durable. Toyo's technique, called the PNC method standing for photo-nitrosation of cyclohexane, was perfected by Ito *et al.* Thus, in the 14 years between 1951, when it imported du Pont's technology for the production of nylon intermediaries, and 1963, when it began to utilise its own PNC technology, Toyo Rayon had mastered the entire process of incorporating a technology, through to developing its successor.

MACHINERY

Whereas the development of the petrochemical industry in Japan has been late and very rapid, the machinery industry has had a long history, developing over a century. Japan entered this industry more than 100 years ago, at the instigation of the government, determined to build boilers and engines for its naval warships, and locomotives and rolling stock for its railways. Production first took place in the government's military establishments — naval shipyards and armaments factories — but spread over into private firms by the end of the nineteenth century.

It was the private firms that began production of internal combustion engines, The two innovators in Japan were the Ikegai and Niigata Machine Companies, firms which followed opposing courses in their technological development, the former employing its own engineers to perfect manufacturing techniques and the latter relying upon foreign technicians. Ikegai was established in 1879, initially producing intake and exhaust valves, and expanding into other parts for machinery, machine tools and diesel engines. A four-horsepower steam engine was the first manufactured, in 1895, followed a few years later by seven- and eight-horsepower petrol engines for use in small fishing vessels. In the decade of the 1910s, with the development of deep-sea fishing and the need for larger, more powerful engines, Ikegai introduced 40- and 50-horsepower petrol engines, capturing the major share of the market.

Ikegai's introduction to diesel engines occurred in 1919 when the Japanese Army assigned it the task of repairing a diesel engine of 120 horsepower imported from Germany. Utilising the experience, Ikegai built for the Tokyo Technology High School a single-cylinder diesel engine of 40 horsepower, which it delivered in 1920. Regular production of this type of engine was established, and two engineers were sent to Europe and the United States in 1921 to learn more from observation of operations in factories there. Subsequent developments were solid-oil spray diesels, copied from a German engine bought in 1924, a diesel-electric engine of 175 kw commissioned by the army, and SD diesel engines for both maritime and electric generating uses. By 1932 enough of the latter had been sold to support an electric generating capacity of 40,000 horsepower.

The Niigata Machine Company also began by first producing, in 1900, petrol engines. Its attention was drawn to diesel engines when some of its managers visited the Paris Machinery Exhibition in 1900 and factories in Europe and the United States. In 1907 Niigata bought a diesel engine of 33 horsepower to experiment on, but decided that its manufacture was beyond its competence. Led by Kato Shigeo, a former civil servant trained in the United States, the company entered into negotiations with two foreign firms, Alis Vicketron and Marris of England and A.B. Diesel of Sweden, with the aim of purchasing their technology. Marris's related to diesel engines for electricity generation, which Niigata began to produce in 1920, with a rating of 300 horsepower, and in 1923, with 550 horsepower. Improvements in engine design, particularly those incorporated in the recycle-type engine produced by Nobel and licensed by Marris, were subsequently adopted.

If Niigata's association with Marris was long, its association with A.B. Diesel was short, lasting only long enough for Niigata to produce in 1919 a ten-horsepower engine for ships. With operating costs 70 per cent higher than competing petrol engines, there was little market for it. The solid-spray diesel engine seemed to offer greater prospects, however; encouraged by the Navy Niigata approached Maschinenfabrik Augsburg-Nüernberg AG (MAN, the same German firm to whom the Koreans were to turn) with the objective of licensing its processes and acquiring its technology. Within two years, Niigata was producing engines of 100 horsepower, capable of being installed on land and shipboard. By 1932, Niigata's manufacturing capacity was double that of Ikegai's (Mitsubishi Heavy Industry, 1970).

IRON AND STEEL

The final industry for which Japan's experience is to be recounted is that of iron and steel. Our Korean case study involved the incorporation of a foreign technology, acquired chiefly from Japan, governing integrated iron- and steel-making; that is the carrying out, within a single manufacturing complex, of the sequence of processes from the massing of the raw materials (iron ore, coal, etc.) through their conversion into iron, into steel, and finally into the shaped (beams, wire, sheet, etc.) products. Our recounting of the experience of the Japanese will concentrate on the same technology, that is the technology governing the integration of iron- and steel-making processes.

The Japanese iron and steel industry emerged from the Second World War obsolete in its state of technology and devastated in its plant and equipment. In the course of mapping out its reconstruction programme, the Economic Stabilisation Board of the government assigned first priority to the two heavy industries, steel and coal. Recognising that it would be better to construct new iron and steel facilities incorporating the latest techniques than to restore pre-war facilities incorporating out-moded techniques, the government first, during the period 1948-51, invited American metallurgical engineers to Japan to examine the existing facilities and to provide instruction in the new technology.

The second act of the government was to provide financial assistance towards the design and construction of the initial integrated works, undertaken by the Kawasaki Steel Corporation in Chiba City and brought into operation in 1953. The technology was imported from abroad: West Germany and the United States provided the technology for the manufacture of pig iron, Austria for top-blown conversion and the United States for heavy-oil burning, casting and rolling. Each foreign supplier provided a complete technological package, including the overall design of the facilities, drawings of the equipment, training of the Japanese engineers and operators, supervision of construction and manufacture, and operating know-how. The strip mills were a particular success, so that several other Japanese steel firms followed Kawasaki, importing the technology in a similar manner.

The application of the technology of integrated operation is only one of the three major characteristics of the post-war steel industry in Japan: the other two are equipment of extremely large scale and location on sites at deep-water ports. These latter characteristics became prominent in the second wave of iron and steel plant construction. The initiator of this wave was the Yawata Iron and Steel Company, the pioneer in the industry (see Iida, 1973). Over 50 years of experience in iron and steel production suited Yawata to the role, as did its most recent technical achievement, the adopting for the first time in Japan of the Linz-Donawitz (LD) converter, an innovation in steel-making utilising pure oxygen for the blow.

It was not Yawata, however, which was first attracted to the innovation. LD converters, which attained their first industrial success in Austria after the Second World War, drew the interest of Nippon Kokan (NKK), which already employed Thomas converters, before any other Japanese steel company. Stimulated by an article published in the West German magazine, *Stahl und Eisen*, late in 1950, NKK sent a fact-finding mission to Europe and, in 1952, started to experiment in secret. A little later in the same year, young engineers at Yawata read an issue of the *Journal of the Iron and Steel Institute* in which there was a feature on the converter and began to think of applications for it in their own company. A company administrator who promptly responded to their enthusiasm was Yawata's chief engineer, Yukawa Masao. In 1953, on his instructions, an existing experimental furnace of one-ton capacity was transformed into one of five tons, permitting both horizontal and vertical blowing (Iida, 1973).

As soon as the test results and survey findings gave an indication of profitability, Yawata sent its steel-making manager, Takeda Kizo, to Europe; in 1955, he started negotiations with Alpine of BOT, the special corporation controlling the rights to the LD process. These negotiations were soon completed, with NKK as the sole representative of the Japanese iron and steel industry.

Yawata was not only keen to utilise the LD process itself, but, as a state-run firm, was also willing to permit other Japanese steel producers to do the same. The company therefore organised, in conjuction with BOT, the Japan BOT Group LD Committee, whose function was to re-license the LD process to other Japanese aspirants, on terms equivalent to those granted to Yawata. An advantage of the re-licensing scheme was that the engineering staffs of the major steel companies in Japan could exchange information and views among themselves, disseminating the technique.

In order to gain operating experience on a full-scale LD converter before constructing its integrated mill, Yawata immediately ordered a set of main components, from Demag and other European equipment manufacturers, and sent several of its engineers to Europe for training. Before the equipment could be produced, in 1956, the Suez crisis broke out, followed by the insurrection in Hungary. Recognising that there would undoubtedly be delays in delivery, Yawata ordered a substitute set of equipment from a Japanese capital goods producer,

Ishikawajima Heavy Industries Ltd. In 1957, the substitutes went into operation, on the date originally scheduled. Demag's equipment, when delivered later, was installed as the second converter unit.

Yawata's first LD converter was installed at its traditional plant at Kukioka, a plant badly laid out, by modern standards, on a congested site. To construct the large-scale plant Yawata had in mind, the company chose a spacious site on the seaboard, the Tobata Area Works. The capacity of the Tobata works was to be 2.5 million tons of crude steel per year. Integrated into a processing chain and synchronised in operation were the following pieces of equipment: two blast furnaces, each capable of producing 1,500 tons in one batch; three 60-ton LD oxygen converters; a blooming and slabbing mill; an 80-inch semi-continuous hot strip mill; an 80-inch reversing mill for cold rolling of hoops; and equipment for galvanising, tinning and bonderising. Compared with past practice in Japan, the blast furnaces were vast in size, as was the cold rolling mill. It was anticipated that the latter would supply the country's entire needs for cold-rolled sheets used in passenger cars, needs that were previously met through imports from the United States.

Yawata's works at Tobata were completed in 1959; in the next six years eight large-scale, integrated iron- and steel-making plants were either built or planned along the coast of Japan: the Nagoya, Sakai, Kimitsu and Oita works of Nippon Kokan; the Mizushima works of Kawasaki Steel Corporation; the Kashima works of Sumitomo Metal; and the Kagowa works of Kobe Steel. These eight works were no replicas of Yawata's integrated works, though; most were even larger in scale, running up to ten million tons in yearly capacity; and all included the various innovations in iron- and steel-making that took place during the 1960s, including, at Nippon Steel's Oita works, the elimination of the blooming mill through a system of continuous casting, with its consequent energy-saving through the avoidance of re-heating.

Most of these innovations were made abroad, but one at least, involving the recovery of heat and pollutants from the gas effluent from the LD converter (called the OG system), was Japanese in origin. The original research was carried out by a boiler manufacturer, Yokohama Industries, which was subsequently absorbed by Kawasaki Heavy Industries. In collaboration with Yawata Iron and Steel, about to install the first LD converter, Yokohama formed a joint committee with the objective of developing the waste heat recovery system. By 1960 the committee had studied the design of the equipment, constructed and operated a two-ton test furnace, developed ancillary devices such as an automatic gas analyser, formulated a scheduling programme which enabled the operation of the converter to be synchronised with that of the blast furnace, and compiled three telephone-directory-sized volumes, the *Test Run Handbook*, of operating procedures. The OG system was first operated in 1962, attached to the 130-ton converter manufactured by Demag and fed by the third blast furnace installed in Yawata's Tobata works.

After its introduction in Yawata's iron and steel works, other Japanese firms adopted the OG system, followed by foreign steel companies, such as Armco and US Steel in the United States, and the Steel Company of Wales in the UK. The United States and the UK, as well as Italy, also imported Japanese technology in the operation of rolling mills. Having initially diffused from the developed countries of the West to Japan, the technology of iron- and steel-making was now diffusing in the opposite direction.

COMPARISON WITH KOREA

In Chapter 9, we will attempt to summarise what we learned about the absorption and diffusion of imported technologies into Korea, but that need not prevent us at the end of this chapter from making a few comparisons with Japan, based upon the superficial account of Japan's absorption and diffusion of the same technologies. In brief, we find the processes of incorporating a foreign technology to be similar in both countries, but the agents through whom the incorporation is accomplished to be different. Japan's lead, in terms of years over Korea, varies from a decade or so in the absorption of operating techniques to a longer period in mastering the 'core' technology.

To start with, both countries seem to have intended to adopt the most modern techniques in existence. In the case of the Koreans, this intention can be documented; in the case of the Japanese, it must be inferred from their actions, both in visiting modern plants in the more-developed Western countries and in quickly imitating the techniques that they encountered there.

Given that both countries selected the most modern techniques, the necessity to import most of the technology and to absorb the novel elements therein automatically arose. In Korea the process of absorption was approached systematically, the government assuring itself that the contracts negotiated with the foreign suppliers contained clauses relating to the acquisition of patents, designs and know-how; to the training, both abroad and on the site, of Korean engineers and managers; to the speedy replacement of expatriates; and to access to improvements in the products and processes. The government also made certain that the terms in the contracts were fulfilled.

We do not know, from the evidence available, the extent to which the absorption of foreign technologies was approached systematically in post-war Japan. We would expect there to be more variation in approach, because the initiating agent in the acquisition of the technology was more likely to be a private firm than the Japanese government. We do not know what the government's policy and behaviour towards the absorption of imported technology was.

Looking at the speed with which the different stages in the process of absorption were carried out, we find a similar pattern in the two countries. Most swiftly learned were the stages of constructing, starting-up and operating the new techniques, followed by the carrying out of improvements and by the design of separate pieces of equipment. Learning the 'core' technology and applying it to the overall design of a facility took still longer; and longer still, so long that it is only now being undertaken in Korea, did process and product innovation.

When we turn to the subject of the agents responsible for the adoption of foreign technologies we begin to see substantial differences between the two countries. In Korea, at least until 1980, the government has been the primary agent; in Japan it seems to have been, in the era since the Second World War, large private firms. The number of foreign suppliers of technology scrutinised by the agents seems to have been greater in the case of Korea, for two reasons; first, there was a larger universe by the time the Koreans, as latecomers, entered the market for technology. The second reason stems from the thesis that it has been the private firms in Japan which have been the chief agents, firms which in many industries are nearly as numerous as the foreign suppliers. The first Japanese firm has usually approached the innovator of the technology. The licence is usually exclusive, so the first imitator in Japan has had to search for a second foreign supplier, among a possibly small number of suppliers. As the process of adoption continued, each successive Japanese firm was matched with a different foreign supplier. At any point in the process, therefore, the Japanese firm wanting to adopt a foreign technology is likely to face no more than a few alternative suppliers, whereas the Korean firm faces many. We would expect the Koreans to be in a better bargaining position as a consequence, and to extract better terms from the supplier finally chosen; but this hypothesis, like others involving the financial aspects of technological choice, cannot be tested with the data we have.

One financial matter that does not require more data than we have available is that of the binding capital constraint. Korea's industrialisation has been constrained by its ability to raise capital abroad, to such an extent that the success of negotiations with potential suppliers of foreign technology has often turned on the provision of capital, both loans and equity. The Japanese firms that have adopted foreign techniques have become large and profitable through previous operations, and so have usually been able to finance imports of technology themselves. Thus technology is a singular import for Japan, whereas it is a joint product, combined with capital, when imported into Korea.

Before we end this comparison of Japan's and Korea's incorporation of foreign technology we should admit that we have left out of consideration grander social and political factors such as national aspirations, linguistic and cultural unity, racial homogeneity, educational background and international tensions, in which, to the Western observer at least, the two countries seem to have been remarkably similar. We should also admit that we are, where Japan is concerned, woefully ignorant of the role that government has played during the post-war era in the incorporation of foreign technology. We will devote part of the final chapter to the role of the Korean government in the selection of supplier and technique, and in the absorption and diffusion of technology; but even for the country which has provided our case material we will have to present our conclusions as merely tentative statements, needing further examination.

9

Conclusion

THE STAGES OF INCORPORATING A TECHNOLOGY

We will now report our chief findings from the study of the process of incorporation of imported technologies in Korea. Our procedure is dictated by the concept of the *process*, described in Chapter 2 on methodology, and will thus move through its stages, from the determination of the needs for the technology, at the beginning, to indigenous research and development at the end. Comparisons will be at the heart of the summary; comparisons between different technologies taken side by side.

THE PLANNING STAGE

So far as the first, planning, stage in the process of incorporating a technology is concerned, the planning of the Korean government and of the industrial firms in our sample seems generally to have been quite accurate and effective. Output targets have been precise enough to enable producers to translate them into demands for their own products, and set long enough beforehand to give them time to respond. More importantly, the targets, once established, have been adhered to, and generally attained. This last achievement is impressive and beneficial for once one set of targets is attained, the next set is all the more plausible and all the more likely to be adhered to. To have an impact on the structure and volume of output, planning must be credible.

Although planning in Korea has generally been successful in

facilitating the incorporation of imported technologies, there have been variations among the industries we studied. In our judgement, the activity was carried out very well with regard to petrochemicals and iron and steel, and less well with regard to machinery and textiles. It must be admitted, however, that the task was much easier in the cases of the first two, because the technologies were being employed for the first time and the scales of operation were very large: the ministry was forecasting for one industry consisting of one firm utilising one technology. In the cases of the last two, machinery and textiles, the ministry was attempting to forecast for industries consisting of many firms employing many technologies and producing hetero-geneous products. The target figures were highly aggregated, giving neither the ministry nor the manufacturing firms clear indices against which to measure performance. It is not certain that more detailed forecasts would have increased the efficiency of planning, because in machinery and textiles one product can often be substituted for another, enabling one target to be missed without constraining subsequent output. 'Targets' have little meaning as numbers to be attained in such cases.

In the case of medium-sized diesel engines, the forecast of demand and installation of manufacturing capacity were gener-ally in excess of eventual sales. Partly this was the result of the over-ambition of a few ministers and directors of development agencies, who intervened in the Economic Planning Board's calculations; partly it was a failure to anticipate the increases in efficiency of smaller-sized diesel engines, which enabled them to be substituted for medium-sized engines in light buses and trucks. The excess capacity existing in diesel engine manufac-ture throughout the period studied has had deleterious effects on costs, on profitability and on the ability of the manufacturer to keep abreast of technical advance.

THE STAGE OF NEGOTIATIONS WITH FOREIGN SUPPLIERS

The second and third stages in the incorporation of imported technologies — surveying alternative techniques and alternative suppliers, and choosing the best combination — may well be considered together, for the two stages overlapped in time. They also provided those studying the process of incorporation with their most surprising results — that the choice of technology is of negligible consequence and that the choice of supplier is of grave consequence.

Early in the enquiry it became apparent that in Korea the choice of technique had been pre-empted. Long before the manufacturing techniques were imported, the Korean government had decided to industrialise by producing in substantial volumes a wide range of modern, sophisticated goods in large-scale plants employing the most advanced technology. Scrutinising the lists of process design and construction firms which had recently undertaken new projects throughout the world, the Korean government discovered that there were usually several alternative suppliers of advanced manufacturing techniques differing in their design and operating characteristics but almost identical in the inputs they consumed and the outputs they produced. In the language of the economists, all employed the same production function. In terms of inputs and outputs, there was no choice of technique, only of technician.

But this did not mean that the Korean government had no choice, rather that technology was irrelevant to the choice. Choice there was, and although in making the choice the Korean government may not have been concerned with adapting the technique to local conditions, it was concerned with securing the technique on the best possible terms for the country. Reconstructing the past, it appears that, once access to the modern technique was assured, foremost among the government's preferences were ample supplies of one resource and one output. The resource that was most keenly sought was foreign exchange, almost certain to be very scarce in a country embarking on such an ambitious programme of industrialisation. The output that was most keenly sought was the product which the technology was designed to produce: the Korean government was determined to secure from the equipment purchased with scarce foreign exchange the maximum rate of production. High profits might be obtained by the producing firms, but only as a consequence of their attaining high rates of output, not as a consequence of their restricting output so as to be able to charge a higher price. Output should be constrained only by the physical capabilities of the equipment and its operators, not by any financial or market considerations.

Lower priority was attached by the Korean government to four other desirable attributes of an undertaking — control over the prices of inputs and outputs, uniform treatment of foreign participants, full acquisition of technical know-how by Korean engineers and managers, and automatic access to subsequent technical improvements. Desirable, but conceded if necessary, seemed to be access to later innovations, government control over the internal administration of the firms operating in Korea, acquisition of financial and marketing knowledge, localisation of capital goods purchasing, and majority ownership by Koreans. Still thought desirable, but assigned the lowest priority in the ranking of the Korean government were competition in the newly-established industry, ready access to export markets for outputs of indeterminate goods, and the temporary although conspicuous presence of expatriates in positions of technician and financial authority.

With this apparent preference order the Korean government entered into negotiation with all possible foreign suppliers. A few foreign firms had previously approached the Korean government; the rest were approached upon the initiative of the Korean government itself. As the negotiations proceeded and the government's terms became stiffer, the foreign suppliers dropped out, one by one. Left at the end of the negotiations was just one foreign firm, willing to accept the stiffest terms of all.

Compared to the initial terms, the final terms were almost always far better for the Koreans: far better in that they seemed to ensure the swifter absorption of the imported technology and far better in that they seemed to confer greater benefits on the Korean economy as a whole. These two consequences are related; swifter absorption of the technology enables output to be produced at a high rate as soon as possible, generates improvements which lower costs and places Koreans in a position to make decisions and earn incomes. The benefits thus accrue on the supply side of the economy — via increases in output and reduced constraints on inputs — and on the demand side — via increases in the incomes of all the Korean participants, be they operators, engineers, managers or shareholders, public or private. Putting it another way, *swift* absorption of the technology has desirable effects, both on output and on employment, and swiftness comes at the outset from negotiating favourable terms with the foreign suppliers.

The two main accomplishments of the Koreans in their negotiations with foreign suppliers of technology — lower costs of acquisition and speedier transmission of know-how — are demonstrated in our cases. It is probably the case of iron and steel that best illustrates the former accomplishment: upon the resumption of diplomatic relations with Japan in 1965 the Korean government secured the allocation of a substantial portion of the Japanese government's official grant and concessional credits to the construction of Pohang's first iron and steel mill. Moreover, so fierce was competition among foreign suppliers of the reducing, converting, casting, rolling and shaping techniques from other developed countries that the Koreans were able to secure them at minimum cost. The lower cost of facilities, relative to the cost paid in developed and other developing countries, is tabulated in Chapter 7; and the bulk of the economies were derived from the lower price of the equipment and technology. Similar cost advantages are cited by Hogan (1985) for the equipment to be installed in POSCO's second iron- and steel-making plant in Quangyang.

The latter accomplishment — the speedier transmission of know-how — is probably best illustrated in the case of petrochemicals in Chapter 4. It is not that the transmission was necessarily faster than in, say, artificial fibres; it is that the case of petrochemicals is the fullest documented. There we can see most clearly the complex nature of the technology, the nature of what had to be transmitted and the agencies through which the transmission occurred.

THE DESIGN STAGE

Firmness, perseverance and dedication have carried the Koreans successfully through the stages of planning and negotiation, but these qualities have been of little avail in the next stage of the process of incorporating foreign technologies — learning how to design facilities and the constituent equipment. Here the Koreans have made the least progress. Here, also, experience has been the most varied; from the manufacturers of artificial fibre, Kolon, and petrochemicals, Hanyang, who are capable of formulating new processing schemes and of altering existing equipment so as to produce novel products; to the manufacturers of iron and steel and diesel engines, who have generally not acquired the skills and experience of design, deliberately in the former case and unintentionally in the latter. It may be that process and equipment design requires collaboration with capital goods producers, in which event the increase in the provision of capital goods domestically, to be considered later in this chapter under the topic of localisation, may still come about.

THE CONSTRUCTION STAGE

If some of the economies in capital cost arose through the successful completion of negotiations with foreign suppliers, others, no less marked, arose through the rapid completion of construction, once begun. Again the most vivid illustration, and probably the most dramatic, comes from the case of POSCO. Not only has POSCO brought its construction to completion faster than firms in other countries, but also it has accelerated from event to event: 38 months were taken to construct the initial plant, 30 months to construct the second, 29 months the third (and that of more than double the capacity of the second) and 24 months the fourth. Statistically, the benefits that accrued to POSCO are impossible to estimate, but the direct savings in interest on the capital committed and the indirect savings via the quicker availability of domestically-produced iron and steel would have been substantial.

THE STAGE OF STARTING-UP AND OPERATING THE EQUIPMENT

A quick rise to full (equals design) capacity output indicates a speedy absorption of the technology, and a successful one as well; a slow rate indicates the opposite. The experience in our four industries is generally one of rapid absorption and successful production, the exceptions being explained mainly by a lack of demand for the products.

For these two stages in the process of incorporating a technology we have data that are comparable across three of the four industries covered by our cases. For artificial fibres we have only qualitative information. Table 9.1, the first of the tables summarising the results of our case studies, provides the data on the speed with which facilities were brought into operation, expressed as the instantaneous rates of output, relative to the

Table 9.1: Summary table: design capacities and rates of output relative to design capacities

Case	Design capacity	Actual output, as a percentage of design capacity, since start-up						
		1 month %	2 months %	6 months %	1 year %	2 years %	5 years %	10 years %
Petrochemicals (Ulsan plant) polyethylene	50,000 metric tons/year	71	94	98	113	139	131	98[a]
VCM	60,000 metric tons/year	40	64	69	93	92	103	86[a]
(Yeocheon plant) polyethylene	100,000 metric tons/year	69	38	12	75[a]	63[a]	115	—
VCM	150,000 metric tons/year	11	22	54	63[a]	76[a]	87	—
Diesel engines	24,000 engines/year (one shift/day)	n.a.	n.a.	n.a.	7[a]	11[a]	68[a]	63[a]
Iron and steel 1st stage	1,030,000 metric tons/year	50	72	104	n.a.	n.a.	110 (6 years)	
2nd stage	1,570,000 metric tons/year	n.a.	n.a.	100 (80 days)	n.a.	n.a.	n.a.	
3rd stage	2,900,000 metric tons/year	n.a.	100 (70 days)	n.a.	n.a.	n.a.	n.a.	
4th stage	2,900,000 metric tons/year	100 (29 days)	n.a.	n.a.	n.a.	n.a.	n.a.	108

[a] Insufficient market for output.

capacity built into the equipment, achieved at various dates after the initial start-up. The clearest pattern to emerge, and the one giving the strongest indication of an ability to absorb the technology, occurred in the case of iron and steel, where full capacity operation was achieved at each successive stage of expansion after shorter and shorter intervals.

Somewhat surprisingly, the opposite pattern, where the attainment of full capacity operation took longer for the second than the first plant, occurred in the case of petrochemicals. To be sure, the second plant, at Yeocheon, had larger capacities than did the first, but the same was true for the facilities producing iron and steel. Of the possible reasons for the slower attainment of full capacity operation in the second petrochemical plant, *vis-à-vis* the first, the demand factor is probably the most significant; the engineers and managers at Yeocheon, in 1980 and 1981, were not under the same pressure to generate output and satisfy market demands as had been the engineers and managers at Ulsan, in 1973 and 1974.

Insufficient demand to spur production is an important factor, although perhaps not of such overwhelming significance, in the cases of diesel engines and the first excursion into the polymerisation of the artificial fibre nylon. In these two cases technical difficulties also arose, and could not be eliminated swiftly because of a lack of experience. In the case of artificial fibres certainly, and in the case of diesel engines probably, the necessary experience has since been acquired, although in the latter case this presumption cannot be supported by statistical evidence, relying as it does solely on the claims of the engineers involved. Nevertheless, the utilisation figures in, say, the column headed '1 year' are markedly higher than those encountered in plants incorporating advanced technologies in other developing countries; overall, we conclude that the Koreans have skilfully started up their facilities and swiftly brought them to fruition.

THE STAGE OF SECURING IMPROVEMENTS

The next stage in the process of incorporating a novel technology is that of improving upon its operation. With regard to improvements we have collected a wealth of descriptive material and some measures of resulting increases in efficiency. The many improvements are listed in the studies of each industry; they impressed the investigators by their variety — improvements in the design and construction of equipment, in the operation of the techniques, in maintenance, in the use of raw materials and energy, in the quality of the products manufactured and in the potential of the installed equipment for still higher rates of output.

All these types of improvements can be measured by a single index, that of reduction in total cost of production. This measurement is reported in Table 9.2 for the manufacture of petrochemicals at Hanyang's first plant at Ulsan, for polymerisation of nylon and polyester at Kolon's two plants at Taegu and Gumi, and for iron- and steel-making in POSCO's facilities at Pohang. No measure is available for diesel engines. The first set of measures, that for petrochemicals, is the most detailed and the most accurate; it shows that a significant reduction in cost occurred through the stretching of equipment, so that it was able to yield outputs greater than those for which it was originally designed.

Obtaining rates of output in excess of those for which the equipment was designed does not generally show up in figures on cost reduction, yet can be of considerable importance. Occasionally one hears of equipment which, with some modifications, is operated at a rate well above that for which it was designed: via improvements its potential to produce output has been substantially increased. Any measure of the *direct* cost of operation will not capture the improvements; one needs a measure of *total* cost, after allowance for fixed costs and overheads. Measures of total cost are even more difficult to extract than those of direct cost, and in multi-product and multi-plant firms are more difficult to estimate accurately. Moreover, rates of production in excess of design are often not observed until several years after the start-up of the equipment, when its capabilities have become fully understood. In only one of the cases we investigated had several years passed, and so the significance of this type of improvement could not generally be assessed. In one case, however, that of the petrochemical, polyethylene, production rates in excess of design were achieved in as short a space of time as a year, and maintained at approximately 30 per cent for the following five years. It may, of course, be that the equipment incorporating the polyethylene technology was over-designed initially and had 30 per cent excess capacity built into it, but this seems rather unlikely in

Table 9.2: Summary table: average annual rates of reduction in unit manufacturing costs achieved through improvements

Case	Period covered	Reduction in unit manufacturing costs (average annual rate, compounded, in per cent)				
		Raw material savings	Energy savings	Localisation of supply	Equipment stretching	Total unit cost
		%	%	%	%	%
Petrochemicals Ulsan plant	1973-6	0.4	0.4	0.1	1.5	2.4
Synthetic fibres Taegu plant Nylon	1974-84	n.a.	n.a.	n.a.	n.a.	5.0
Gumi plant Nylon	1974-84	n.a.	n.a.	n.a.	n.a.	8.3
Polyester	1974-84	n.a.	n.a.	n.a.	n.a.	7.5
Iron and steel	1973-83	n.a.	n.a.	n.a.	n.a.	4.4 to 4.8

such a well-known and frequently employed technique. Credit must be given to the operating firm for extracting more output from its equipment.

The stretching of equipment was probably also significant in the securing of reductions in average unit cost of manufacture for artificial fibres and iron and steel, although this conclusion can only be subjective, since the cost data cannot be disaggregated. Moreover, the overall estimates of cost reduction for artificial fibres and iron and steel in the last column of Table 9.2 cannot be taken too precisely, since they were obtained only by deflating current costs for the effect of inflation, and since they did not make any allowance for increases in the variety and quality of the products manufactured. This latter type of improvement may be quite substantial, although absent from these two sets of measures. Certainly it would add support to our contention that, in these three cases, the effect of improvements in the employment of the imported techniques by the Korean firms has been impressive indeed.

THE STAGE OF DEVELOPING NEW PRODUCTS AND TECHNIQUES

The final stage in the incorporation of imported technology is the research and development that leads to its being superseded by a superior technology. In our investigations we did not encounter any such supercession; nor did we expect to, since all the technologies employed were, at the time of their adoption, highly advanced, representing the highest state of the art in the developed countries.

In each of the industries we studied there have been major innovations between the time when the Korean firms first installed their facilities and now. All these innovations were carried out in the developed countries. In petrochemicals and iron and steel, the innovations took the form of new processes, namely the polymerisation of polyethylene at low pressures (producing so-called 'linear' low-density polyethylene) and the continuous casting of steel. The two Korean firms, Hanyang and POSCO, kept themselves informed of these developments and installed them on the next occasion that capacity was expanded.

In artificial fibres and diesel engines, the innovations have

241

taken the form of new or improved products, such as fish nets, tyre cords and artificial turf in the case of nylon and engines with better combustion properties and higher horsepower-to-weight ratios in the case of diesel engines. The Korean artificial fibre firm, Kolon, adopted the new products soon after they emerged in the developed countries, but the diesel engine manufacturer, Daewoo, was frozen in the increasingly obsolete design. Awareness of the innovation there was, and appreciation of its effect on engine design and performance, but the ability to imitate the innovation was lacking.

In our studies, however, we did encounter research and development groups in every firm. Although not engaged in fundamental research, out of which an innovation might eventuate, the groups were generally performing useful functions, chiefly through investigating the characteristic and production modes of products that were novel extensions of their existing product lines. Co-polymers at Hanyang; aromatic polyamide and ultra-fine yarn at Kolon; new construction equipment to be powered by diesel engines at Daewoo: these were the sorts of developments that were being advanced by the research groups. To us, the allocation of technical resources to these types of research and development seemed proper.

THE ABSORPTION OF IMPORTED TECHNOLOGY

As measures of the rate of absorption, the speed and intensity of use and reductions in costs through improvements have much to recommend them; yet they are only partial measures, covering only two of the several stages involved in incorporating a foreign technology. Table 9.3 is devoted to all the stages of incorporation, from planning and negotiation to the conduct of research and development for new products or techniques, and displays a nearly uniform pattern. The data in Table 9.3 can be read vertically, down each entire column, in order to observe differences across industries in the extent to which Koreans have participated in each of the stages: they can also be read horizontally, across each row, in order to observe differences across stages. These two readings suggest that the Koreans have entered more in the stages of construction, start-up and operation and improvement than in the earlier stages of design, and in the later stage of research and development; and that there are

Table 9.3: Summary table: absorption of foreign technology by Korean engineers, according to the stage of the process of incorporation

Case	Stage in the process of incorporating the technology						
	Planning and negotiation	Process design	Equipment design	Construction	Start-up and operation	Improvement	R & D
Petrochemicals							
Ulsan plant (1945-85)	s	o	o	s	s	x	o
Yeocheon plant (1975-85)	s	s	s	s	s	x	s
Synthetic fibres							
Taegu plant							
Nylon line 1 (1960-85)	s	o	o	s	s	s	o
Nylon line 5 (1970-85)	s	s	s	s	s	s	s
Gumi plant							
Nylon line 3 (1983-5)	x	x	x	x	x	x	x
Diesel engines	s	o	o	s	s	s	o
Iron and steel							
1st stage (1965-85)	s	o	o	s	s	s	o
2nd stage (1974-85)	s	o	o	s	s	x	o
3rd stage (1976-85)	s	o	s	s	s	x	s
4th stage (1979-85)	x	x	x	x	s	x	s

Key: o = no. Koreans participating; s = some participation; x = all Korean.

243

not great differences in participation across industries.

More interesting than comparisons down entire columns or across entire rows are comparisons across rows within a single industry. For the three industries (petrochemicals, artificial fibres and iron and steel) with multiple rows, signifying more than one incorporation of a technology, the general pattern is of increasing participation from earlier to later installations. This progress in participation is seen most prominently in the case of iron and steel, in which there has been a general movement from partial to complete reliance on Korean engineers in the majority of the stages. If we think of absorption in a dynamic sense, as an increase, from installation to installation, in participation throughout the process of incorporating a technology, than all three cases demonstrate an ability on the part of Koreans to absorb foreign technology. This is our major conclusion regarding the absorption of new techniques.

THE DIFFUSION OF IMPORTED TECHNOLOGY

In the four cases we studied there was no diffusion of manufacturing techniques. This was the result of deliberate action on the part of the Korean government: had the Korean government chosen to encourage the construction of small-scale plants there would have been more diffusion, but the government preferred, rightly in our estimation, to exploit the substantial economies inherent in large-scale operation. As a consequence, adoptions of imported technology have been limited, chiefly to one firm. Had we chosen different industries, characterised by many competing firms employing simple technologies on a small scale, we would have been able to draw some conclusions on the diffusion of imported manufacturing techniques; but our choice of industries, characterised by single firms employing sophisticated technologies on a large scale, precluded this.

Knowledge of the capabilities of the products manufactured through the imported technology has diffused to customers. What diffused was chiefly information on the nature and performance of the products they were buying, through such media as conferences of producers and users, trade journals and visits by technical salesmen. So far as we could judge, this diffusion of this limited technological information proceeded adequately.

Of more significance, in our opinion, has been the diffusion of the technology to institutions supplying resources to the adopting firm. The main supplying institution is the industry manufacturing capital goods in Korea. Encouraged by the government's policy of stimulating local production of capital goods, firms adopting foreign technology did communicate their needs and commissioned the purchase of domestic capital goods, usually those of a simple nature but occasionally those of considerable complexity. Complex capital goods were ordered from domestic suppliers when time was short and when the supplier was willing to work closely with the customer, welcoming the customer's engineers in its own factory.

The data for capital goods supplied to the petrochemical firm Hanyang and the iron- and steel-making firm POSCO are summarised in the top and bottom rows of Table 9.4. Revealing is the success that Hanyang had in obtaining replacements for worn-out capital equipment, the easiest form of domestic capital goods manufactured since users are already familiar with the equipment and since the producers have at hand prototypes (the original pieces of equipment, manufactured abroad) with which to work.

POSCO's success in shifting the source of supply of new capital equipment in successive expansions of its plant is impressive. The increase in the percentage supplied domestically was largest in the fourth stage, which, significantly, was (for the blast furnace and the continuous casting line) a replica of the third.

These same conclusions — a relatively greater success in reproducing or copying existing equipment than in building novel equipment, and an increasing degree of localisation with successive installations — have been reached by the authors of a detailed study of the procurement of power plant equipment in Korea (Lee, Jin-Joo and Sharan, 1985, Tables II.4 and II.5 pp. 30-2). From twelve observations, two of small-scale thermal power plants, seven of large-scale thermal plants and three of nuclear plants, the authors found that the domestic portion of total expenditures on engineering design and on capital equipment fell as one moved from smaller plants incorporating simpler technology to larger plants incorporating more complex technology. Moreover, with the passenge of time, the portion of total expenditures undertaken domestically on similar sized plants of identical technology tended to rise.

Table 9.4: Summary table: degree of localisation of supply

Case	Period covered	Type of resources provided locally	Basis of comparison	Measure of localisation %
Petrochemicals Ulsan plant	4 years 1974-7	Replacement of original (foreign) capital equipment	Saving in capital cost	45
Diesel engines (engine D0846M)	1975-84	Components, parts and materials	Purchases of domestic components, etc. as percentage of total purchases by value	40 (1975) 50 (1977) 66 (1979) 77 (1981) 89 (1983) 90 (1984)
Iron and steel 1st stage	1970-3	New capital equipment	Value of locally-manufactured equipment, as a percentage of total value of capital equipment	12.5
2nd stage	1974-6	Same	Same	15.5
3rd stage	1976-8	Same	Same	22.6
4th stage	1979-81	Same	Same	35.0

The remaining rows in Table 9.4 refer not to the localisation of capital equipment but to the localisation of intermediate products used in final manufacture. The gradual replacement of foreign by domestic components is a familiar characteristic of assembly industries in developing countries, and so the increase in domestic supply of diesel engine components is not surprising. What is complimentary to the Korean component manufacturing industry is the high proportion reached in recent years.

Not appearing in Table 9.4 but encountered in two separate cases, were once-and-for-all substitutions of domestically-produced for imported raw materials. Ethylene dichloride (EDC), produced at Yeocheon, displaced imported EDC in the synthesis of vinyl chloride monomer (VCM); and caprolactam, produced at Ulsan, displaced imported caprolactam in the polymerisation of nylon. The extent to which these two examples of the localisation of production were conditional upon the diffusion of VCM and nylon technologies was negligible, however, since the technologies for both EDC and caprolactam manufacture and use had to be imported in their entirety.

The last direction of diffusion of imported technologies has been abroad, to countries less developed than Korea. In two of the four case studies, artificial fibres and iron and steel, we encountered examples of the transfer of Korean construction and operating in conjunction with the transfer of the 'core' technology by its original American or Japanese supplier. The historical pattern of transfer abroad — the Korean firm supplying the more easily learned part of the technology and the original foreign supplier, with whom the Korean firm had established bonds when it, the Korean firm, first incorporated the technology, supplying the more difficult part — is the same that Japan had followed in its first exercises in technology transfer abroad some ten years previously (see Ozawa, 1971, for a contemporary report).

IMPLICATIONS FOR PUBLIC POLICY

Returning to the earlier section of this chapter on planning and negotiation we seize again upon the conclusion that the Korean government intervened, with considerable dispatch and with a favourable outcome, in the process of incorporating a foreign technology. The foregoing is probably the chief discovery of this

247

study. When we began our inquiry, we did not realise how dependent the success of the absorption of the foreign technology was upon precise terms obtained by the Korean government in its negotiations with the foreign suppliers. The Korean government could have behaved in different ways, as do governments of other developing countries: it could have been passive, accepting whatever terms the foreign supplier offered; or it could have negotiated just as firmly but for different terms, terms which might have enriched a small fraction of its citizens while leaving the remainder no better off. We believe that in either of these cases the absorption of the imported technology would have been less successful, and the benefits to the entire economy less substantial. To put this as succinctly as possible, we are persuaded that a major determinant of the ability of a developing country to absorb an imported technology is the preferences of its government, as reflected in the terms that it imposes upon the foreign suppliers. If these terms are output- and employment-oriented, the country's ability to absorb the technology will be enhanced; if these terms are profit- and publicity-oriented, the country's ability will be reduced (Enos, 1985).

We feel quite confident in drawing this conclusion regarding the strategic importance of the adoption of the foreign technology. Of the verity of the remaining conclusions we are less confident: to the extent that the study has failed to uncover important aspects of the absorption and diffusion of imported technologies the conclusions will be questionable; to the extent that the study has been restricted in its coverage of industries the conclusions will be limited; and to the extent that the study has concentrated on relatively sophisticated technologies employed in large-scale plants the conclusions will be particular and not general. It might have been possible to have drawn more upon other studies, directed towards other industries, and covering primitive and intermediate technologies, but we prefer generally to rely upon our own analysis. What we have relinquished in breadth we hope we have more than compensated for in accuracy. In other words, our conclusions stem from our discoveries and our analysis, which have been reported in full in the text and for whose correctness we take full responsibility. They do not take account of the studies and conclusions of other research workers.

Nevertheless, we do have conclusions covering all the stages in the process of incorporation of imported technologies, even the last, research and development. But, starting with the first stage devoted to planning, we would conclude that three of the principles which have guided Korean planning have been wise; i.e. that the Korean government set the targets for the various sectors of the economy, in a manner that has been both consistent and detailed and in a spirit that has been ambitious; that individual plants have been large enough to exploit economies of scale; and that the most modern technologies, proved elsewhere in operation, have been employed.

Although we have enunciated these principles of planning separately we would argue that they are closely connected. Ambitious planning encourages countries to project current product demands into the future with the presumption that a relatively high rate of growth will be maintained. New projects are scheduled on the basis of expected rather than present volumes of output. The Korean government has tended to initiate projects before the demand for the project's output has materialised, but to try to complete their construction and bring them into operation at that point in time when the extra demand will be matched by the extra supply. In the meantime, during the construction, the difference between domestic demand and domestic output has been filled by imports. In other words, the Koreans have built up to demand, but not ahead of it.

Since industrial plants come in relatively large sizes, adding relatively large increments to domestic output, the graph of total industry capacity through time has resembled a flight of stairs, with alternative flat and vertical portions. In planning over a long period of time, a government can reach a certain altitude on the capacity-time graph with many small steps or with a few large ones, the former requiring a sequence of small plants at short intervals and the latter a sequence of large plants at infrequent intervals. If there are substantial economies of large-scale production, and if imports are readily available, it is profitable for the country to choose the latter sequence.

An additional advantage accrues to the choice of large-scale plants if the government, like that of Korea, is determined to adopt the latest proven technology. This technology will almost certainly be imported from one of the developed countries, where it has been designed to supply large markets, both domestic and foreign. Experience will therefore have been obtained in the construction and operation of large-scale plants, experience which can be drawn upon in the construction and operation of similarly-scaled plants in the developing country. Constructing and operating a small-scale plant in the developing country might well be a novel experience, for which the past would provide little guide. In this way, the choice of a modern technique reinforces the argument for installing large-scale plants, for taking giant steps, and vice versa.

The second stage in the process of incorporating a foreign technology starts with surveying alternative technologies and alternative suppliers. As we saw in the case of Korea, a rapidly developing country which has consistently gone for the latest proven technique, the survey has reduced chiefly to one of alternative suppliers, each capable of providing quite similar technical schemes, as well as a range of auxiliary services such as soliciting overseas finance, training engineers, operators and managers, providing marketing channels for excess output, and even constructing and installing capital equipment.

We conclude that the Korean government would be well advised to persevere with its policy of surveying all possible foreign suppliers of technology when adding to industrial capacity. To neglect a possible supplier at the beginning of negotiations with others is to reduce the developing country's options. Nevertheless, there is one exception to this principle of maximising the domain of choice, an exception which is appearing more frequently as Korea accumulates industrial capacity; it is that of rewarding previous foreign suppliers of technology who have faithfully met the conditions originally agreed upon. One obvious reward is granting the foreign supplier the right to supply the next technology, or to be a partner in the next plant using the previous technology. This is a delicate decision for any government of a developing country: to consider alternative suppliers when an existing supplier has acted in the country's interest. Will it continue to act in the country's interest? Would a new foreign supplier accept terms that would be even more in the developing country's interest? Would the new supplier conform strictly to the terms if it suspected that it too might ultimately be superseded? We doubt if any general answer can be given to these questions; each case may have to be treated separately.

Another factor that will intervene increasingly in the survey of alternatives in rapidly industrialising countries like Korea is the appearance of potential domestic suppliers of formerly imported technologies. Once having mastered a technique, a domestic firm may want to expand, drawing upon its own organisation for the necessary economic and technological resources. In this event, various policies would be conceivable; first of all, to treat the domestic firm exactly like any potential foreign supplier; second, to consider the domestic firm along with foreign suppliers but grant it privileges or exemptions; or, third, to initiate negotiations with the domestic firm, bringing foreign suppliers into consideration only if satisfactory terms could not be agreed upon. Of these three policies we would prefer the first, provided the domestic firm had approximately the same capabilities as its foreign competitors. If the domestic firm had had less experience than its foreign competitors, as is more likely to be the case, the second policy would seem preferable because it still keeps the government's options open.

The policies adopted in the foregoing part of the process of incorporating a technology will, of course, vitally affect the decision reached at the end of the second stage, namely choosing the combination of technology/supplier. As we have argued, for Korea the choice is chiefly that of supplier of a modern technique, although the choice will still be among numerous contenders. In the cases we examined the number was between half a dozen and a dozen initially, quickly reducing to two or three, or occasionally one. Since negotiations are laborious and time-consuming, a speedy elimination of less desirable candidates is always an objective; speed is probably best secured by setting the initial terms for negotiation quite high. The terms to which potential suppliers will have to agree in order to continue in contention will change with the developing country's level of development: dominant on Korea's negotiations during the 1960s and early 1970s were the raising abroad of most of the project finance and the obtaining of guarantees of full-capacity operation, but other terms may dominate negotiations in the 1990s. Future terms will be difficult to predict, although assured access to international markets may well be one of them. In any event, the developing country will find that it is always worth while to negotiate with potential suppliers so as to extract the best possible terms: technologies themselves are neither profitable nor unprofitable; it is the terms on which they are obtained that determine the profitability. As in any negotiation, it is where the bargain is struck that matters.

With the following stages of the process of incorporating an imported technology absorption can begin. Designs are drawn; equipment is ordered and installed; operating, maintenance and managerial cadres are formed; raw materials are accumulated; and products are produced and sold. The role of the government becomes less important, its influence steadily diminishes. To be sure, the government will usually scrutinise the progress of the absorption, whose time-table will have been set during the final negotiations with the selected supplier, but the work will chiefly be undertaken by the foreign supplier, the construction firms, local and foreign, regional and local governmental agencies, and the operating firm. What the central government can do, and what the Korean government has generally done, is to perform four tasks: first, to keep fully aware of the progress of the absorption of the technology; second, to assure that all the different branches of government — those issuing import licences, those granting permits, those training individuals, etc. — synchronise their activities; third, to establish a system of incentives and penalties — e.g. prices for, and allocations of, inputs needed by the new operating firm and the products manufactured by it; and, fourth, to instill in all the non-governmental bodies the same sense of purpose that the government itself has.

The second and third of these four tasks are sufficiently familiar that we need not expand upon them, but the first and last deserve comment, if only for the reason that the governments of so many developing countries fail to perform them. All too often, the signing and pronouncement of the contract between the foreign supplier of the technology and the vehicle for its implementation in the developing country ends the government's interest. The hard, tedious work of implementation is neglected, or even abdicated, being left to the foreign supplier and domestic operating firm to carry out alone. Because the foreign supplier and the domestic operating firm may not be able to mobilise all the resources necessary to implement the project, or because their objectives are not consistent with the country's interest, these two non-governmental agencies may not secure the desired outcome. So we conclude that it is highly desirable that a government which itself is imbued with the urge to develop its economy and the drive and perseverance to achieve development should put pressure on the producing firms to fulfil the terms of their agreements. By being on the scene, by expediting requests and applications, by setting high standards of performance, by demanding compliance to terms agreed upon, and by meeting its own commitments, a government staffed by honest and dedicated men can speed the absorption of technology and the production of goods.

The next stages in the process of incorporating an imported technology — improving upon it, and developing a superior technology to replace it — are not easily separated in principle. It is difficult, if not impossible, to tell where improvements in the existing technology cease and the creation of a new technology starts. Of more use is a separation by institution, or agency, or firm. The firm that has innovated will naturally improve the technology, having both the opportunity and the incentive. There is not much that a government can, or need, do to affect the internal operations of the innovating firm, but it can do much to encourage improvements by affecting the firm's external environment, chiefly by means of its overall price and output policies. If the innovating firm is faced with a high and stable demand for its products it will have an incentive to make those improvements which raise the capacity and assure steady operation of its plant; if the innovating firm is faced with a gently declining price for its output, relative to all other prices, it will have an incentive to make those improvements which lower its average cost of production. Our evidence from the innovating forms in Korea is that it is possible to secure improvements in the imported technologies and that these improvements take the forms both of increasing the capacity of equipment already installed and reducing its average cost. Moreover, these improvements seem to have been more readily forthcoming when the forms felt the pressures of unsatisfied demand for their products and erosion of the initially high prices they received. Pressure to produce, and to produce ever more efficiently, can be a spur to improvement.

The innovating firm is not the only firm that can make improvements in the imported process: there are two other types of firms that can also contribute. The first of these is the foreign supplier itself, which will undoubtedly be making improvements in the process to which it holds the rights. Since it will be in the interest of the innovating firm in the developing

253

country that these improvements are made available to it, automatically and cheaply, this is one of the conditions that should be included in the initial contract between the foreign supplier and the importing country.

The second type of firm that can also contribute to improvements in the imported technology is any domestic firm subsequently entering the industry. If this firm adopts the same or a similar technology, it too will have the opportunity and incentive of the initial producer: perhaps even more of an incentive, since it will not have the secure market position that the innovating firm is likely to enjoy. Imitating firms can be encouraged to improve upon the technology by means of the same policies — policies affecting output and price — as directed towards the innovator, provided imitation has itself been encouraged and the technology has diffused.

Coming to the penultimate stage in the incorporation of imported technology, we may discuss public policy towards research and development, where its objective is to supplant the imported technology itself. Again, as in the case of improvements in technology, it is convenient to look at the institutions which might carry out the research and development. The most likely organisation would be the supplier of the original technology and its partner in the developing country, a rival producer, research laboratories (public or private) and the universities. Policies would differ depending upon which institution was to be encouraged, but a serious issue is which institution or set of institutions is to be given the greater encouragement. One could argue that the original supplier and its domestic partner should receive the most aid, because these are the institutions which have the most experience with the technology. One could argue that it is their rivals, because they have the greatest incentive. One could argue that it is research laboratories, because they contain the requisite skills and are not limited in scope to a single industry. Finally, one could argue that it is the universities, because they contain the same skills as the laboratories and are, moreover, linked to industry by their employed graduates and consulting arrangements.

Rather than concerning oneself with which institution should be singled out for attention one might well ask whether or not resources should even be devoted to trying to supplant the imported technology. The very resources that would be consumed in the task — scientists, engineers, technicians, laboratory equipment, money and time — are extremely scarce in most developing countries. These resources will have a very high opportunity cost, for their value in alternative uses — in diffusing the original technology, say, or absorbing a different imported technology — will be substantial. Moreover, research and development yield an uncertain return, whereas the return to the allocation of the same resources in securing process and product improvements has a much higher probability of success. Therefore we might conclude that developing countries would be better advised to channel their technical skills into improving existing lines of endeavour, at least until they have such abundant supplies that they are no longer extremely scarce. The time to start building research laboratories to advance the state of the art may only be when there are so few opportunities for scientists and engineers and technicians within the domestic economy that appreciable numbers are seeking work. Then they can be employed on such specialised activity.

The last stage of incorporating an imported technology — its diffusion throughout the economy — may start before the technology has been completely absorbed in its first application, so public policies regarding diffusion may have to be formulated and implemented simultaneously with policies regarding absorption. These policies regarding diffusion will be much more diverse, affecting many more economic agents, and extending over a much wider area. They will have to be directed towards other industries, so as to strengthen the bonds and increase the flow of information between the producing firm and its suppliers and customers; they will have to be directed towards the schools and universities, so as to guarantee the training of skilled personnel and the dissemination of technical knowledge; they will have to be directed towards other firms in the same industry as the producing firm, so as to enable them too to take the greatest possible advantage from the imported technology. Such a wide variety of policies defies summary description; perhaps the only advice to give is that it is desirable to formulate them and efficacious to carry them out.

For a country like Korea, which has deliberately chosen to adopt modern technology and to exploit its inherent economies of scale by commissioning large plants, the question of whether or not to encourage the entry of additional, competing firms does not arise for several years, until the need for a second plant is felt. Since the industry initially consists of a single firm

— the innovator — there is no possibility of diffusion of the technology during this interval. It is only when the second plant is considered that the possibility of diffusion within the producing industry arises; then there are two alternative routes that the diffusion can follow, either via the construction and operation of a second plant by the innovator or via the construction and operation of an initial plant by its new competitor. Since the differences in the rates of diffusion are not likely to be very great, the speed of diffusion is not likely to be a criterion in judging whether or not to facilitate entry. The government's objectives will be to attain the desired structure of industry, as well as to purchase the desired technologies and other scarce resources on attractive terms; the path of diffusion of the previously imported technology will follow as a consequence.

Looking at the experience of Korea, we found examples of both alternative choices of industrial structure. On some occasions the government decided to favour the innovating firm with the right to install the second plant in the industry, thereby permitting it to retain its monopoly in production; on other occasions the government decided to favour competing suppliers. Industry structure became dependent upon the performance of the innovating firm and the promises of potential competitors, promises which potential competitors have been obliged, in Korea, to convert into future performance. Perhaps it is right that the Korean government should continue to weigh the performance of already-privileged firms with the binding promises of potential entrants, making its decision case by case. Nevertheless, as time passes and Korean industrial output grows, the favour might fall more often on the potential entrant. What might be lost in the slower absorption of the technology would be more than compensated for in the increased efficiency and reduced market power fostered by competition.

This is the last inference we draw for public policy. That the discussion should have concentrated on public policy rather than private policy, and on public policy towards government activities rather than public policy towards private activities, is natural: governments can generally exert a closer degree of control over their own operations than over those of private firms; and government behaviour sets the standard for others to attain. Implicit throughout the discussion has been an interventionist attitude on our part, based on our experience in

Korea. We have found the Korean government to be a beneficial force in the economy, acting in the public interest towards the achievement of national objectives. Had the Korean government not acted in this way, we might well have perceived a minor role for public policy; but as it is, we have assumed that the role of government should be the major one, and that, consequently, public policy should be extensive. There is no stage in the process of incorporating an imported technology that a conscientious and patriotic government should neglect; there is no stage that should not have its appropriate public policy.

References

Adelman, I., ed. (1969) *Practical Approaches to Development Planning: Korea's Second Five-year Plan*, Baltimore: Johns Hopkins Press. ‹

Adelman, I. and Morris, C.T. (1973) *Economic Growth and Social Equity in Developing Countries*, Stanford California: Stanford University Press.

Adelman. I and Robinson, S. (1978) *Income Distribution Policy in Developing Countries: A Case Study of Korea*, New York: Oxford University Press.

Amsden, Alice H. and Kim, Lin-Su (1982) 'Korea's Technology Exports and Acquisition of Technological Capability', World Bank Productivity Division, Development Research Department, Washington, D.C.

Amsden, Alice H. and Kim, Lin-Su (1984) 'A Technological Perspective on the General Machinery Industry in the Republic of Korea', Division of Research, Harvard Business School, Working Paper 9-784-075, Boston, Mass. (forthcoming in Fransman, Martin, ed.)

Bailey, N. (1957) *Mathematical Theory of Epidemics*, London: Griffin.

Baranson, J. (1978) *Technology and the Multinationals*, Lexington, Mass.: Lexington Books.

Bell, R.M. (1984) 'Learning and the Accumulation of Industrial Technological Capacity in Developing Countries', in M. Fransman and K. King (eds), *Technological Capability in the Third World*, London: Macmillan.

Berman, J.A. (1976) *Transfer of Manufacturing Technology within Multinational Enterprises*, Cambridge, Mass: Ballinger.

Cole, D.C. and Lyman, P.N. (1971) *Korean Development: the Interplay of Politics and Economics*, Cambridge: Harvard University Press.

Davies, S. (1979) *The Diffusion of Process Innovations*, Cambridge, UK: Cambridge University Press.

Denison, E.F. and Chung, W.K. (1976) *How Japan's Economy Grew So Fast*, Washington, D.C.: The Brookings Institution.

Doyle, L.A. (1965) *Inter-Economy Comparisons. A Case Study*, California: University of California Press.

Engineering News Record; annual surveys of large international engineering related firms, engaged in design and construction.

Enos, J.L. (1958) 'A Measure of the Rate of Technical Progress in the Petroleum Refining Industry', *Journal of Industrial Economics*, June.

—— (1985) 'A Game-Theoretic Approach to Choice of Technology in Developing Countries', in J. James and S. Watanabe, *Technology, Institutions and Government Policies*, London: Macmillan, pp. 47-80.

Franks, C., Kim, K. and Westphal, L. (1975) *Foreign Trade Regimes and Economic Development: South Korea*, Washington, D.C.: National Bureau of Economic Research.

Gouverneur, J. (1971) *Productivity and Factor Proportions in Less Developed Countries: The Case of Industrial Firms in the Congo*, Oxford UK: Oxford University Press.

Griliches, Z. (1957) 'Hybrid Corn: An Exploration in the Economics of Technological Change', *Econometrica*, October, pp. 501-22.

Habu, L.F. (1958) *The Chemical Industry during the Nineteenth Century.*

—— (1971) *The Chemical Industry 1900-1930 and 1935.*

Haruo, Suzuki (1968) *Chemical Industry*, Toyokeizai-Shinbunsha.

Hirata, M. (1982) 'Present State of Energy Conservation and the Government Policy in Japan', *Canada-Japan Energy Conservation Conference* (1982).

Hirsch, W.Z. (1956) 'Firm Progress Ratios', *Econometrica*, April.

Hogan, W.T. (1985) 'Pohang Steel Continues to Grow', *Iron and Steel Engineer*, April, pp. 32-8.

Hollander, S. (1965) *The Sources of Increased Efficiency: A Study of du Pont Rayon Plants*, Cambridge, Mass.: MIT Press.

Iida, Kenichi (1973) *History of Iron and Steel Technology in Japan*, Tokyo: Sanichi-Shobo.

Jenkins, Gareth L. (1974) *Non-Agricultural Choice of Technique: An Annotated Bibliography of Empirical Studies*, Oxford: Institute of Commonwealth Studies.

Jones, L.P. and Sa-Kong, Il. (1980) *Government, Business and Entrepreneurship in Economic Development: the Korean Case*, Cambridge: Harvard University Press.

Kamien, M.I. and Schwartz, N.L. (1982) *Market Structure and Innovation*, Cambridge, UK: Cambridge University Press.

Katz, Jorge *et al.* (1978) 'Productivity, Technology and Domestic Efforts in Research and Development', IDB/ECLA Research Programme in Science and Technology Working Paper no. 13, Buenos Aires, July.

Kim, Lin-Su (1980a) 'Stages of Development of Industrial Technology in a Developing Country: a Model', *Research Policy*, 9, pp. 254-77.

—— (1980b) 'Organizational Innovation and Structure', *Journal of Business Research*, pp. 225-45.

—— (1982) 'Technological Innovations in Korea's Capital Goods Industries: A Micro Analysis', ILO Working Paper WEP 2-22/WP92, Geneva.

Kim, Lin-Su and Utterback, J.M. (1983) 'The Evolution of Organizational Structure and Technology in a Developing Country', *Management Science*, 29, 10, pp. 1,185-97.

Kim, Lin-Su and Young-Bae Kim (forthcoming) 'Innovation in a Newly Industrializing Country: A Multiple Discriminant Analysis', *Management Science.*

Lee, J.-J. (1981) 'Development of Engineering Consultancy and Design Capability in Korea', in A. Araoz (ed.), *Consulting and Engineering*

Design in Developing Countries, Ottawa: International Development Research Center.

Lee, Jin-Joo and Sharan, H.N. (1985) 'Technological Impact of the Public Procurement Policy: The Experience of the Power Plant Sector in the Republic of Korea', UNCTAD programme on technology issues in the energy sector of developing countries, UNCTAD/TT/60, Geneva: United Nations.

Lee, Won-Pyo (1985) 'Steel Industry in Korea', paper presented at the meeting of the International Iron and Steel Institute's *Technical Conference on Steel Statistics,* Brussels, 6-9 May 1985.

Mansfield, E. (1971) 'Technical Change and the Rate of Limitation', *Econometrica,* pp. 741-66.

Meyer, J.R. and Herregat, G. (1974) 'The Basic Oxygen Steel Process', in L. Nabseth and G.F. Ray (eds), *The Diffusion of New Industrial Processes,* Cambridge: Cambridge University Press, pp. 146-99.

Michell, T. (1984) 'Trade, Industrialization and Employment in the Republic of Korea', ILO World Employment Programme, Geneva.

Mitsubishi Heavy Industry (1970) *History of Mitsubishi Heavy Industrial Co. Ltd.*

Moritani, Masanori (1984) *Advanced Technology and the Japanese Contribution,* Tokyo: Nomura Securities Co. Ltd.

Moxon, R.W. (1979) 'The Cost, Conditions and Adaptation of MNC Technology in Developing Countries', in R.G. Hawkins (ed.), *The Economic Effects of Multinational Corporations,* Greenwich, Connecticut: JAI Press.

Nabseth, L. and Ray, G.F. (1974) *The Diffusion of New Industrial Processes: An International Study,* Cambridge: Cambridge University Press.

Nelson, R.R. (1981) 'Research on Productivity Growth and Productivity Differences: Dead Ends and New Departures', *Journal of Economic Literature,* 19, 3 (September), pp. 1,029-64.

Nelson, R.R. and Winter, S. (1980) 'The Schumpeterian Tradeoff Revisited', *American Economic Review,* vol. 70, pp. 114-32.

Oster, S. (1982) 'The Diffusion of Innovation among Steel Firms: The Basic Oxygen Furnace', *The Bell Journal of Economics,* vol. 13, no. 1 (Spring), pp. 45-56.

Ozawa, Terutomo, 'Transfer of Technology from Japan to Developing Countries', UNITAR Research Reports no. 7, New York: United Nations Institute for Training and Research.

Ramaer, J.C. (1979) 'The Choice of Appropriate Technology by a Multinational Corporation: A Case Study of Messrs. Philips, Eindhoven', in A. Robinson (ed.), *Appropriate Technologies for Third World Development,* London: Macmillan.

Ray, G.F. (1984) *The Diffusion of Mature Technologies,* Cambridge: Cambridge University Press, Chapter 2 ('Oxygen Steelmaking', pp. 21-7) and Chapter 3 ('Continuous Casting of Steel', pp. 28-37).

Ray, George *et al.* (1985) *Technological Trends and Employment: 2 Basic Process Industries,* Aldershot, Hampshire: Gower.

Rosenberg, Nathan (1976) *Perspectives in Technology,* Cambridge, UK: Cambridge University Press.

REFERENCES

Simmonds, N.W. (1979) *Principles of Crop Improvement*, London: Longmans.
Stewart, F. (1978) *Technology and Underdevelopment*, 2nd edn, London: Macmillan.
Stobaugh, R.B. (1971) 'The International Transfer of Technology in the Establishment of the Petrochemical Industry in Developing Countries', UNITAR Research Report no. 12, New York: United Nations Institute for Training and Research.
Teece, D.J. (1976) *The Multinational Corporation and the Resource Costs of International Technology Transfer*, Cambridge, Mass: Ballinger.
Tilton, J.E. (1971) *International Diffusion of Technology: The Case of Semiconductors*, Washington, D.C.: The Brookings Institution.
Tipten, F.B. Jr. (1981) 'Government Policy, and Economic Development in Japan: A Sceptical Revaluation', *Economic History*, vol. 41, no. 1 (March), pp. 139-50.
Toyo Rayon Co. (1977) *Fifty Years' History of Toyo Rayon*.
Turner, T. (1977) 'Two Refineries: A Comparative Study of Technology Transfer to the Nigerian Refining Industry', *World Development*, 5, 3 (March), pp. 235-56.
Utterback, J.M. and Kim, Lin-Su (forthcoming) 'Invasion of a Stable Business by Radical Innovation', in P.R. Kleindorfer (ed.), *Productivity, Technology and Organizational Innovation*, London: Plenum Press.
Veldhuis, K.H. (1979) 'Transfer and Adaptation of Technology: Unilever as a Case Study', in A. Robinson (ed.), *Appropriate Technologies for Third World Development*, London: Macmillan.
Westphal, L.E., Rhee, Yung-W., Kim, Lin-Su and Amsden, Alice H. (1984) 'Exports of Technology by Republic of Korea', *World Development*, 12, 5/6, pp. 505-33.
Westphal, L.E., Kim, Lin-Su and Dahlman, C.J. (1984) 'Reflections on Korea's Acquisition of Technological Capability', World Bank, Development Research Department, Economics and Research Staff Paper, April (forthcoming in Nathan Rosenberg (ed.), *International Transfer of Technology: Concepts, Measures and Comparisons*, New York: Pergamon Press).
Yotopoulos, P.A. and Nugent, J.B. (1976) *Economics of Development: Empirical Investigations*, New York: Harper and Row, Table 9.1, pp. 152-3.

Index

Note: Information is assumed to be about Korea unless otherwise specified. The alphabetisation is word by word, but initials are alphabetised as though they are acronyms.

Canada 107
capability 24
capacity 20, 103
    and production 55-6, 73, 154-6,
        157
    using 164, 236-8, 239-41
capital 35, 48, 62, 101, 142, 144,
    172-3, 177, 178, 230
caprolactam 50, 117, 119, 142
    imports 50, 51
    localisation of supplies 247
    polymerisation to nylon 53
    production 47, 91-2, 222
change 9, 74, 162; see also
    improvements
Changwon Machine Industry Base
    36
characteristics see national
    characteristics and personal
    characteristics
Cheil Synthetic Textiles Co. 54
chemical industry
    R&D expenditure 44, 45
    see also petrochemical industry
Chemstrand 115
Chemtex 142
    and Kolon 115-16, 117, 122-5,
        131, 144, 145
Chile 107-8
Chinese Steel Corporation 212
chlorine removal 83-4
choices 17, 233
Chosun Machine Works 148
Chung, W.K. 46
Chungju Fertiliser Company 60, 63,
    91; see also Korea General
    Chemical Corporation
cleaning materials 96
co-operation 145, 146, 167-8,
    174-5
co-polymer of VCM and EVA 87,
    88-91, 105
Cole, D.C. 28
Columbia 172
comparability 16-17, 133-40
comparisons 107-8, 173, 175,
    212-16, 228-30
competition 109-11, 142-3, 145,
    166-7, 222, 230, 255
compression 87
computer ribbon 141
condensate 77-80
confidentiality 111, 112; see also
    secrecy
conflict 14
consortiums 177-8

contracts 36-7, 40-2, 63-5, 88, 101,
    111, 131, 149-51, 173, 178-9,
    208, 212, 221, 222
    of employment: anti-pirating
        clauses 143-4, 210
cosmetic tissue see tissue
costs 87, 109, 110-11, 133, 136-40,
    156-7, 162-4
    compared for different industries
        185-6
    measuring 13, 239
    reductions/savings in 97-8,
        205-7, 234-5, 239-41
course(s) 10-11, 12-13

Dae Han Synthetic Fibre Co. 54
Dae Nong Petrochemical Ind. Co.
    49
Daewoo Corporation 148
Daewoo Heavy Industries 88, 132,
    148-9, 154-69, 172-5, 211, 242
    employees' training and
        experience 158-61, 164, 165
    history 148-51, 156-61, 162-6
    position in industry 28
    production figures 237
    products 148, 164-6
    share ownership 148
    see also Hankook Machine
        Industrial Co.
Daewoo Industrial Company 149
Daewoo Machinery Company 148
Dahlman, C.J. 24, 26, 39-40, 43,
    44, 55, 180
Dart 62n4
Davies, S. 26
decision-making 11, 178
definitions 5-14, 16, 26, 63, 69
DEMAG 177, 226-7, 228
demand 57-8, 60, 64, 73, 88, 112,
    144, 154-6, 160-1, 238
    and absorption 160-1
    see also markets
Denison, E.F. 46
design 99-100, 175, 235-6
design capacity 20, 103
DHI see Daewoo Heavy Industries
diesel engines 149-50, 157-8, 223,
    224
    demand for 154-7
    mounting 156
    not final products 156
    production 55-6
        methods 151-3, 159-64, 174,
            242
        problems with 232

263